LONGMAN LINGUISTICS LIBRARY

THE ENGLISH VERB
Second Edition

LONGMAN LINGUISTICS LIBRARY

General editors
R. H. Robins, University of London
Martin Harris, University of Essex

General Linguistics
An Introductory Survey
Third Edition
R. H. ROBINS

A Short History of Linguistics
Second Edition
R. H. ROBINS

Structural Aspects of Language Change
JAMES M. ANDERSON

Text and Context
Explorations in Semantics and Pragmatics of Discourse
TEUN A. VAN DIJK

Modality and English Modals
F. R. PALMER

Grimm's Grandchildren
Current Topics in German Linguistics
THOMAS HERBST,
DAVID HEATH,
HANS-MARTIN DEDERDING

Explanation in Linguistics
The Logical Problem of Language Acquisition
EDITED BY NORBERT HORNSTEIN
AND DAVID LIGHTFOOT

Introduction to Text Linguistics
ROBERT-ALAIN DE BEAUGRANDE
AND WOLFGANG ULRICH
DRESSLER

Spoken Discourse
A Model for Analysis
WILLIS EDMONDSON

Psycholinguistics
Language, Mind and World
DANNY D. STEINBERG

Dialectology
W. N. FRANCIS

Principles of Pragmatics
GEOFFREY N. LEECH

Adjectives and Comparison in English
A Semantic Study
JAN RUSIECKI

Generative Grammar
GEOFFREY HORROCKS

Norms of Language
Theoretical and Practical Aspects
RENATE BARTSCH

The English Verb
Second Edition
F. R. PALMER

Pidgin and Creole Languages
SUZANNE ROMAINE

The English Verb

Second Edition

F. R. Palmer

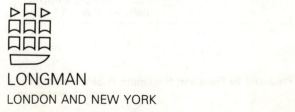

LONGMAN

LONDON AND NEW YORK

Longman Group UK Limited
Longman House, Burnt Mill, Harlow,
Essex CM20 2JE, England
and Associated Companies throughout the world

Published in the United States of America
by Longman Inc., New York

First published as *A Linguistic Study of the English Verb* 1965
Revised as *The English Verb* 1974
Second edition 1988

British Library Cataloguing in Publication Data

Palmer, F. R.
The English verb. – 2nd. [i.e. 3rd] ed.
– (Longman linguistics library)
1. English language – Verb
I. Title
425   PE1271

ISBN 0-582-01470-0 CSD
ISBN 0-582-29714-1 PPR

Library of Congress Cataloging in Publication Data

Palmer, F. R. (Frank Robert)
The English verb.

Bibliography: p.
Includes indexes.
1. English language – Verb.   I. Title.
PE1271.P3   1988   425   86-27169
ISBN 0-582-01470-0
ISBN 0-582-29714-1 (pbk.)

Produced by Longman Singapore Publishers (Pte) Ltd.
Printed in Singapore.

Contents

Preface		xi
Pronunciation table		xii
1	**Introduction**	1
	1.1 General considerations	2
	1.1.1 Grammatical description	3
	1.1.2 Speech and writing	4
	1.1.3 Form and meaning	8
	1.2 Linguistic units	8
	1.2.1 Word and phrase	9
	1.2.2 Sentence and clause	10
2	**The verb phrase**	12
	2.1 Preliminary considerations	12
	2.1.1 Finite and non-finite	12
	2.1.2 Concord	14
	2.2 The auxiliaries	14
	2.2.1 The forms	15
	2.2.2 Negation	16
	2.2.3 Inversion	18
	2.2.4 'Code'	19
	2.2.5 Emphatic affirmation	20
	2.2.6 DO	21
	2.2.7 Non-assertion	22
	2.2.8 DARE and NEED	23
	2.2.9 Primary and modal auxiliaries	25
	2.3 Types of verb phrase	26
	2.3.1 Simple and complex phrases	27
	2.3.2 Auxiliary and full verb	28

3   Tense and phase   32
   3.1 Characteristics of the primary auxiliaries   32
       3.1.1 The paradigms   32
       3.1.2 The four categories   35
       3.1.3 Outline of uses   36
   3.2 Tense   37
       3.2.1 Time and tense   37
       3.2.2 Time relations   39
       3.2.3 Reported speech   40
       3.2.4 Related issues   43
       3.2.5 Unreality   44
   3.3 Phase   46
       3.3.1 Time relations   46
       3.3.2 Results   47
       3.3.3 HAVE as past   51
       3.3.4 Problem uses   52

4 Aspect   54
   4.1 Duration   54
       4.1.1 Points of time   54
       4.1.2 Other durational uses   55
   4.2 Future and habitual uses   56
       4.2.1 Adverbial specification   57
       4.2.2 Non-habitual present   58
   4.3 Habitual   60
       4.3.1 The simple present   61
       4.3.2 Limited duration   62
       4.3.3 Sporadic repetition   63
   4.4 Future   64
       4.4.1 Progressive   64
       4.4.2 Non-progressive   65
       4.4.3 Future and habitual   67
   4.5 Progressive perfect   68
       4.5.1 'Results'   68
       4.5.2 A complex pattern   69
   4.6 Non-progressive verbs   70
       4.6.1 Verbs of state   71
       4.6.2 Private verbs   72

5 Voice   77
   5.1 Passive   77
       5.1.1 Active–passive correspondence   77
       5.1.2 Agentless passives   78

5.1.3 Passive and transitivity 79
5.1.4 Restrictions on the passive 81
5.1.5 The functions of passive 83
5.2 Passive gradience 85
5.2.1 Pseudo-passives 85
5.2.2 Semi-passives 87
5.2.3 Statal passives 88
5.3 GET 89
5.4 Lexical passives 90
5.4.1 Case relations 90
5.4.2 'Adverbial' passives 92

6 The modals of possibility and necessity 94
6.1 Characteristics of the modals 94
6.1.1 The paradigms 94
6.1.2 Types of modality 96
6.1.3 Tense, negation, voice 98
6.1.4 Neutral modality 102
6.1.5 Possibility/necessity and negation 103
6.1.6 Non-assertion 104
6.1.7 Other forms 106
6.2 May and can 107
6.2.1 Epistemic 107
6.2.2 Deontic 109
6.2.3 Dynamic 112
6.2.4 Problem types 116
6.3 Might and could 117
6.3.1 Past tense 117
6.3.2 Tentative 119
6.3.3 Problem types 120
6.4 BE ABLE TO 121
6.5 MUST and NEED 122
6.5.1 Epistemic 122
6.5.2 BE BOUND TO 124
6.5.3 Deontic 125
6.6 HAVE (GOT) TO 128
6.6.1 Epistemic 129
6.6.2 Neutral 129
6.7 OUGHT TO and SHOULD 131
6.7.1 Deontic 131
6.7.2 Epistemic 134
6.7.3 'Evaluative' SHOULD 134
6.8 DARE 135

7 The modals WILL and SHALL   136
  7.1 Modal WILL AND SHALL   136
      7.1.1 Epistemic WILL   136
      7.1.2 Dynamic WILL   138
      7.1.3 BE WILLING TO   140
      7.1.4 Deontic SHALL   141
  7.2 Future WILL/SHALL   142
      7.2.1 Conditionality   142
      7.2.2 'Modal' future   143
      7.2.3 Future tense   144
  7.3 BE GOING TO   146
      7.3.1 Current orientation   146
      7.3.2 Contrasts with WILL/SHALL   147
  7.4 Conditionals   149
      7.4.1 The basic patterns   149
      7.4.2 Other types   153
      7.4.3 Conditionals and modals   155

8 Marginal verbs   158
  8.1 BE   158
      8.1.1 Full verb   158
      8.1.2 IS TO   160
  8.2 HAVE   162
      8.2.1 Full verb   162
      8.2.2 'Affected' subject   164
      8.2.3 Summary   168
  8.3 DO   169
  8.4 USED TO   170
  8.5 BETTER, RATHER, LET'S   170

9 The catenatives   172
  9.1 Classification   173
      9.1.1 Basic structures   173
      9.1.2 Aspect, phase, tense and voice   174
      9.1.3 Identity relations   178
      9.1.4 Prepositions in the structure   185
      9.1.5 Semantics   187
      9.1.6 Homonyms   188
  9.2 Catenative classes   191
      9.2.1 Futurity   191
      9.2.2 Causation   195
      9.2.3 Report   196
      9.2.4 Perception   198

9.2.5 Process   200
9.2.6 Achievement   202
9.2.7 Attitude   202
9.2.8 Need   204
9.2.9 Appearance and chance   204
9.3 Further issues   205
9.3.1 Related and contrasted structures   206
9.3.2 Simple and complex phrases   208
9.3.3 Verbal nouns and adjectives   208
9.3.4 Status of the subordinate clause   211

10 Phrasal and prepositional verbs   215
10.1 Classification   216
10.1.1 Grammar and lexicon   216
10.1.2 Preposition and adverbs   217
10.1.3 Formal contrasts   219
10.2 Phrasal verbs   222
10.2.1 Transitive forms   222
10.2.2 Intransitive forms   223
10.2.3 Semantics   224
10.2.4 Idioms   226
10.3 Prepositional verbs   229
10.3.1 Free prepositions   229
10.3.2 Semantics   231
10.3.3 Intransitive forms   231
10.3.4 Transitive forms   235
10.3.5 'Postpositions'   237
10.4 Phrasal prepositional verbs   238

11 Morphology   240
11.1 The auxiliaries   240
11.1.1 Irregular forms   240
11.1.2 Negative forms   241
11.1.3 Weak forms   242
11.2 Full verbs: -*ing* and -*s* forms   248
11.3 Full verbs: past tense and -*en* forms   249
11.3.1 Regular -*ed* formation   249
11.3.2 Secondary -*ed* formation   250
11.3.3 Back vowel formation   253
11.3.4 -*en* suffix   255
11.3.5 Idiosyncratic forms   256
11.4 BE, HAVE and DO   257
11.5 Forms with *to*   257

References and citation index   259
Verb index   260
Subject index   265

Preface

This book is, in effect, a second revised version of *A Linguistic Study of the English Verb*, published in 1965; the first revision appeared as *The English Verb* in 1974. There has been considerable rewriting and reorganization of all the chapters, except the last (now 11 instead of 9), but the major changes are in the treatment of voice (Ch. 5), of HAVE (8.2) and, above all, of the modals, which are now discussed in two chapters (6 and 7) instead on one. The analysis of the modals is based on my *Modality and the English Modals* (1979), though the presentation is different.

Like its predecessors it is intended both for students of linguistics and for all who are interested in the description of modern English.

University of Reading
January 1987   F. R. P.

Pronunciation table

CONSONANTS			VOWELS	
VOICELESS		**VOICED**		
/p/	pig	/b/	big	/iː/	sheep
/t/	ten	/d/	den	/ɪ/	ship
/k/	cot	/g/	got	/e/	bed
/f/	fat	/v/	vat	/æ/	bad
/θ/	thin	/ð/	then	/ɑː/	calm
/s/	soon	/z/	zero	/ɒ/	pot
/ʃ/	fish	/ʒ/	pleasure	/ɔː/	caught
/tʃ/	cheap	/dʒ/	jeep	/ʊ/	put
/h/	hot	/m/	sum	/uː/	boot
		/n/	sun	/ʌ/	cut
		/ŋ/	sung	/ɜː/	bird
		/l/	led	/ə/	above
		/r/	red	/eɪ/	day
		/j/	yet	/əʊ/	coal
		/w/	wet	/aɪ/	lie
				/aʊ/	now
				/ɔɪ/	boy
				/ɪə'/	here
				/eə'/	there
				/ʊə'/	poor
				/eɪə'/	player
				/əʊə'/	lower
				/aɪə'/	tire
				/aʊə'/	tower
				/ɔɪə'/	employer

Quirk et al. 1985

To Andrew and George

Chapter 1

Introduction

In recent years interest in English grammar has greatly increased, but there have been more books and articles on the verb than on the noun, the adjective or any other class of word. One reason, obviously, is that the verb, or rather the verb phrase, as defined in this book, is so central to the structure of the sentence that no syntactic analysis can proceed without a careful consideration of it. Another is the great complexity of the internal semantic and syntactic structure of the verb phrase itself.

For almost any language the part that concerns the verb is the most difficult. Learning a language is to a very large degree learning how to operate the verbal forms of that language, and, except in the case of those that are related historically, the pattern and structure of the verb in each language seem to differ very considerably from those in every other language. Most of us, as native speakers of a language, are as a result reasonably convinced that our own language has a fairly straightforward way of dealing with the verbs and are rather dismayed and discouraged when faced with something entirely different in a new language.

The verbal patterns of languages differ in two ways, first of all formally, in the way in which the linguistic material is organized, and secondly in the type of information carried.

On the formal side the most obvious distinction is between those languages whose verbal features are expressed almost entirely by inflection and those which have no inflectional features at all, those which, in traditional terms, used to be distinguished as 'inflectional' and as 'isolating' languages. Extreme examples of these are Latin or classical Arabic on the one hand and Chinese on the other. English, in this respect, is

much closer to Chinese than it is to Latin; or at least this is true
as long as we are thinking about *words*. If we ask how many
different forms of the verb there are in Latin, the answer will be
over a hundred, and the same is true for classical Arabic. For
English, on the other hand, there are at most only five forms:
the verb 'to take' has only *take, takes, taking, took* and *taken*.
But this contrast is misleading because it is in terms of single-
word forms. For if the verbal forms of English are taken to
include such multi-word forms as *is taking, has been taking, may
have taken*, etc, there are possibly over a hundred forms of the
English verb.

More important, and more difficult for the learner, is the
nature of the information carried by the verbal forms. Speakers
of European languages expect that their verbs will tell them
something about time; and that there will be at least a future,
a present and a past tense referring to a future, a present and
a past time. But there is no natural law that the verb in a
language shall be concerned with time. There are languages in
which time relations are not marked at all, and there are
languages in which the verb is concerned with spatial rather than
temporal relations. Even in languages where time seems to be
dealt with in the verb, it is not always a simple matter of present,
past and future; English does not handle present, past and future
as a trio in the category of tense (3.2.1). More troublesome is
the variety of other features indirectly associated with time that
are indicated by the verb. In English, for instance, the verb may
indicate that an action took place in a period preceding, but
continuing right up to, the present moment, as well as simply in
the past. In other languages, such as the Slavonic languages, what
is important is whether or not the action has been completed. *I
read a book last night* will be translated into Russian in two
different ways, depending upon whether or not I finished the
book.

1.1 General considerations

It is not the aim of this book to raise or to answer questions of
linguistic theory for their own sake, though it contains a considerable amount of discussion that is of theoretical relevance. Any
book of this kind must, moreover, make assumptions about its
subject – that we can, for instance, usefully identify the verb and
that statements about the meaning of linguistic items are themselves meaningful. Some general comments, however, on the
linguistic standpoint and the basic concepts are appropriate.

1.1.1 Grammatical description
This is a (partial) descriptive grammar of English. Its aim, that is to say, is simply to describe the facts of English. It will not make recommendations about the ways in which English should be spoken or written; it will not suggest, for instance, that *If I was rich* is incorrect and should be replaced by *If I were rich*, or that *You can leave now* should be corrected to *You may leave now*.

Many grammars and handbooks written over the last two centuries and some that are still in use in parts of the world contain normative or prescriptive rules such as those that condemn split infinitives, recommend the use of *whom* or reject *It's me* as ungrammatical. There is no place for any of these in this book. Yet that is not to say that there are no rules in English. On the contrary, there are rules such as the one that requires *The boys are coming* rather than **The boys is coming*. But these are descriptive rules, based on the observable facts of the language (and there may be some variation according to matters such as dialect or style).

There is, then, no clash between description and correctness provided that it is clearly understood precisely what kind of English is being described. One variety that is referred to is 'standard English', or more strictly, 'standard British English'. This is to some degree a fiction, because different people have different views about what is standard. But the advent of radio and television means that there is fairly general agreement (and, curiously, where there are objections to 'incorrect' speech on the mass media, they more often relate to the prescriptive rules mentioned earlier, not to more legitimate descriptive differences).

Inevitably, the material for this book is what the author believes is standard, or what he believes he uses when he speaks standard English, though some of the examples are taken from recorded texts (especially in Chs 6 and 7).

Even this, however, will not produce a precise account of what is and what is not grammatical in English. For there are forms that are marginal; native speakers are not always clear about what they could or could not say. For instance, there is some doubt about the status of:

He would have been being examined.

Many people would accept this, but only just, yet it is marked as 'wanting' in one well-known description of English (Palmer and Blandford 1939: 131).

An examination of actual texts may establish that some

dubious forms actually occur, but a grammar cannot reasonably be based on such texts alone. Apart from the fact that some forms may, quite by accident, not occur unless the corpus is vast (perhaps even infinite), it will also be the case that some of the forms that occur will be rejected not only by the investigator but even by the original speaker (or writer) as slips of the tongue or mistakes. Inevitably, some judgments have to be made, and it will not be surprising or undesirable if the judgments of the reader of this book are not always the same as those of the writer.

In general, then, most of the forms presented here for exemplification are accepted as grammatical. Others, however, are less straightforward and conventions are required to indicate their status:

[i]   Forms that are ungrammatical are marked with an asterisk:

    *He has could been there.

[ii] Forms that are doubtful are marked with a question mark:

    ?He could have been being examined.

[iii] Forms that are grammatical, but not under the interpretation required in the analysis, are marked with an exclamation mark. For instance, all the following are possible:

    He began talking.
    He began to talk.
    He stopped talking.
    !He stopped to talk.

The section in which these are discussed (9.3.1) is concerned with the constructions associated with catenatives, and whereas *talking* and *to talk* can be used in a particular (catenative) construction with BEGIN, only *talking* can occur with STOP in that construction; the last sentence, though quite grammatical, is of a different construction and irrelevant to the argument.

1.1.2 Speech and writing

It is a reasonable question to ask of a linguist whether he is attempting to describe the spoken or the written language. With a few exceptions most grammarians until fairly recently have been concerned almost exclusively with the written language and their works are often superbly illustrated by copious examples from English literature (*eg* Jespersen 1909–49). This concentration on the written language has sometimes been associated with the assumption that speech is inferior, because it is ephemeral rather than permanent, and because it is often ungrammatical or corrupt. Not surprisingly, perhaps, there has also been a reaction to this point of view; there have been linguists who have taken the opposite view and argued that only speech is language.

It is easy to show at the level of the sound and writing systems of the language, the phonology and the graphology, that spoken and written languages are very different. Apart from the fact that they are in different media, one in sound and the other in marks upon paper, there is often no one-to-one correspondence between the units of one and the units of the other, at least in the case of languages that have a long tradition of writing. It is not simply that there are such words as *cough, tough*, etc in which there seems to be no relation between the spelling and the pronunciation. The differences go deeper than that. In English there are only five vowels in the writing, but it would be difficult to analyse the sound system in any way that would reduce the number of vowels to less than six. Equally important is the fact that in speech there are the features of stress and intonation, which have only to a very limited degree counterparts in the written language. In this respect the reverse of the traditional belief is true: writing is a poor representation of speech.

Even the grammar of the spoken language is different from the grammar of the written. In the written language the form *has* is irregular, for **haves* is to be expected, whereas *does* is quite regular as seen from comparing *go/goes*: in the spoken language both are irregular, since they are [hæz] and [dʌz] instead of **[hævz] and **[duːz]. Conversely there is in speech a perfectly regular negative form of *am*, which is, however, used only in questions, exactly analogous to the negative forms of *can* and *shall*. The negative forms differ from the positive in that (i) the vowel is [ɑː] instead of [æ], and (ii) the last consonant of the positive form is missing:

can [kæn]	*can't* [kɑːnt]
am [æm]	*aren't* [ɑːnt]
shall [ʃæl]	*shan't* [ʃɑːnt]

Yet although there is no problem about writing *can't I?* and *shan't I?* there is hesitation about the written form for the negative of *am*; the only possible representation seems to be *aren't I?* (not **an't I?*), but this looks more like the negative of *are*.

However, for the purposes of this book the distinction is not particularly important. We are not concerned with phonology except incidentally, while morphology is dealt with in Chapter 11. For the rest of the grammatical analysis (which is mainly syntactic) the differences between speech and writing are smaller (or, perhaps, one should say that there are greater correlations between the two). In particular, the writing conventions of the language, the orthography, can be used to identify the forms of the spoken language. It will, naturally, not be an accurate indication of the phonology or (to a lesser degree) of the morphology, but it will indicate fairly accurately most of the grammatical structure that we are concerned with. Indeed it is no coincidence that the term grammar is derived from the Greek word meaning 'to write', for an essential part of writing is that it reflects the grammatical system of the language.

It is, therefore, reasonable to claim that this is essentially a study of the spoken form of the language, yet at the same time to use the written form to identify the words and sentences that we are talking about. One work on the English verb (Joos 1964) used as its source material the transcript of a trial. This was essentially the analysis of the spoken form of English, yet the text available was wholly in written form. It need hardly be added that the reader will find the orthographic form of the examples easier to read than if they had been in a phonetic script. This is not simply a matter of familiarity, but also reflects the fact that a phonetic script supplies details that are unnecessary for the grammatical analysis.

It could be argued, however, that the orthography is defective in that it does not mark stress and intonation. This is a just criticism since stress and intonation are clearly grammatical; and there are other prosodic features that are left unstated. But these features are grammatical in two different senses. In the first place they often correlate with grammatical features that belong to the written language. For instance there is a distinction between:

> *I didn't do it because it was difficult.*
> *I didn't do it, because it was difficult.*

The first sentence means that I did it, but not because it was difficult, the second that I did not do it, because it was difficult. What is negated is *because it was difficult* in the first, *I did it* in the second. The comma indicates this in the written form. In speech the distinction is made even clearer by the use of appropriate intonation (probably a single fall-rise intonation in the first, but two intonation tunes in the second, a rise and then a fall). Secondly, however, intonation involves grammatical issues of a different kind. Statements and questions are normally regarded as grammatically different, and distinguished as declaratives and interrogatives respectively in, for instance, *I shall come tomorrow* and *Shall I come tomorrow?*, but the status of

I shall come tomorrow with a rising intonation in speech, is not clear; the order of the words is that associated with a statement, but the intonation indicates that it is a question. It could well be argued that intonation is as relevant as word order in the distinction between declarative and interrogative. But there are other distinctions that can be made with intonation. *I shall come tomorrow* with a fall-rise intonation can be taken to mean that it is tomorrow, not some other day, that I shall come. But is this too to be treated as a grammatical distinction?

These prosodic features will be largely excluded from consideration. Intonation, for example, can be largely ignored in the study of the verb. The reason for this is twofold. In the first place, the grammar that belongs to intonation is to a large extent independent of the rest of the grammar of the language. It is possible to deal with most of the characteristics of the verbs of English, to talk about the tenses and the other grammatical categories, progressives, perfect, active and passive, the modal auxiliaries, the catenatives, etc, without saying much about the intonation. Secondly, it is difficult, if not impossible, to analyse intonation in the kind of framework within which more traditional grammar is handled. The reason is that the relation between the intonation tunes and their functions is incredibly complex. For most grammatical features there are specific phonological exponents. For instance, past tense is marked by the addition of an alveolar consonant (*liked* [laikt], *loved* [lʌvd]), a zero ending (*hit*) or change of vowel (*took, bought*, etc). What does not happen is that an alveolar consonant is sometimes the exponent of past tense, sometimes of future, sometimes of negation, sometimes of a modal auxiliary. Yet a single intonation tune has a vast variety of different functions, depending on a number of factors, some within the language, others situational and outside the language.

The term 'stress' is, unfortunately, used in at least three different (though related) senses. It is used to distinguish otherwise identical nouns and verbs such as CONVICT and EXPORT, the noun being said to have stress on the first syllable, the verb on the second. It is also used to indicate, in a particular utterance, the presence, or equally the absence, of stress on a syllable that is a stressed syllable in the first sense; it is in this second sense that *shall* or *was* can be stressed or unstressed (11.1.3). It is further used to refer to the 'nuclear' or 'sentence' stress which marks the focal point of an intonation tune. As suggested earlier, these features will be largely ignored here, but the term 'stress' will sometimes be used in the second sense only, while nuclear stress will be referred to as 'accent' and indicated with an acute accent as in (see 10.1.2):

That's the flag he ran úp.
That's the hill he rán up.

1.1.3 Form and meaning

As with the controversy over speech and writing there have been disagreements about the relation of form and meaning to grammar. Some older grammarians assumed that grammar was essentially concerned with meaning and defined their grammatical categories in semantic terms, nouns in terms of 'things', gender in terms of sex, singular and plural in terms of counting. Most modern linguists have firmly maintained that grammar must be formal, that grammatical categories must be based on form not on meaning.

It is easy enough to show that categories based on form and categories based on meaning are sometimes incompatible. There is an often quoted pair of words in English, *oats* and *wheat*, of which the first is formally plural and the second formally singular. But there is nothing in the nature of oats and wheat that requires that they should be treated (in terms of meaning) as 'more than one' and 'one' respectively.

The argument can become a sterile one, for it is impossible to undertake a grammatical analysis that has in no way been influenced by meaning, and it is equally impossible to undertake an analysis purely based on meaning. What is needed, and what all grammars have ever provided, is an analysis that is formal in the sense that it illustrates formal regularities and can be justified formally in that formal evidence is always available, but also semantic in the sense that it accounts for semantic features that correlate with formal distinctions.

It is almost certainly the case that any semantic distinction can be matched somewhere in the language by a formal one and that any formal regularity can be assigned some kind of meaning. It is not, then, a matter of form versus meaning, but of the weighting to be given to obvious formal features and to fairly obvious semantic ones.

1.2 Linguistic units

The terms 'word', 'phrase', 'clause' and 'sentence' are all familiar and used extensively in this book, but some comments on them are needed.

1.2.1 Word and phrase

The word appears to be an obvious element in the written language; it is the element that is marked by spaces. There are, however, no spaces in speech; it is certainly not the case that there is a brief gap or pause between the words of the spoken language. Nevertheless, it is reasonable to accept the written word as the basis of a grammatical discussion, even when dealing with the spoken language, for the conventions of writing are not wholly arbitrary, and, to a very large extent, the word of the written language is a basic grammatical unit.

Even if this is accepted there are some issues concerning the definition of the word. To begin with, it is obvious that any grammatical study is concerned with words as 'types' rather than 'tokens'. The point here is that the word *and* may occur twenty times on a page, but all would be said to be the 'same' word. They are the same in that they are the same type, although they are different tokens.

There is another distinction that is more important and more likely to confuse. In one sense *cat* and *cats* (types) are different words, but in another sense they are the same word, being the singular and plural forms of the lexical item CAT. This distinction is most easily handled in terms of 'word form' and 'lexeme' (or 'lexical word'), word forms being written in italics and lexemes in small capitals, as has just been done.

This distinction, with its potential confusion, is also found with terms such as 'noun' and 'verb'. 'The noun *cat*' is different from 'the noun CAT'. *Take, takes, taking, taken* are all verbs, but only in the sense of being verb forms of the verb (lexeme) TAKE. It may be noted that traditionally the lexeme is referred to as 'the verb "to take"', but this is not particularly helpful. It is still necessary to distinguish the form (the '*to*-infinitive' – see 2.1) *to take*, which is distinct from the other forms, and the lexeme TO TAKE. Moreover, there are good reasons for not choosing this form as the indication of a lexeme. First, some verbs (the modals) have no *to* form (*to shall, *to ought, etc). Secondly, this form consists of two words instead of one. Its choice is a result of basing English grammar on Latin; for, in Latin, the infinitive is a single word and conveniently used as the name of the lexeme.

Throughout this book the term 'verb' will be used for lexemes and 'verb form' for forms. But for practical reasons the distinction will not be made with other parts of speech (except in Chapter 10 – see below). Theoretically a distinction can be made for adverbs, between, for instance, *soon* and SOON, but since there is only one form for each lexeme it usually makes no difference whether there is reference to *soon* or to SOON in *John will soon come*. In Chapter 10, however, where the compound verbs consist of verb plus particle, the identification of the verb as a lexeme requires that the particle shall be identified in the same way – *eg*. HANG UP, not HANG *up*.

The only alternative to the word as the basis of grammatical analysis is the morpheme. Thus it is possible to distinguish two morphemes in *dogs* – *dog* and *s* (or [dɒg] and [z] in speech). But there have been great problems in morphemic analysis, especially with word forms such as *took*. There is no simple way of identifying two morphemes here; if the solution is in terms of *take* and past tense or, better perhaps, TAKE and past tense, that is, in effect, to analyse in terms of a word and a grammatical category.

The term 'phrase' is used in 'noun phrase' and 'verb phrase'. The precise definition of 'verb phrase' is given in 2.3.1, but it should be noted that it is being used in a traditional sense and not in the sense given to it in transformational-generative grammar. The term 'noun phrase' is used to refer to sequences in which there is a head noun modified by adjectives, determiners, etc; it is noun phrases, not nouns, that function as the subjects or objects of sentences.

1.2.2 Sentence and clause
The term 'sentence' is used, unfortunately, in modern linguistics in two different but related senses. Consider:

John expected that he would see his father.

In one sense this is a single sentence (and so marked in the orthography by a full stop). In another sense it is two sentences, one of them, *he would see his father*, being both a sentence in its own right and also part of the other sentence. This feature is known in traditional grammar as 'subordination' and in more recent terminology as 'embedding'.

The use of a single term 'sentence' in both senses has some justification in that, though in one sense the second sentence is part of the first, it is also a whole in its own right, with the same kind of structure. The relation is thus quite different from the relation between sentence and phrase where sentences are made up of phrases (and phrases similarly of words). With sentences the same units are used, but at different levels of subordination.

Traditional grammars distinguish clause and sentence, so that a sentence may be composed of one or more clauses (and in the example above there is one sentence, but two clauses). This is clear and simple, provided it is remembered that the clause-sentence relation is not like that of phrase-clause; this traditional terminology will be used here.

Within the sentence a further distinction can be made between main and subordinate clauses. There are two kinds of subordinate clause, one requiring the same kind of verb phrase as a main clause, the other containing no finite form (see 2.1.1):

While he talked, he banged the table.
While talking, he banged the table.

Traditional grammars sometimes used the term 'phrase' for the latter kind of clause. This is misleading and confusing. If a distinction is to be drawn it is in terms of finite and non-finite clauses. (For a more detailed discussion of the issues raised in this chapter, see Palmer 1984.)

Chapter 2

The verb phrase

The topic of this book is restricted to those characteristics of the English verb that can be handled within the verb phrase. It does not deal with those that are best dealt with in terms of sentence structure, except where they are directly relevant to the features of the verb phrase. The issue of, for instance, transitive, intransitive and ditransitive verbs is considered only because it is relevant to the discussion of the passive. There is, however, a chapter on the catenative verbs which, it might be argued, involve sentence structure, on the grounds that these can be handled in terms of complex verb phrases (see 2.3.2).

2.1 Preliminary considerations

There are a few points of terminology and detail to be considered, but most of this chapter is concerned with the auxiliaries (2.2).

2.1.1 Finite and non-finite

The lexeme TAKE has the forms *take*, *takes*, *took*, *taking* and *taken*. The first three are finite forms and the last two non-finite. The traditional definition of 'finite' is in terms of a verb form that is marked for person, but this would characterize only *take* and *takes* but not *took*. For English, it is better to use occurrence in a simple sentence as the sole test of finiteness, *eg*:

> *I take coffee.*
> *He takes coffee.*
> *I/he took coffee.*
> **I/he taking coffee.*
> **I/he taken coffee.*

If the verb phrase consists of a sequence of forms, only the first will be finite, the remainder non-finite, as in:

He has taken coffee.
He was taking coffee.
He wants to take coffee.

There is no very general agreement about the names of the five different forms. One distinction is between present and past tense forms. The past tense form is one that, for regular verbs (but see Ch. 11), ends in *-ed*. There are two present tense forms, one with, the other without *-s*; these will be called the 'simple form' and the '*-s* form'. The non-finite form *take* can be given the traditional name 'infinitive', though there is a need to distinguish the 'bare infinitive' without *to* and the '*to*-infinitive' with *to*. For *taking* and *taken* the most suitable names are simply '*-ing* form' and '*-en* form'. The former avoids the difficulties about participles and gerunds (see 9.3.3). The latter is justified in that it uses the same kind of label. Many *-en* forms (the traditional 'past participles'), however, do not end in *-en*, but often in *-ed*. But *-en* is an ending confined to these in contrast with the past tense, and thus provides an unambiguous label.

If two forms of the infinitive are distinguished, there are four non-finite forms, with four basic structures defined in terms of them. That is to say, any verb can be classified in terms of the non-finite form it requires to follow it. This is of particular importance for Chapter 9. The four basic structures with examples of verbs that require them are:

(1) Bare infinitive   CAN   HELP
(2) *to*-infinitive   OUGHT   WANT
(3) *-ing* form   BE   KEEP
(4) *-en* form   BE   GET

There will be a brief discussion in 3.1.1 of some verb phrases that contain no finite forms at all. These involve the use of the infinitives and the *-ing* form only and are dealt with under the heading of Infinitivals and Participials. Examples are *having said*, *to have made* in such sentences as:

Having said that, he walked away.
He cannot be said to have made a success of it.

These sequences occur either in subordinate clauses or as part of a complex phrase (Ch. 9). Also considered in 3.1.1 are the imperatives (the forms used in requests and commands). The imperatives only partly follow the pattern of the other verbal forms.

2.1.2 Concord

There is no place here for the traditional paradigm of the type *I take*, *Thou takest*, *He takes*, etc. All that need be noted is that there are certain very limited features of concord or agreement of the verbal form with the subject of the sentence. There are, in fact, three kinds of concord of which only the first is at all generalized.

[i]   All the verbs of the language with the exception of the modal auxiliaries (2.2.1 and 11.1.1) have two distinct present tense forms. One of them, the *-s* form, is used with the pronouns *he*, *she* and *it*, and singular noun phrases. The other, the simple form, is used with all other pronouns, *I*, *you*, *we* and *they*, and with plural noun phrases. We cannot define the two verbal forms as singular and plural respectively, unless we treat the first person singular pronoun *I* as plural, since it is found only with the simple form.

[ii] The verb BE alone has two distinct past tense forms, *was* and *were*. These could be regarded as singular and plural respectively, since the first is found with the pronoun *I* as well as the pronouns *he*, *she* and *it* and singular noun phrases. The other is found only with *we*, *you* and *they* and with plural noun phrases.

[iii] The verb BE alone in the language has a special form for the first person singular of the present tense – *am*.

2.2 The auxiliaries

Although the ultimate test of an auxiliary verb must be in terms of its syntagmatic relations with other verbs in the verb phrase, it is a striking and, perhaps, fortunate characteristic of English that the auxiliary verbs are marked by what Huddleston (1976:333) has referred to as their 'NICE' properties. This refers to the fact that they occur with negation, inversion, 'code' and emphatic affirmation (NICE being an acronym formed from the initial consonants of these terms). In particular, it will be seen that auxiliary verbs are to be clearly distinguished from a group of verbs that are here called the 'catenatives' (Ch. 9), verbs such as WANT, SEEM, KEEP. These verbs have something in common with auxiliaries both in the semantics and their syntactic relationships with other verbs, but do not share the NICE properties. The remaining verbs, those that are not auxiliaries, are referred to as 'full' verbs.

Each of the NICE properties will be discussed in a separate section (2.2.2, 2.2.3, 2.2.4, 2.2.5). The function of DO and the status of DARE and NEED are subsequently considered in the light of these features (2.2.6, 2.2.8).

2.2.1 The forms
There are eleven auxiliaries, with twenty-eight forms in all:

	finite	non-finite
BE	*is, are, am, was, were*	*be, being, been*
HAVE	*has, have, had*	*have, having*
DO	*do, does, did*	
WILL	*will, would*	
SHALL	*shall, should*	
CAN	*can, could*	
MAY	*may, might*	
MUST	*must*	
OUGHT	*ought*	
DARE	*dare*	
NEED	*need*	

It will be noted that the first three, BE, HAVE and DO, have -*s* forms, the remainder do not. This is a morphological distinction between the primary auxiliaries and the modal auxiliaries or modals; the distinction is discussed in some detail in 2.2.9.

Only the first two, BE and HAVE, have non-finite forms. In particular they alone have infinitives. The infinitive is, therefore, not always available as the name of the verb (the lexeme). Reference to the auxiliary verbs 'to will' and 'to shall' is now a linguistic joke (Vendryes 1921:29); the latter, of course, is non-existent, and the former, though historically related to the auxiliary verb, is synchronically to be considered as a different (full) verb. Errors of this nature are, unfortunately, still made. Even in a more recent grammar there is reference to the auxiliary verb 'to do' (Zandvoort 1957:78); yet the auxiliary verb has no infinitive form (in spite of *does go* there is no **to do go*). There are also verbs with infinitive forms *to can* and *to must*, and, according to the dictionary, *to may*, but these are unconnected with the auxiliaries. *To dare* and *to need* exist, but this results from the fact that DARE is both an auxiliary and a full verb, and these infinitives are to be treated as forms of the full verb (see 2.2.8).

The use of small capitals to identify lexemes avoids the problems created by the use of the *to*-infinitive. Even for the modals, it is possible to refer to WILL, SHALL, CAN, MAY, etc.

Notice also that *had* does not occur among the non-finite forms
of HAVE. The full verb HAVE has both a finite past tense form *had*
and a non-finite *-en* form *had*, but the auxiliary has the past tense
form only. This is clear from:

He's had his lunch.
**He's had gone.*

Having and *being* occur as forms of the auxiliary. *Being* alone
occurs within the basic paradigms (3.1.1, 6.1.1). Both occur in
initial position in the phrase where they mark participials (3.1.1).

2.2.2 Negation

The first test of an auxiliary is whether it is used in negation, that
is to say, whether it occurs with the negative particle *not*, or more
strictly, whether it has a negative form (11.1.2). Examples of
sentences with auxiliaries used for negation are:

I don't like it.
We aren't coming.
You can't do that.
He mustn't ask them.
They mightn't think so.

Positive sentences may or may not contain an auxiliary:

I can come.
We must go.
I like it.
We saw him.

An auxiliary verb, then, has forms that are used together with
the negative particle, or, to put it a better way, has paired
positive and negative forms. The difference between an auxiliary
and a full verb in this respect is seen clearly in the negative
sentences corresponding to the four given above. The first two
are:

I can't come.
We mustn't go.

But there are no similar forms corresponding to the last two. The
following are not possible:

**I liken't it.*
**We sawn't him.*

In modern English it is not even possible to say:

*I like not it.
*We saw not him.

Instead, the corresponding negative sentences, like all negative sentences, contain an auxiliary, one of the forms of DO:

I don't like it.
We didn't see him.

More striking is the fact that other verbs which might seem to be auxiliaries, but are, in fact catenatives, verbs such as WANT and BEGIN, are found only with the forms of DO in negative sentences:

I want to ask you.
I don't want to ask you.
*I wantn't to ask you.
He began to cry.
He didn't begin to cry.
*He begann't to cry.

These verbs are catenatives, the subject of Chapter 9.

There are some verbs that have not been included in the list of auxiliaries that seem to be used with the negative particle. Examples of sentences containing such verbs are:

I prefer not to ask him.
I hate not to win.

However, verbs such as PREFER and HATE do not have negative forms like those of the auxiliaries:

*I prefern't to ask him.
*I haten't to win.

In fact the two sentences must be regarded as positive sentences, the form not being associated not with prefer and hate but with to ask and to win. For there are corresponding negative sentences that also contain an auxiliary:

I don't prefer not to ask him.
I don't hate not to win.

The problem is dealt with in greater detail later (9.3.2).

MAY provides a slight problem. There is no negative form *mayn't, but only may not:

*He mayn't come.
He may not come.

Mightn't occurs but is not used by most speakers of American English. But although MAY does not, in respect of negation, function like the other auxiliaries, it satisfies the other tests and has the characteristics of the modals as stated in Chapter 6.

2.2.3 Inversion

The second test of an auxiliary is whether it can come before the subject in certain types of sentence, the order being auxiliary, subject and full verb. The most common type of sentence of this kind is the interrogative. Examples are:

> *Is the boy coming?*
> *Will they be there?*
> *Have you seen them yet?*
> *Ought we to ask them?*

In these the auxiliary comes first, before the subject. The verb phrase is discontinuous, divided by a noun phrase, the subject of the clause. The examples given are all questions, but the test of an auxiliary is not in terms of question. For in the first place, a question may be asked without the use of inversion at all, but merely by using the appropriate intonation, commonly (though not necessarily) a rising intonation:

> *He's coming?*
> *They'll be there?*
> *You've seen them?*

Secondly, inversion is found in sentences that are not questions, especially with *seldom* and *hardly*, and in certain types of conditional sentence:

> *Seldom had they seen such a sight.*
> *Hardly had I left the room, when they began talking about me.*
> *Had I known he was coming, I'd have waited.*

Inversion, then, as the test of an auxiliary is restricted to questions and sentences with initial *hardly, seldom, scarcely, never, nowhere*, words that are described as 'semi-negatives' (2.2.2).

With the four sentences that were considered in the previous section, the test of inversion and its parallelism with negation becomes clear:

> I can come.   Can I come?
> We must go.   Must we go?
> I like it.   *Like I it?
> We saw them.   *Saw we them?

Once again the forms of DO are used:

Do I like it?
Did we see them?

The test shows again that WANT and BEGIN are not auxiliary verbs:

Do I want to ask you?
Did he begin to cry?
*Want I to ask you?
*Began he to cry?

There is a different kind of inversion that does not require an auxiliary verb, as illustrated by:

Down came a blackbird.
Into the room walked John.
In the corner stood an armchair.

The essential feature of these is that there is an adverbial in sentence-initial position. This type of structure will be excluded. A more idiosyncratic exception to the general rule about auxiliaries and inversion is found in a colloquial use of GO:

How goes it?
How goes work?

Alternative forms with little or no difference of meaning are:

How's it goint?
How's work going?

These sentences are used as part of a conventional formula for greeting. Sentences using DO – *How does it go?* are not used in this context.

2.2.4 'Code'

The third characteristic of an auxiliary is its use in what Palmer and Blandford (1939:124–5) called 'avoidance of repetition' and Firth (1968:104) called 'code'. There are sentences in English in which a full verb is later 'picked up' by an auxiliary. The position is very similar to that of a noun being picked up by a pronoun. There are several kinds of sentence in which this feature is found. A type that illustrates it most clearly is one that contains . . . *and so* . . .:

I can come and so can John.
We must go and so must you.
I like it and so do they.
We saw them and so did he.

In none of these examples is the whole verb phrase repeated in
the second part. In all of them the only verbal form after . . .
and so is an auxiliary. Where the first part contains an auxiliary,
it is the auxiliary alone that recurs. Where the first part contains
no auxiliary, once again one of the forms of DO is used. By the
same test WANT and BEGIN are excluded from the class of auxiliary
verbs:

> *I want to ask you and so does Bill.*
> *He began to cry and so did she.*

There are other types of sentence in which the auxiliary is used
in this way. A common use is in question and answer:

> *Can I come?*   *You can.*
> *Must they go?*   *They must.*
> *You saw them?*   *I did.*

Very often there will already be an auxiliary in the question
sentence since inversion is common in questions. But, as the last
pair of sentences shows, if a question is asked without inversion
and without an auxiliary (being marked only by the intonation)
a form of DO is required in the reply.

It is possible to invent quite a long conversation using only
auxiliary verbs. If the initial sentence, which contains the main
verb, is not heard, all the remainder is unintelligible; it is, in fact,
truly in code. The following example is from Firth:

> *Do you think he will?*
> *I don't know. He might.*
> *I suppose he ought to, but perhaps he feels he can't.*
> *Well, his brothers have. They perhaps think he needn't.*
> *Perhaps eventually he may. I think he should, and I very much
> hope he will.*

The 'key to the code' is *join the army*.

2.2.5 Emphatic affirmation

Finally, a characteristic of the auxiliaries is their use in emphatic
affirmation with the accent upon the auxiliary. Examples are:

> *You múst see him.*
> *I cán do it.*
> *We wíll come.*
> *He hás finished it.*

This use of the auxiliaries is not easy to define formally. For any
verbal form may take the accent, *eg:*

I líke it.   *I can cóme.*
We sáw them.   *We must gó.*
I wánt to ask you.
He begán to cry.

What is essential about the use of the auxiliaries is that they are
used for emphatic affirmation of a doubtful statement, or the
denial of the negative:

I cán come.   (You are wrong to think I cannot)
You múst come.   (You do not want to)
We díd see them.   (You thought we did not)

Once again forms of DO occur. Often these forms would have
occurred in the previous utterance which would be a question or
a negation, *I dó like it* being the emphatic affirmative reply to
either *Do you like it?* or *You don't like it.* But this is not necessarily so; the previous sentence might have been *You like it?* or
Perhaps you like it?

2.2.6 DO

DO is a special type of auxiliary, in that it is used only under those
conditions where an auxiliary is obligatory. It occurs only, that
is to say, with negation or inversion or code or emphatic affirmation. It is thus the neutral or 'empty' auxiliary used only where
the grammatical rules of English require an auxiliary:

I don't like it.
Do I like it?
I like it and so does Bill.
I dó like it.

What does not occur is DO in a sentence such as:

*I do like it.   (with *do* unstressed)

(This occurs, however, in some West Country dialects of English
instead of the simple form of the verb.)

Equally DO does not occur where there is already another
auxiliary (which is thus available for negation, etc):

*He doesn't can go.
*Does he will come?
*I may go and so does he.
*He dóes be coming.

The only exception is in the imperative (3.1.1) where it may
occur with BE:

Do be reading when I arrive.

These remarks do not apply to the full verbs BE and HAVE though there are restrictions with them too (8.1.1, 8.2.1).

2.2.7 Non-assertion

Although negation and interrogation have been treated as two of the NICE properties of the auxiliaries, they are usefully handled along with some other features under the heading of 'non-assertion' (Quirk *et al.* 1972:53). An important distinguishing feature of non-assertion is the choice of a whole set of non-assertive words including *any, much, long, far*, which are used instead of *some, a lot of, a long way, a long time*. This is simply illustrated by comparing simple positive forms with negatives and interrogatives:

He has some/a lot of money.
**He has any money.*
?He has much money.
He doesn't have any/much money.
Does he have any/much money?
He went a long way, stayed a long time.
He didn't go far, stay long.
Did he go far, stay long?

(*He went far, stayed long* is less likely in normal speech, but not impossible).

In addition to negation and interrogation, these non-assertive forms also occur with 'semi-negatives'. These include the adverbs noted in 2.2.3, *seldom, never, scarcely, nowhere*, and *no-one, nobody, none, nothing*:

He has scarcely any money.
No-one has much money.
They never stay long.
We seldom went far.

These do not count as negative, however, for the NICE properties, as shown by:

He doesn't go.
**He not goes.*
He never goes.
He seldom goes.

There is, however, one other type of sentence for which the semi-negative must be recognized – the sentence with the so-called 'tag-question':

John's coming, isn't he?
John isn't coming, is he?

These are fairly complex in their variety, especially in terms of
intonation. It is enough to consider those that ask for confir-
mation of a suggestion (most probably, with a falling and then
a rising intonation). With these there is always a reversal of the
positive/negative polarity of the two clauses: if the statement is
positive the tag is negative and vice versa. For this purpose too
semi-negatives functions as negatives requiring positive tags:

No one saw you, did they?
He has never tried, has he?
He has scarcely time, has he?
They are nowhere around, are they?

There is one type of question that needs special notice – the
negative interrogative, *eg*:

Isn't John coming?

This is not a question about the negative *John isn't coming*, but
a particular type of question ('one expecting the answer "Yes"').
It is close to, but not identical with:

John is coming, isn't he?

There is no direct way of questioning the negative or asking a
question expecting the answer 'No'. The closest again uses a tag:

John isn't coming, is he?

Negative interrogatives are still non-assertive.

Non-assertion is particularly important in the analysis of the
modals, especially when dealing with distinctions between MAY,
and CAN, MUST and NEED (6.1.6). It is also relevant for the brief
discussion of NEED and DARE in the next section.

2.2.8 DARE and NEED
DARE and NEED provide some difficulty because:

[i]   in terms of the NICE properties some of their forms are
      forms of auxiliaries, others of full verbs;
[ii] the distribution of the auxiliary forms is defective.

They are clearly shown to be auxiliary verbs in negation and
inversion:

He daren't go.
You needn't ask.

Dare we come?
Need they look?

Moreover, not only are these verbs used here in negation and inversion, but they also have the characteristic of modal auxiliaries in not having an *-s* form. There are no forms **daresn't* or **needsn't*; nor do we say **Dares he . . .?* or **Needs he . . .?* At the same time the full verbs DARE and NEED occur in:

He doesn't dare to go.
You don't need to ask.
Do we dare to come?
Do they need to look?

That they are here full verbs and not auxiliaries is clear from the presence of one of the forms of DO in the negative and inverted form.

Another difference between the auxiliary and the full verb is the structure with which it is associated. The auxiliary is associated with structure 1, being followed by the bare infinitive (see 2.1.1), while the full verb is associated with structure 2, being followed by the *to*-infinitive.

With inversion and negation, then, both the auxiliaries and the full verbs may be used (the latter, of course, with DO). In all other cases only the full verb occurs. This is especially to be noted for the positive non-inverted forms:

He dares to ask me that!   *You dare to come now!*
He needs to have a wash.   *They need to get a new car.*

The reasons for thinking that these are full verbs and not auxiliaries are:

[i] the forms have a final *-s* for the third person singular;
[ii] the structure is 2 (*to*-infinitive), associated with the full verb, and not 1 (bare infinitive), associated with the auxiliary.

These reasons would not in themselves be sufficient criteria for excluding the forms from the auxiliaries since the primary auxiliaries have *-s* forms and the modal OUGHT is associated with structure 2, but since a distinction between full verb and auxiliary is relevant here they are sufficient to link the forms to the full verbs DARE and NEED, rather than the auxiliaries whose characteristics (no *-s* and structure 1) are shown in the negative and inverted forms.

With code and emphatic affirmation the auxiliary forms do not occur unless there is also negation or inversion:

Dare I ask him?   No, you daren't.
I needn't come and neither need you.

(There can be no **Yes you dare* or **. . . and so need, you.*) The full verbs can, of course, occur with DO.

The functions of the auxiliaries and the full verbs are shown in the following table (using only NEED, though a similar statement could be made for DARE):

	AUXILIARY	FULL VERB
positive		*He needs to come.*
negative	*He needn't come.*	*He doesn't need to come.*
inverted	*Need he come?*	*Does he need to come?*
'code'		*He needs to come and so do I.*
emphatic affirmative		*He dóes need to come.*

In fact the auxiliary forms of these verbs occur not only with negation and inversion, but with any type of non-assertion:

> *No one need know.*
> *He hardly dare ask.*
> *He need never know.*
> Cf: *John needs to know.*
> *He even dares to ask.*

They can also occur where the context is negative in meaning but not in form:

> *All he need do is ask.*
> Cf: *All he needs to do is to ask.*

This, of course, has the sense 'He need do nothing more than ask.'

There appears to be a mixture of the characteristics of full verb and auxiliary DARE in negation and inversion when DO is used but the bare infinitive (structure 1) also occurs:

> *I don't dare ask.   I don't dare to ask.*
> *Does he dare ask?   Does he dare to ask?*

The same is true of NEED, but much less commonly:

> *I don't need ask.*   (more commonly . . . *to ask*)
> *Does he need ask?*   (almost always . . . *to ask*)

2.2.9 Primary and modal auxiliaries

Although the discussion so far has been concerned with auxili-

aries as a single class, there is an important distinction between
the primary auxiliaries, and the secondary or modal auxiliaries
(or simply the 'modals').

BE and HAVE plus DO in its special functions are primary auxiliaries: WILL, SHALL, CAN, MAY, MUST, OUGHT, DARE and NEED are
the modals (the last two may also be full verbs).

There are several important formal differences.

[i]   Only the primary auxiliaries have -s forms: is, has and does:
      there are no modal forms *wills, *shalls, *cans, *mays,
      *musts and *oughts. Dares and needs exist, but are forms
      of the full verbs DARE and NEED and not the auxiliaries (see
      2.2.8).

[ii] The modals have no non-finite forms; they therefore cannot
      co-occur, and are restricted to initial position in the verb
      phrase. There are no forms such as *can may go, *must can
      go, etc. By contrast BE and HAVE (but not DO) have finite
      forms and so can co-occur and can occur other than in initial
      position in the verb phrase: has been singing, has been hurt,
      must be singing, must have sung. There are, however, strict
      limitations on their co-occurrence, with a restriction to the
      bare infinitives be and have (the to-infinitives after OUGHT),
      the -ing form being and the -en form been.

On the basis of the distinction between primary and modal
auxiliary it is possible to set up two sets of paradigms. The first,
the primary paradigms, involve both the form with no auxiliary
and those with primary auxiliaries only the second, the modal
paradigm, is based upon the primary paradigms with the addition
of a modal verb in initial position in the verb phrase. These
paradigms are set out in full in 3.1.1 and 5.1.1.

There are basically, then, four types of verb for the purposes
of this book, two kinds of auxiliary, other verbs that combine in
a somewhat similar way (the catenatives, which are the subject
of Ch. 9) and the full verbs, which fit none of these categories:

1. Primary auxiliaries BE, HAVE, DO.
2. Secondary or modal auxiliaries WILL, SHALL, CAN, MAY, MUST,
   OUGHT, DARE, NEED.
3. Catenatives KEEP, WANT, LIKE and SEE and many others.
4. The remaining full verbs.

2.3 Types of verb phrase

There are two further issues that concern all the types of verb
phrase being discussed here.

2.3.1 Simple and complex phrases

Sequences of verb forms such as *has been running, may have run, keeps wanting to run* will all be referred to as 'verb phrases'. But the term 'verb phrase' could be restricted to phrases within a single clause and it could have been argued that, in the last example above, there is subordination involving three clauses and, therefore, three verb phrases *keeps, wanting* and *to run*.

However, the use of 'verb phrase' to cover all these sequences is very useful because of the close relationships between the forms in the sequences. All will in fact be referred to, then, as 'verb phrases' but with a distinction between 'simple' and 'complex' phrases, the latter involving subordination and more than one phrase in the other sense of that term. There are, however, some problems with the distinction, no matter how it is described. For the immediate discussion of the problem it is easier to think in terms of one verb phrase versus several.

One way of treating a form such as *has taken* is to say that it is the perfect form of the verb lexeme TAKE. That assigns to the two-word sequence the same kind of grammatical status as that of single words in another language (*eg* Latin *amavi* 'I have loved'). Yet at the same time *taken* is a form of the full verb TAKE, and *has* is an auxiliary, and while the full verb indicates the lexical meaning the auxiliary refers to the grammatical category 'perfect' (or rather 'phase', see 3.1.3). But there is only one verb phrase here, and that verb phrase contains only one full verb (though it may also contain one or more auxiliaries). In contrast, *remembered coming* is not a form of the lexeme COME, but a sequence of forms of the lexemes REMEMBER and COME. Moreover, there is some structural similarity between:

I remembered coming.
I remembered that I came.

In the second of these there is subordination. That involves two clauses and therefore two verb phrases.

More problematic are forms such as *may have run*, which contain modal auxiliaries. Although the idiosyncratic NICE properties link modal auxiliaries with primary auxiliaries, it could be argued that syntactically, at least, they do not function like the primary auxiliaries, but like the catenatives. If so there would be two phrases here, not one.

There are, however, other criteria that may be used to establish whether there is a single verb phrase or a sequence of verb phrases. First, it may be assumed that tense (and any other verb category) will occur only once in a phrase. If tense is marked more than once there will be more than one phrase. Secondly, the same may be true of negation; a single phrase will not be negated more than once. Thirdly, a sentence with a single clause can be passivized quite simply; passivization then identifies a single clause and a single phrase. (See 2.3.2).

However, as suggested above, it is simpler to use the terms 'simple' and 'complex' phrase; sequence of phrases in the sense just used are described as complex phrases. These criteria are used, therefore, to distinguish simple and complex phrases. They do not, however, provide an absolute distinction between simple and complex phrases, but they are sufficient to confirm the distinction between primary auxiliaries, modals and catenatives. Phrases involving primary auxiliaries are fairly clearly simple, while those with catenatives are complex (though not all pass all the tests). Phrases with modals lie somewhere between the two, sharing characteristics of both simple and complex phrases.

We need recognize no grammatical relations between the elements of the verb phrase except subordination (and the 'identity relations' of 9.1.3). Indeed the notion of verb phrase allows us to avoid many problems of a quite insoluble kind. Some scholars have interpreted the later elements of the verb phrase as being complements, objects, etc of the preceding element, so that *is swimming* is likened to *is happy*, though not, one hopes, so that *has gone* is likened to *has a dog*. Even Jespersen (1909–49. Pt V: 171) argued that *can* takes the following form as its object; thus *swim* is the object of *can* in *can swim*, in spite of the fact that we cannot say **can cricket*. There is no virtue in this line of argument. Nothing is gained by talking of objects, etc; everything that can be said is said in terms of the structure of the verb phrase.

It is rather more tempting to see objects, etc in the complex phrase where *keeps talking* looks like *keeps quiet* and *likes swimming* looks like *likes chocolate*. But even here there are counter arguments (see 9.3.3). The notion of the complex phrase remains a useful one; both the semantics and the syntax of the forms can be fully accounted for in terms of its structure.

2.3.2 Auxiliary and full verb
Although in this work and in most description of the English verb the auxiliaries are distinguished from the other verbs, notably the catenatives, it has been argued (*eg* Huddleston 1976:333) that the distinction cannot be maintained and that all auxiliaries should be treated as 'full' verbs ('full' verbs in this sense including the catenatives). In effect this means that any sequence of auxiliary

and another verbal form should be treated as a verb with a subordinate clause and that there would be no difference, therefore, in the overall syntactic structure of any of the following:

John is coming.
John may come.
John wants to come.
John said that he came.

The arguments depend in part upon the linguistic model being used, but also upon the fact that there is no clear line between auxiliaries, catenatives and other verbs that may have subordinate clauses.

The argument is not a very fruitful one, and not particularly relevant to the purpose of this book, but it may be as well to look briefly at the issues.

The first point concerns the status of the NICE properties. These can clearly be used to identify the auxiliaries, but it is argued that they are merely idiosyncratic features of a group of verbs and not therefore good grounds for making an important distinction. There is also the fact that BE and HAVE even when they are full verbs and not auxiliaries (8.1.1, 8.2.1) still have the NICE properties.

Against this three points may be made.

[i]   The four NICE properties define almost exactly the same set of verbs; this is hardly an unimportant characteristic.

[ii] The auxiliaries have much in common semantically: the primary auxiliaries are the exponents of basic verbal categories and the modals the exponents of modality, which is associated with the verb in many languages.

[iii] The properties themselves have something in common in that they are largely concerned with basic discourse functions of denying, questioning, answering and affirming.

These considerations suggest that they are important. The fact that the full verbs BE and HAVE also have these properties is not, perhaps, a strong counter-argument. Such verbs are often idiosyncratic in languages and it would not be very strange if they adopted the characteristics of the auxiliaries, when they themselves were lexically identical with them.

A second point concerns the paradigms and the possible sequence of forms. Although *has been talking* is possible *is having talked* is not. Attempts have been made to provide a semantic explanation for this, but the fact is that the latter sequence is completely ruled out in the way that semantic anomalies are not. There is also the point that modals may occur only as the first form of the sequence – *may be coming* but not **is maying come*. The counter-argument that this results from the fact that the modal verbs have no non-finite forms is hardly convincing. It is more reasonable to suppose that, conversely, they have no non-finite forms because they do not occur except in initial position.

Thirdly, there are what have been called the TNP tests – those of tense, negation and passivization. For tense the issue is that where a full verb is used with another, both may be independently marked for tense (or more strictly for time) *eg*:

John seems to have seen Mary yesterday.
John intended to come tomorrow.

Here there is a sequence of present-past and past-future. There appears to be no possibility of double time marking in:

John has come.
John is coming.

However, it is possible to say:

John was coming tomorrow.

It is even possible to say:

Yesterday John was coming tomorrow.

This would appear to be an example of double time marking. But if this is evidence for two full verbs it is difficult to see how the forms *started* is explained in:

They had to leave early as they started work the next day.

There is double time marking here (*started* is both past and future), but only one verb. Tense/time is not then a very clear test, though, for the most part, there is no double time marking when auxiliary verbs are used.

The argument for negation is similar. All of the following are possible:

John prefers to come.
John doesn't prefer to come.
John prefers not to come.
John doesn't prefer not to come.

But there is only one negative with the primary auxiliaries:

John isn't coming.
John hasn't come.

(*John isn't not coming, *John hasn't not come are, perhaps, just possible, but only as deliberately unnatural forms.) Some of the modals, however, appear to allow separate and double negation. In this respect they are more like full verbs (see 6.1.3).

A final test is that of 'voice neutrality', ie whether, if the whole verbal complex is treated as the verb phrase involved in the passivization, the resultant passive form with its switched noun phrases has not changed the meaning. The primary auxiliaries certainly seem to be voice neutral:

John has seen Bill.
Bill has been seen by John.
John is writing a book.
A book is being written by John.

But there is no voice neutrality in:

John wants to meet Mary.
Mary wants to be met by John.
*Mary is wanted to meet by John.

In fact, the passivization test works fairly well. The modals are on the whole voice netural:

John may have seen Mary.
Mary may have been seen by John.

Yet there is no voice neutrality if will is used in its volition sense (7.1.2):

John won't meet Mary.
Mary won't be met by John.

The TNP tests are, then, rather inconclusive.

There is one final and quite important point. In general an auxiliary is independent of the subject of the sentence in the sense that there are usually no restrictions on the choice of subject in terms of the auxiliary verb; what restrictions there are depend on the first full verb. Thus:

The water runs down the street.
The water is running down the street.
The water may run down the street.
*The water intended to run down the street.

This suggests that it is the full verb that is the head or main verb of the verb phrase and that auxiliaries are modifiers (and indeed that is part of what may be meant by 'auxiliary verb').

Chapter 3

Tense and phase

This chapter and the next two are concerned with the categories associated with the primary auxiliaries and the primary paradigm. Tense and phase are discussed here, aspect in Chapter 4 and voice in Chapter 5.

3.1 Characteristics of the primary auxiliaries

The first section of the chapter discusses the primary paradigms and the categories involved.

3.1.1 The paradigms

The basic primary paradigm for the verb TAKE is:

(1)	takes			
(2)	took			
(3)	is		taking	
(4)	was		taking	
(5)	has	taken		
(6)	had	taken		
(7)	has	been	taking	
(8)	had	been	taking	
(9)	is			taken
(10)	was			taken
(11)	is		being	taken
(12)	was		being	taken
(13)	has	been		taken
(14)	had	been		taken
(15)	has	been	being	taken (?)
(16)	had	been	being	taken (?)

The columning is deliberate; tense is marked in the first column, while the second, third and fourth columns indicate partial markers of phase, aspect and voice respectively.

There are two important characteristics of the forms that justify their treatment in this paradigmatic fashion. First, they are a closed class: these are the only sequences formed from BE and HAVE followed by *-en* and *-ing* forms and containing only one full verb. There are, however, other sequences involving BE and HAVE with *to*-infinitives which are excluded from this paradigm:

> *He is to come tomorrow.*
> *He has to come tomorrow.*

These are more like modal verbs than primary auxiliaries and are discussed in 6.6 and 8.1.2.

Secondly, each form in the paradigm is essentially a whole. They cannot be analysed either formally or semantically in terms of the individual (word) forms of which they are composed, except in the morphological description of these (word) forms. Analysis in terms of the syntactical structures with which they are associated (*ie* that BE is followed by the *-ing* form and by the *-en* form and that HAVE is followed by the *-en* form only) is insufficient, since this will not rule out the following, which are not possible:

> **is been taking*
> **is being been taken*
> **was had taken*
> **was having taken*
> **is being had been having taken* etc

Moreover, the grammatical categories in terms of which the forms of the paradigm are to be analysed (3.1.2) and the semantic features associated with these categories cut right across word division in these forms. The position is different from that of sequences involving catenatives, where the analysis of, *eg: He kept asking her to help him get it finished* may be handled entirely in terms of the semantic and syntactic characteristics of the verbs KEEP, ASK, HELP and GET.

Forms 15 and 16 are marked with a question mark; there is some doubt if they are possible. They are marked in one grammar (Palmer and Blandford 1939:131) as 'wanting', yet another offers (Hill 1958:220)

> *John had been being scolded by Mary for a long time when the neighbours came in.*

There is a place for them semantically, but they often seem to be avoided, presumably because of their complexity.

The paradigm stated is one of several. Further paradigms may be set up by taking into account:

[i] the different forms associated with number and person, the paradigm here being for the third person singular (for the first person singular replace *takes* by *take*, *is* by *am*, and *has* by *have*, and for all other forms replace *takes* by *take*, *is* by *are*, *was* by *were*, and *has* by *have*);

[ii] the forms used in negation, inversion, etc (replace *takes* by *does take* or *do take* and *took* by *did take*).

The paradigms required for non-finite verbal forms (the infinitivals and participials) and for phrases containing imperatives have fewer forms. The paradigm of infinitival forms contains exactly half the number found in the basic paradigms, one form corresponding to each consecutive pair (there being no tense distinction – see 3.1.2). For the participials the number is further reduced in that there are no forms containing two consecutive *-ing* forms. The possibilities are, then:

	INFINITIVALS	PARTICIPIALS
(1/2)	*to take*	*taking*
(3/4)	*to be taking*	(no *being taking*)
(5/6)	*to have taken*	*having taken*
(7/8)	*to have been taking*	*having been taking*
(9/10)	*to be taken*	*being taken*
(11/12)	*to be being taken*	(no *being being taken*)
(13/14)	*to have been taken*	*having been taken*
(15/16)	*to have been being taken* (?)	*having been being taken* (?)

Phrases containing imperatives are still further limited in number in that there are none containing HAVE forms. Semantically there seems no reason to exclude *Have taken*, *Have been taking*, etc, but these forms do not exist. But the four other forms are to be found – *Take*, *Be taking*, *Be taken* and (possibly) *Be being taken*. (It might, admittedly, be difficult to attest all the forms with TAKE which is here chosen solely as a model, particularly the last two, but there is nothing odd about *Be dressed* and (with less certainty) *Be being dressed*.)

The infinitivals and participials may all be preceded by *not*; these are the negative forms. But the negative and emphatic forms of the phrases with imperatives require special treatment. Neither BE nor HAVE provide any negative imperative forms;

haven't occurs, but not as an imperative, while **ben't* simply does not occur (8.1.1). *Don't* is the only negative form; all the negative forms of the paradigms contain *don't* – *don't take, don't be taking, don't be taken*, (?) *don't be being taken*. In addition there are the emphatic *dó take, dó be taking, dó be taken*, (?) *dó be being taken*. Apart from the first, which is regular, these are unexpected since emphatic imperatives could simply be marked by accenting *be* – and *bé taking, bé taken*, (?) *bé being taken* are possible. Yet it is not surprising that the emphatic forms here, as elsewhere, have the same characteristic (occurrence of DO) as the negatives. A set of examples to illustrate the negative and emphatic forms is:

> *Don't be reading when I come in!*
> *Do be reading when I come in!*
> *Be reading when I come in!*

3.1.2 The four categories

The sixteen forms in the basic paradigm of the primary pattern can be divided into two sets of eight in four different ways, each division being in terms of a formal feature (which is later linked to a semantic one). Each form is thus characterized in four different ways, and distinguished from all the others in these terms. If sixteen forms are admitted there are no gaps: all the possibilities occur; but, as was seen, only fourteen of them can be positively accepted.

First, the forms may be classified in terms of tense, past and present. Present tense (phrase) forms are defined as those containing present tense (word) forms. The word forms are, of course, defined morphologically, *takes, is* and *has* being present and *took, was* and *had* past. In the paradigm the odd-numbered forms are present and the even-numbered ones past; the difference of tense is marked in the first column of the table (3.1.1).

Secondly, a distinction in terms of aspect, progressive and non-progressive, may be made, progressive forms being those that contain both a form of BE and an *-ing* form (occurring in column three). Every second pair in the paradigm (beginning with 3 and 4) is progressive. The terms 'continuous' and 'non-continuous' are sometimes used. So too are 'habitual' and 'non-habitual' (habitual = non-progressive) but these are to be rejected as misleading (see 4.2.2).

Thirdly, the forms are to be classified in terms of phase (see Joos 1964:126, 138), perfect or non-perfect, the perfect forms being those that contain a form of HAVE, which is always followed

by an -*en* form (in column two). The first four and the third set
of four (9 to 12) are non-perfect, and the others perfect.

Finally, the traditional category of voice, active and passive,
distinguishes those forms that contain both a form of BE and an
-*en* form (passive) from those that do not (active). The first eight
are active and the last eight passive. There is some superficial
resemblance between the passive and the perfect since both are
defined in terms of one of the two auxiliaries plus an -*en* form.
But the place of the -*en* forms in the phrase is different, as is
shown by the columning of the paradigm. The form associated
with the perfect is always second while that associated with the
passive is always last (in column four), with in each case the
relevant form of the auxiliary preceding it. Structurally, then, the
two are quite different.

This analysis provides a basis, indeed the only satisfactory
basis, for more detailed analysis of the forms. In particular it
should be noted that there is no place for a 'future tense' (3.2.1).

3.1.3 Outline of uses

[i]   The progressive indicates action in progress, *ie* activity
      continuing throughout a period of time. In this sense it can
      be said to be durational. By contrast, the non-progressive
      merely reports an action (rather than an activity), without
      suggesting or indicating that it has duration. This is shown
      by comparing:

      He walked to the station.
      He was walking to the station.

      The first sentence simply gives the information that he
      walked to the station; the second indicates that the walking
      is continued through a period of time. There is no sugges-
      tion that there are two kinds of activity, one without and
      one with duration, but simply that attention is drawn in the
      one case to its durational aspect. The reasons for drawing
      attention to this are various; a common one is to show that
      the period of time during which the activity took place
      overlapped a briefer period or a point in time:

      When I met him, he was walking to the station.
      He was walking to the station at ten this morning.

[ii] Tense and phase are initially best handled together, in order
      to make the point, not usually made, that both are essen-
      tially concerned with time relations. The time features are
      most simply illustrated by considering progressive forms,
      which involve a period of time:

I'm reading at the moment.
I've been reading since three o'clock.
I was reading when he came.
I'd been reading for an hour when he came.

The present non-perfect refers to a period of time in the present, a vague period that includes both past and future time but overlaps the present moment. The past non-perfect refers to a similar time in the past, which may overlap an indicated point of time in the past; it does not extend to the present. The perfect forms indicate periods of time that specifically began before and continued up to (possibly overlapping) a point of time, the present moment in the case of the present tense, and a point of time in the past in the case of the past tense. The four possibilities may be shown diagrammatically:

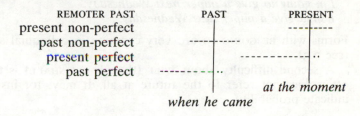

With the perfect the initial point of the period may be indicated, *eg*, by *four an hour*, or *since Tuesday*, as well as the later point.

3.2 Tense

Tense appears to have three distinct functions, first to mark purely temporal relations of past and present time, secondly in the sequence of tenses that is mainly relevant for reported speech and thirdly to mark 'unreality', particularly in conditional clauses and wishes. But a clear distinction must first be drawn between tense and time, and it will be necessary to consider whether the three functions are really different.

3.2.1 Time and tense

The traditional statement of tense in terms of present, past and future, exemplified by *I take*, *I took* and *I shall take*, has no place in the analysis presented here. The basic reason for this is quite simply that while *I take* and *I took* are comparable within the analysis, in that they exemplify the formal category of tense as established in the primary paradigm, *I shall take* belongs to the modal paradigm, and ought not to be handled together with the other two.

There are other reasons to justify the decision not to make a simple grammatical distinction between future and present/past. One is that some forms of the primary paradigm may refer to the future:

I'm giving a paper next Wednesday.
I give my paper next Wednesday.

Moreover, even in terms of future time reference, there is little justification for the selection of WILL and SHALL as the markers of future tense, for there are four common constructions used to refer to future time, the two already exemplified plus those illustrated by:

I'm going to give a paper next Wednesday.
I shall give a paper next Wednesday.

Forms with BE GOING TO are very common in colloquial speech (see 7.3).

A second difficulty about WILL (though not SHALL) is that it often does not refer to the future at all. It may, for instance, indicate probability:

That'll be the postman.

or it may refer to characteristic habitual activity:

She'll sit for hours watching television.

Even when it refers to the future it may suggest not mere futurity, but willingness as in:

Will you come?

This is different from *Are you coming?* see 7.2.3. It is, moreover, characteristic of the other modal auxiliaries that they may refer to the future (though with additional reference to ability, probability, etc) as in:

I can/may/must/ought to come tomorrow.

There is clearly an overriding case for handling WILL and SHALL with the other modal auxiliaries and not together with the distinction of past and present tense that belongs to the primary paradigm.

3.2.2 Time relations
The most important function of tense is to indicate past and present time. The distinction is very clear in:

> *He's reading the paper at this moment.*
> *He was reading the paper when I saw him this morning.*

But there are three reservations to make.

[i]   Present time must be understood to mean any period of time that includes the present moment. It includes, therefore, 'all time' as in:

> *The sun rises in the east.*
> *Water boils at 100° Centigrade.*

Past time excludes the present moment. Past time may seem to be the 'marked member' of the pair, in that it specifically excludes the present moment. Present time is any period of time, short, long or eternal that includes the present moment.

[ii] There is one exception only to the statement in [i], the so-called historic present. There are many examples of this in literary English, but it is also to be found in speech, *eg*:

> *He just walks into the room and sits down in front of the fire without saying a word to anyone.*

The traditional explanation of this usage, that it recalls or recounts the past as vividly as if it were present, is adequate. It seems highly probable that it is not specifically English but a characteristic of many, if not all, languages that make time distinctions in the verb.

[iii] The use of tense is complicated by its relation to the temporal characteristics of phase and by the habitual and future uses of the forms (which are dealt with in later sections).

The adverbials that are used with tense (present and past) are of four kinds. First, there are those that may be used with past tense only, *last week, yesterday, last year, a long time ago*. Secondly, there are those that may be used with present tense only; *now, at this moment, at the present time*. Thirdly, there are those that may be used with either, though the period of time to which they refer includes the present moment. These are *today, this week, this year* etc, as in:

He was working today.
He's working today.

When these are used with the past, the activity is shown as taking place within the period indicated by the adverbial, but before the present moment. Fourthly, there are adverbials that indicate past or present time according to the time at which the utterance is made, and for this reason may be used with past or present forms. Examples are *this morning, this afternoon* and *this summer*. *This morning* is present if it is still morning, but past if the morning is over. In the afternoon *this morning* will occur with past tense forms. To complicate matters, these adverbials also function like the previous set. *This morning*, for instance, can be used not only with present tense forms but also with past tense forms, while it is still morning, to refer to an earlier event that same morning.

3.2.3 Reported speech
Most commonly when someone reports what someone else has said he does not simply repeat the actual words but uses what is usually termed 'indirect speech'. Thus there is a difference between the first and second pair:

> *John said 'I like chocolate'.*
> *John said 'I'm reading "Vanity Fair"'.*
> *John said he liked chocolate.*
> *John said he was reading 'Vanity Fair'.*

It is a normal rule in English with indirect speech, that, if the verb of reporting is in the past tense, any present tense form in the original utterance will be reported in the past tense, as shown by the examples above.

This is usually explained in terms of 'sequence of tenses'. Yet this rule is not automatic since it is possible in such circumstances to retain the original, present tense, form, not to change to the past:

> *John said he likes chocolate.*
> *John said he's reading 'Vanity Fair'.*

To explain this, it is necessary to consider the fact that it is not only tense that is involved in the change, but also adverbials of time, adverbials of place and personal pronouns. This can be illustrated by an utterance by Mary and its report by John:

> (Mary)   *I'm working here today.*
> (John)   *Mary said she was working there yesterday.*

The explanation lies in what may be called 'deictic shift'. There are, in most, perhaps all, languages, a number of deictic expressions whose precise interpretation depends on who is speaking and to whom, plus where and when the act of speaking takes place. The most obvious deictic expressions are:

Time: *now, today*, present tense, *then, yesterday*, past tense.
Place: *here, this, there, that*.
Person: *I, you, he, she, it, they*.

The point about deictic shift is that the original speaker (here Mary) uses the deictics appropriate to her, and the speaker who reports what was said (here John) uses the deictics appropriate to him. Instead of Mary's *I*, present tense, *here* and *today*, John uses the deictics *she*, past tense, *there* and *yesterday* (provided he is speaking in a different place and on the following day).

In English, although there must be a change in the other deictics, there is a choice for the second speaker between changing to past tense or retaining the original present tense. This depends on whether the statement being reported is still true for him. If it is, he may (but is not required to) retain the present tense. Thus in the examples above the retention of the present tense would imply that the speaker believes that John still likes chocolate and that he is still reading 'Vanity Fair'. It follows, of course, that the present tense cannot be retained if the time adverbials are changed to past:

*Mary said she's working there yesterday.
(Mary said she's working there today.)

Similarly consider:

I'm looking forward to the summer.
I'm looking forward to Christmas.

In November (after the summer, but before Christmas) only the second could be reported with the present tense:

He said he was looking forward to the summer.
!He said he's looking forward to the summer.
He said he was looking forward to Christmas.
He said he's looking forward to Christmas.

Quite often the use of the present tense form indicates that what is said is something that the speaker believes to be true (in general rather than in time relations). Consider (Jespersen 1909–49, IV:156):

The ancients thought that the sun moved round the earth; they did not know that it is the earth that moves round the sun.

The first sentence uses the past tense because the speaker does not believe it to be true, but the second has the present tense because the speaker (and others) accept it as true. Even with a generally accepted truth like this, however, it is not obligatory to use the present tense. There would be nothing strange about *. . . was . . . moved . . .* in the example given.

If there are two verbs in the original utterance one may involve switch, the other not, depending on the speaker's attitude. This is even possible where one is in a subordinate clause:

I'll visit you when the weather is finer.
He said he would visit us when the weather was finer.
He said he will visit us when the weather is finer.
He said he would visit us when the weather is finer.

In the last example the speaker does not suggest that he believes the visit will take place, but he foresees the weather being finer.

If the verb of the original statement is already in the past it is normally reported in the same form:

I was reading when she came.
He said he was reading when she came.

But a past non-perfect tense form may also be reported by a past perfect form which then functions as a 'past-past' (see also 3.3.3):

I saw him yesterday.
He said he had seen him the day before.

Although the events referred to can be seen as past-past because they were already past for the original speaker speaking in the past, they can equally be seen, from the second speaker's point of view, as simply past. He is free, that is to say, to see them as simply past or as past-past. Unless he wishes to emphasize that they are past-past, *ie* that they were past for the original speaker, he would normally report them with the simple past, not using deictic shift.

The past perfect also, of course, reports the present perfect, and it is the only form available to report the past perfect:

I've already seen him.
I'd already seen him.
He said he'd already seen him.

There are, then, only two possible forms with deictic shift (the

past and the past-past/past-perfect) corresponding to four possible forms in the original:

ORIGINAL	REPORTED
I see	
I saw	*he saw*
I have seen	*he had seen*
I had seen	

3.2.4 Related issues

Deictic shift may also be used to explain what is sometimes called
'future in the past' as in:

> *John was coming tomorrow.*

The essential point here is that it was said or believed in the past
that John would be coming tomorrow. Although there is no
actual verb of reporting, one can be 'understood', and the
sentence is then exactly like:

> *John said/believed that he was coming tomorrow.*

This is commonest with the progressive form. It is less easy to
contextualize:

> ?(Yesterday) *John came tomorrow.*

However, this might be possible if the original belief or statement
was 'John comes tomorrow'. A more natural example of a simple
past is:

> *At that time they didn't come till next week.*

However, where there is no verb of reporting, it is not only
past tense that may be used to indicate the temporal characteristic of the statement. This is clear from sentences such as those
that relate to the proverbial boasting of the fishermen:

> *Yesterday the fish was four feet long.*
> *It's always been four feet long.*
> *It had always been four feet long.*

Other verbs that express time relations may be similarly used
(WILL, BE GOING TO, USED TO):

> *Tomorrow the fish will be four feet long.*
> *Tomorrow the fish is going to be four feet long.*
> *The fish used to be four feet long.*

Nor is this confined to verbs that indicate time. Verbs of process (9.2.5) may equally be involved:

When he grew old, the fish began to be four feet long.
When he grew old, the fish stopped being four feet long.

These are not all strictly examples of deictic shift. But they are all concerned with the status of the proposition expressed from the point of view of the speaker.

Rather different, perhaps, but still involving time/tense relations and the speaker is what may be called 'displaced' time marking as in (Lakoff 1970:839):

The animal you saw was my dog.
The man you'll be talking to will be the Mayor.

The sentences are quite normal even if the animal still is my dog, or the man already is the Mayor. Here we have not only past tense, but also *will* for future time reference (7.2). BE GOING and USED are not normally used in the same way, though they may be possible if the time is not already marked in a relative clause:

The man next to me used to be the Mayor.
The man next to me is going to be the Mayor.

These are ambiguous. The most likely interpretation is that the man who is or was next to me used to be or is going to be the mayor, but they could also mean that it used to be or is going to be the case that the man next to me is the mayor. The time reference in the verbs may relate either to the man being the mayor, or to my sitting next to him.

3.2.5 Unreality
The past tense is also used for what may be called 'unreality', though there are three types:

[i]   It is used to express a tentative or polite attitude in questions and requests:

I wanted to ask you about that.
Did you want to speak to me?

These are a little more tentative or polite than:

I want to ask you about that.
Do you want to speak to me?

This 'tentative' use of the past tense is not common with primary paradigm forms, but is much more common with the modals (6.1.1).

[ii]   It is always used in the *if* clause of 'unreal' conditions (7.4):

> *If he came, he would find out.*

The 'real' condition is:

> *If he comes, he will find out.*

Similar to this are clauses introduced by *supposing* and some relative clauses that must be regarded as also being part of 'unreal' conditions:

> *Supposing we asked him, what would he do?*
> *Anyone who said that would be crazy.*

Belonging to this pattern is the almost fossilized *If I were you*. Only in this form is *were* used regularly with *I* in spoken English. *If I was you* might be regarded as substandard English, but in other cases *was* or *were* are both possible. There is a choice between:

> *If I were rich . . . If I were to ask him . . .*
> *If I was rich . . .   If I was to ask him . . .*

It is only in unreal conditions that this form *were* occurs. In past real ('hypothetical') conditions (see 7.4.2) only *was* will occur with *I, he, she, it* and singular nouns:

> *If he was here, he was in the garden.*
> **If he were here, he was in the garden.*

[iii] It is found in wishes and statements of the type *It is time . . .*:

> *I wish I knew.*
> *It's time we went.*

Sentences beginning *If only* are perhaps to be handled here, though they might equally be treated as unreal conditions:

> *If only I understood what you are saying.*

It has been suggested (Joos 1964:121) that the use of unreality and the past time use of the past tense are essentially the same, that the past tense is the 'remote' tense, remote in time or in reality. There is some attractiveness in this idea, for tense could then be seen to have but a single use (for the sequence of tenses, too, can be easily explained in terms of time and deictic shift). Nevertheless there is a clear semantic difference between past time and unreality, and, unless some answer can be given to the question why they are associated in a single form, nothing is gained by the use of a single label.

Traditional grammarians would object that the unreality use is essentially the subjunctive, but the notion of a subjunctive mood is a simple transfer from Latin and has no place in English grammar, since all the potential subjunctives turn out to be past tense in form (or to be the simple uninflected form as in *God save the Queen*). Even the formal *If I were you* does not prove the existence of a subjunctive. For this 'subjunctive' *were* is a normal past, like *loved* or *took*, in that it has just the one form: by contrast the more common past tense of BE has two forms, *was* and *were*, and in this respect it is unique. What requires explanation, then, is not *were*, but *was*. *Were* is a morphologically irregular, but otherwise normal, past tense form like *loved, took*, etc. But *was* is completely anomalous because it is the only form in English that marks singular past tense (indeed it is the only verb form that wholly marks singular in any tense, since the *-s* form of the verb applies only to third person). Talking about the subjunctive fails to explain this.

The use of sequence of tenses or deictic shift, with past tense verbs of reporting, has already been discussed but only when the tense of the verb of reporting marks past time. Where a past tense form is used for unreality, deictic shift appears to be optional:

> *You might think he'd finished it.*
> *I could say I was coming.*
> *You might think he's finished it.*
> *I could say I'm coming.*

Strictly, this is not deictic shift in that time relations are not involved. But the same principle is involved: the actual speaker is able to choose whether or not to associate himself formally with the 'unreality' of what is being reported.

3.3 Phase

Phase is best seen as the marker of a complex set of time relations. Though there are several possibilities, all of them share the characteristic that what is involved is a period of time that began before, but continued right up to, a point of time which may itself be present or past according to the tense used.

3.3.1 Time relations
There is no problem with activity going on throughout the period of time as in:

I've been reading for an hour.
I'd been reading for an hour when he came.

With the first (present tense) the activity began an hour before, and continued right up to, the present; in the second (past tense) it began an hour before, and continued right up to, the past point of time indicated by the adverbial clause.

The adverbials associated with tense are the same with the perfect forms as with the non-perfect. That is to say *last week, yesterday* occur with past (perfect) tense forms, *now, at this moment* only with present (perfect) tense forms, *today, this week* with either, while the use of *this morning, this afternoon* etc depends upon the actual time of speaking. What is important here is that the adverbials that are used only with past tense forms are used only with the past perfect, but not with the present perfect, even although the present perfect appears to have reference to the past in that it refers to activity that began in the past. It is not normal to say:

*I've been reading yesterday.

In addition to the adverbials used with tense, there are some that are specifically associated with the perfect. These are the adverbial clauses and phrases beginning with *since* (*since Tuesday, since we met*). They indicate the starting point of the period of time.

Adverbials beginning with *since* are used only with perfect forms, except, rarely, with progressive forms used for limited duration (4.3.2):

I've been reading since three o'clock.
I'd been reading since three o'clock.
*I'm reading since three o'clock.
*I was reading since three o'clock.

Adverbials beginning with *for* (*for an hour*, etc) are also often used with perfect forms, but they are not restricted to them. The restrictions on adverbials of this kind are to be stated in terms of aspect.

3.3.2 'Results'
In spite of the simple picture set out in the previous section there is a problem where it is clear that the activity does *not* continue throughout the relevant period of time. This is likely with action verbs, since their activity is without marked duration:

I've cut my finger.

He's painted his house.
Have you seen him?

A common explanation of such examples is that the perfect is used where the activity has results in the present. This is, however, rather misleading unless results include nil results as shown by:

I've hit it twice, but it's still standing up.
I've written, but they haven't replied.

A more accurate explanation is in terms of current relevance (Twaddell 1965: 6), that in some way or other (not necessarily in its results) the action is relevant to something observable at the present. The past perfect may similarly be treated in terms of activity occurring before, but relevant to, a point of time in the past.

Examples such as these in no way refute the suggestion made earlier that phase refers, like tense, to features of time, and that the perfect indicates a period of time preceding but continuing up to a later point of time (present or past). This can be illustrated from the present perfect, though similar considerations hold for the past perfect too. Examples of present perfect (non-progressive) forms are:

I've seen John this morning.
I've mended it three times today.
He's written the letter.

In all three cases, the activity took place in the past. The same actions could have been reported by past tense forms:

I saw John this morning.
I mended it three times today.
He wrote the letter.

What this shows is that the periods of time indicated by the present perfect and the past (non-perfect) overlap, and that an action performed in the past may be included in either of them. The interpretation in terms of time reference that accounts for *I've been reading* equally accounts for the perfect forms exemplified here: the actions took place in a period of time that began in the past and continued right up to the present.

The problem is to establish what determines the choice of the present perfect rather than the past in these cases, but the question is best asked in the form, 'Why is the activity placed in the period of time indicated by the present perfect rather than the period indicated by the simple past, since it occurred within them both?' The answer is in terms of current relevance. A period of time that includes the present is chosen precisely because there are features of the present that directly link it to the past activity. The temporal situation being envisaged by the speaker is one that includes the present; the present perfect, is, therefore, used. Examples are:

I've bought a new suit.
I've finished my homework.
They've left the district.

In all of these there are features of the present which form part of the whole relevant situation set out in time. The new suit may be displayed at the time of speaking, or the implication may be 'I shan't be untidy any more'. The child who says 'I've finished my homework' is probably asking to be allowed to go out to play now. The information 'They've left the district' tells us that we shan't find them, that it's no use calling on them any more. Other examples, with comments, are:

I've cut my finger.   (It's still bleeding)
He's broken the window.   (It hasn't been mended)
I've told you already.   (You are stupid *or* I won't tell you again)
They've fallen in the river.   (They need help *or* Their clothes are wet)
You've had an accident.   (I can see the bruises)

The insistence on the interpretation of phase in terms of periods of time is partly justified by the fact that it makes possible a single statement for all the perfect forms, and does not need to handle current relevance as a special meaning of the perfect, unrelated to its other uses. But it is wholly confirmed by a consideration of the adverbials that are collocated with the present perfect and past tense forms, for an adverbial that indicates purely past time is not used with a present perfect. This rules out *They've come last Monday*, though an adverbial that indicates a period that includes the present is possible – *They've come this week*. An explanation simply in terms of results or current relevance cannot account for this, for it would not exclude *They've come last Monday* with the meaning that they came on Monday and are still here. English might be the richer if this were possible, for as it is a single phrase cannot combine the two pieces of information about (i) arrival at a specific time in the past and (ii) the current relevance of this. It is because the

present perfect indicates a period of time that includes the
present that it is not possible further to specify by an adverbial
a past time at which the activity took place.

Often it is the choice of the adverbial alone that determines
the choice between present perfect and past. There is no question
of current relevance, but only whether the period of time being
indicated includes the present moment or not. It is possible to
say *I've seen him three times today*, and *I saw him three times
yesterday* but not **I've seen him three times yesterday*. Similarly
I've seen him this morning is possible only if it is still morning;
if the morning is over, the period of time indicated is wholly in
the past and a present perfect form cannot be used.

There is one fundamental difficulty about current relevance:
it is not easy to define what is and what is not relevant. British
speakers of English seem to use the perfect wherever there seems
to be any kind of relevance, but some American speakers, at
least, use it more sparingly. For a British speaker it would not
be normal to ask a child coming to the table:

Did you wash your hands?

But for many, if not most, Americans, this is quite acceptable.
There is no reason to suppose that the function of phase is
different in American speech, only that the interpretation of
relevance is stricter.

It is unusual to use the perfect when talking about the dead:

?Queen Victoria has visited Brighton.
?Shakespeare has written a lot of plays.

Yet there is nothing odd about the passive:

Brighton has been visited by Queen Victoria.
A lot of plays have been written by Shakespeare.

The reason is obvious. In the first set we are talking about people
who are dead, and there can be no current relevance. In the
second set we are talking about present-day Brighton or the pres-
ently extant quantity of plays. But subject position does not
necessarily indicate what we are talking about and so what may
be relevant. There would be nothing odd about:

Even Queen Victoria has visited Brighton.
Shakespeare has written most of the best plays we know.

Here we are not talking about Queen Victoria or Shakespeare
but about Brighton and the best plays, and the perfect is not at
all abnormal.

What has been said in this subsection about present perfect
forms is equally valid for past perfect forms, though with current
relevance relating to a past point of time:

I'd cut my finger.   (It was still bleeding)
He'd broken the window.   (It hadn't been mended)
I'd already told you.   (I wouldn't tell you again), etc

The perfect with the progressive has a similar interpretation, but
is discussed in detail in 4.5.

3.3.3 HAVE as past
In spite of the clear distinction of perfect and past noted in 3.3.1
HAVE marks past tense rather than perfect phase in two kinds of
structure.

[i]   The formal past perfect is used also as a 'past past'. This
is clearly shown in the contrast of:

I had already seen him when you arrived.
I had seen him an hour before you arrived.

The first is clearly past perfect – I saw him in a period of
time preceding but up to the time of arrival, and there is
current relevance. But the second merely places seeing
him before the arrival – previously to a past point of time,
ie 'past past'. There is a clear contrast with present perfect
which cannot be interpreted as a past:

I've already seen him.
*I've seen him an hour ago.

There is a similar use in reported speech (3.2.3) and in
unreal past conditionals (7.4.1).

[ii]   Non-finite forms of HAVE may mark tense or phase. This
is clear from the adverbials that are possible with the
infinitivals and participials:

To have finished already/yesterday.
Having finished already/yesterday.
(*I have finished yesterday.)

This is equally valid of HAVE used with modals (see 6.1.3):

He may have finished already/yesterday.
He ought to have finished by now/yesterday.

But these remarks in no way invalidate the very clear
distinction between phase and tense with the finite forms.

3.3.4 Problem uses
There are three uses of the perfect that need some comment.

[i]   Very recent activity is indicated by *just* with the perfect:

> *I've just seen him.*
> *He's just gone.*
> *I've just been waving goodbye to him.*

These are, presumably, current relevance perfect forms since the activity does not continue up to the present time. The use of *just* here can be accounted for if it is seen as a present time adverbial, to indicate a brief period of time preceding, but up to the present moment. The adverb is, in fact, used unambiguously as a present time marker in:

> *They're just arriving.*

But it is also used as a past time adverb:

> *I just saw him leave.*
> *He just went out of the door.*

The function of *just* is thus like that of *today*. Yet semantically it is a little odd for there is little or no current relevance in the examples first quoted: the sentences are no different from:

> *I saw him a moment ago.*
> *He went a moment ago.*

Here the present perfect cannot be used. It is, then, to some degree a formal fact that *just* is used with the present perfect. In British English there is a much greater tendency to use the present perfect than in American English where the simple past is common. The problem does not arise with the past perfect since this is both 'past perfect' and 'past past' (3.3.3).

[ii] The perfect with accent on the auxiliary (and usually with a fall-rise intonation) is used to refer to past experiences:

> *I háve read Oliver Twist.*
> *She hás visited Paris.*

The use of the perfect is to be explained on the grounds that past experiences are part of a person's present make-up – that reading 'Oliver Twist' is included among the experiences that make me what I am.

[iii] The verb BE is used with a special meaning with the perfect, and with the perfect alone occurs with *to*:

> *I've been to London.*
> *He'd been to my house.*

It is not possible to say:

> *I am to London   (or *I was to London).
> **He was to my house.*

With the perfect and followed by *to* the verb has the meaning of having gone and returned. There is a difference, then, between:

> *He's gone to London.*
> *He's been to London.*

In the former he is still in London; in the latter, he has returned. Quite commonly the verb occurs in the use mentioned in [ii], to refer to past experiences:

> *I háve been to London*   (but it was years ago).

Chapter 4

Aspect

Although it can be argued that there is a basic use of the progressive, there are some problems with its use to refer to habitual and future actions and with its occurrence with certain ('non-progressive') verbs. There is also a need to discuss the combination of aspect and phase.

4.1 Duration

It has already been suggested (3.1.3) that the progressive indicates action in progress, *ie* activity continuing throughout a period of time and that in that sense it is durational; in contrast, the non-progressive merely reports the action.

4.1.1 Points of time

The simplest and clearest use of the progressive is when it is used to indicate activity going on at a point of time, *ie* both before and after it.

This explains its use in the present where the activity clearly overlaps 'now':

Please be quiet, I'm reading.

The speaker has been reading and intends to continue. There is a similar use in the past tense, but the point of time is then usually indicated and there is, as a result, a clear contrast with the non-progressive, which would usually indicate that the action followed the time indicated, as in:

When I saw him, he was running away.
When I saw him, he ran away.

In the second the act of running away was preceded by (and probably an effect of) my seeing him. Simultaneity is possible, however, as in:

As the clock struck ten, he died.
He died at ten o'clock.

The non-progressive specifically excludes overlap, as is shown where a number of actions are reported:

When I arrived, he shouted three times.

All three shouts followed my arrival. In fact, English has no simple way of showing that there were three shouts and that the shouting both preceded and followed my arrival.

If the meaning of the lexical verb itself includes a sense of duration, the non-progressive may be used even if there clearly is some duration:

I read all morning.
I worked for a long time.
He slept all night.

Contrasted with these are:

I was reading at ten.
I was working when he arrived.
I was sleeping at the time.

Yet if there are two overlapping periods of time, rather than one point of time and a period extending on both sides of it, either the progressive or non-progressive may be used, especially with verbs that normally indicate continuing activity:

John read, while Bill worked.
John read, while Bill was working.
John was reading, while Bill worked.
John was reading, while Bill was working.

4.1.2 Other durational uses

There are other conditions under which the progressive may be used, all related to, but not identical with, the sense of duration or activity in progress.

[i] The progressive often suggests that the activity was unfinished, the non-progressive that it was completed:

I was painting the house this morning.
I painted the house this morning.

This contrast is not, however, always maintained. The second sentence might be used simply to report what had been done, but could still elicit the reply:

What? The whole of it?

There would not normally be a similar distinction in the present, partly because the non-progressive form is seldom used to report (but see 4.3.1), partly because a point of time (the present moment) is always implicit with the progressive so that the activity overlaps it and is therefore incomplete at the time of speaking.

[ii] The use of the progressive does not necessarily imply unbroken activity, as shown by:

I'm reading 'The Mayor of Casterbridge'.

This may suggest either that I am at this moment sitting with a book in front of me, or that I have read part of the book and intend to read some more, but that at the moment I am not actually reading it. We may similarly compare:

I'm writing a letter.
I'm writing a book.

It is at least likely that the letter is actually being written at the time of speaking, whereas the book has merely been begun.

[iii] The progressive is used with such adverbials and adjectivals as *more and more, faster and faster:*

It's getting bigger and bigger.
More and more people are buying television sets.
He's working less and less.

The adjectivals and adverbials indicate an increase or decrease in the activity or some aspect of the activity, and therefore imply duration. But perhaps this is 'limited duration' – see 4.3.2.

4.2 Future and habitual uses

Both non-progressive and progressive forms can be used to refer to action at the time indicated, to action in the future or to habitual (or repeated) action. But the precise conditions under which they may have these uses are not entirely simple and have created some confusion.

4.2.1 Adverbial specification

There is a clear contrast between present, future and habitual/repeated activity in:

> *He's giving a lecture at the moment.*
> *He's giving a lecture tomorrow.*
> *Whenever I want him, he's giving a lecture.*

In the absence of the adverbials, *He's giving a lecture* would normally be interpreted in its present sense, and for this reason it has been suggested that the future and habitual senses are not part of the meaning of the progressive, but are fully indicated by the adverbials (Twaddell 1965:6). Yet this is misleading, as can be seen from a comparison of:

> *He reads 'The Times'.*
> *He's reading 'The Times'.*

The first of these would normally be taken to indicate habitual activity, the second non-habitual (present) activity, but the contrast is not indicated by any adverbial. The presence of *always* would, however, make both habitual:

> *He always reads 'The Times'.*
> *He's always reading 'The Times'.*

What this shows is that some forms require adverbials in order to specify certain meanings, while others do not. The simple present does not normally need an averbial to have the habitual sense, but the progressive does. This has been called 'adverbial specification' (Crystal 1966).

No less important is the fact that the presence of an adverbial may actually exclude the more usual sense of a form. Thus a future adverbial will over-rule the durational sense of the progressive:

> *He's getting his reward tomorrow.*
> *They're arriving on Thursday next.*

These simply refer to future events (getting the reward, arriving) without an indication of duration or activity in progress.

There are, moreover, some specialized habitual uses of the progressive that are not predictable from the adverbials – those of 'limited duration' and 'sporadic repetition' (4.3.2, 4.3.3). For reasons such as these, it is essential to look at the habitual and future uses of the progressive forms, with and without adverbials.

4.2.2 Non-habitual present

Because the simple (*ie* non-progressive, non-perfect) present often seems to have a habitual use, it has been suggested that in the present the simple/progressive contrast implies habitual/non-habitual (Hill 1958:207–11). This is true in many cases, but is misleading. In general, the simple form merely reports an activity, while the progressive specifically indicates duration or some feature closely associated with it.

There is, moreover, a reason why the simple present is so commonly used in the habitual sense: the fact that it is only rarely required for its 'simple', 'reporting', non-habitual sense. There are two obvious reasons for this. First, we rarely need to report a present activity, because, if the speaker can observe it (at the present time), so too in most circumstances can the hearer. Past activity, on the contrary, is often reported by a speaker who observed it (or heard about it) to a hearer who did not. With the past tense, therefore, unlike the present, non-habitual activity is commonly referred to, as well as habitual activity:

> *I saw my mother yesterday.*
> *I saw my mother every day.*

A second point is that present activity is usually incomplete, and therefore, even when there is no specific reference to the duration of the activity, its incompleteness implies the use of the progressive. In, for instance, *What are you doing?* the speaker avoids the suggestion that the activity is complete.

The progressive is, thus, the commoner form for reference to present activity. Indeed it is the norm: unless there are obvious reasons to the contrary the progressive is used. (With the 'non-progressive' verbs, however, (4.6), the reverse is true.) But there are a number of situations in which the non-progressive, the simple present, is used.

[i] It is the form normally used in a commentary, especially on the radio where the commentator is reporting something that the listeners cannot see. This use is exactly parallel to the use of the simple past to report past activity:
> *. . . and he passes the ball to Smith, and Smith scores!*
> *He bowls, and he just misses the wicket.*
> *He hits him again, right on the jaw.*

[ii] It is used in demonstrations, where the audience can see what is happening, but the demonstrator reports it as well to make sure there is no misunderstanding. Once again he is merely reporting the activity and is not indicating its duration; the simple present is the only appropriate form:

(Conjuror) *I place the rabbit in the box and close the lid.*
(Cookery demonstration) *I take three eggs and beat them in this basin.*
Then I add sugar . . .

[iii] Another use is where the words themselves form part of the activity they report. These are the so-called 'performative' verb forms (Austin 1962:4). Again they merely state the occurrence of the activity:

I name this ship . . .
I pronounce you man and wife.
I declare the meeting closed.

A rather similar use is of verbs of statement which are used merely to reinforce the fact that the speaker makes his statement:

I say he should go.
I call it an outrage.

These utterances imply not 'I am saying . . .' or 'I am calling . . .' but '. . . that's my opinion' and '. . . that's my name for it.'

[iv] Less easy to explain are:
He talks like an expert.
Look at the way he walks!
Why do you say that?

The common characteristic of all these utterances is that they contain an adverbial to indicate either the manner or the cause of the activity. It is in the manner or cause that the speaker is interested; the duration of the activity is not in question. Again the simple present is appropriate. In some cases it might be argued that there is habitual activity:

Why do you cut it like that?

But it is equally clear that in many cases the activity is not habitual, that the speaker is concerned only with a single present activity. There can be contrast between a present and a past activity, neither of them apparently habitual, as in:

Yesterday he talked nonsense. Today he talks like an expert.
He walked all the morning. Look at the way he walks now.

> *You said something different a few minutes ago. Why do*
> *you say that now?*

Similar considerations hold for:

> *John enters through the window.*   (Stage directions)
> *It says in the Bible . . .*

The stage directions are similar to a commentary; the play
simulates present activity. The words in the Bible are
simply statements and there is no indication of any duration. It must be admitted that the present is timeless in
some cases, in that it extends without limit on both sides
of 'now'. This may partly account for the use of the simple
present in stage directions and in the report of written statements. More will be said on this point in dealing with the
habitual. But what has been shown here is that most of the
non-habitual uses of the simple present fit quite normally
into the pattern, and ought not to be treated as special uses
of the form. On the contrary, there is more plausibility in
treating habitual usage as secondary to the basic use, in
spite of its much greater frequency with this particular
form.

The simple present, causes difficulty to the teacher of
English if he tries to illustrate the verb forms situationally;
for in order to illustrate the use of the present progressive,
he is likely to perform actions and describe them:

> *Now I am opening the door.*
> *Now I am writing on the blackboard.*

The difficulty arises from the fact that in the situation the
teacher is demonstrating, and so would normally use the
simple forms:

> *Now I open the door.*
> *Now I write on the blackboard.*

But these forms would be unhelpful, or even misleading,
to learners of English. The difficulty can, in part, be overcome by making such sentences replies to *What am I doing?*
But that may create a more artificial situation.

4.3 Habitual

Every one of the forms may be used in a habitual (as well as non-
habitual) sense. Examples of all of them (active only) are:

(1) *He bowls, and . . .*
    He always bowls well.
(2) *He's writing a book.*
    He's always writing a book.
(3) *He went to work yesterday.*
    He always went by bus.
(4) *He was reading, when I arrived.*
    He was reading, whenever I saw him.
(5) *He has come to see me.*
    He has come to see me every day.
(6) *He had called on them, when I saw him.*
    He had called on them every week, when they died.
(7) *He's been reading since three.*
    Whenever I've seen him, he's been reading.
(8) *He had been reading all day.*
    Whenever I saw him, he'd been playing golf.

As these examples show, the distinction made by progressive/non-progressive is valid for the habitual use no less than the non-habitual: the activity may or may not be durational.

4.3.1 The simple present
With all the progressive forms illustrated above the habitual sense requires an adverbial. But this is not true of the present simple (non-progressive) forms. Indeed with (1) it is the habitual sense that requires no adverbial:

He bowls well.

By contrast, the non-habitual sense is established only by clearly indicating the fact that it is part of a cricket commentary.
  The simple present is not, however, simply used for habitual (or repeated) actions, but is also used for inductive generalizations and what have been called 'timeless truths'. Possible examples are (two of each):

I always take sugar in tea.
The milkman calls on Sundays.

Oil floats on water.
Water boils at 100°C.

The Severn flows into the Atlantic.
The sun rises in the East.

There is, however, no very clear distinction between these three types. Certainly *The sun rises in the East* could be seen in terms of repeated habitual action (and can even be qualified by an adverbial such as *every day*). Inductive generalizations are slightly different in that they will not occur with such adverbials and that they can also be expressed by *will*:

> *Oil will float on water.*

(With the others *will* carries a different meaning, usually that of futurity.)

What is important is to contrast these simple present forms with the progressives. With progressive forms the sentences refer to activity going on (with duration) at present:

> *I'm going to work.*
> *The oil is floating on the water.*
> *The Severn is flowing into the Atlantic.*   (I can see it moving)

With the past tense by contrast, the non-progressive form, like the progressive, requires an adverbial if it is to be interpreted (out of context) in a habitual sense:

> *He went to London.*
> *He went to London every day.*

The first simply reports the single action of going to London.

There are, however, some specialized functions of the progressive in a habitual sense that are not directly predictable from the adverbials, limited duration and sporadic repetition.

4.3.2 Limited duration
The progressive is used to indicate habitual activity in a limited period of time (Twaddell 1960:8) in:

> *He's going to work by bus.*
> *We're eating a lot more meat now.*
> *We've been getting up early this week.*
> *I'd been visiting him every day.*

The activity is habitual, but it is over a limited period. In the first example the inference is probably that the man's car has broken down, and that he is now forced (temporarily) to take the bus. If he always went by bus, the non-progressive would be normal:

> *He goes to work by bus.*

The period of time is normally shown to be limited by adverbials, especially *these day* or *in those days*. There are contrasts between:

We eat a lot of meat. (And always have)
We're eating a lot of meat these days.
I went to work by bus. (All my life)
I was going to work by bus in those days. (Now I have a car)

The present progressive often differs very little in its use from the present perfect, and may even be used with *since*, in spite of the fact that adverbials of this kind mark a period of time characteristic of the perfect:

We're eating more meat since the war.
He's going to work by bus since his car broke down.

In both cases a perfect would equally be possible – *we've been eating, he's been going.* With the perfect the period of time is, of course, often limited; *since* marks the limitation. But one important difference is that the present progressive implies the continuance of the activity, even though for a limited period, through present time into the future. The perfect does not. In the case of the man whose car has broken down, if the car is now back at his disposal. *He's been going* will be used rather than *He's going.*

A special use that can, perhaps, be treated under the heading of limited duration is that of showing increasing or decreasing activity, or increase or decrease of some feature of the activity; this has already been mentioned (4.1.2):

More and more people are buying television sets.
They are visiting us more and more often.
They were stealing more and more of his money.
I've been giving him less and less every week.

4.3.3 Sporadic repetition
The progressive is also used to indicate habitual activity that is repeated and sporadic:

She's always breaking things.
The car's always breaking down.

What is happening happens very often, but it does not happen at set times. If there is reference to repeated points of time, indicating regularity, the non-progressive is used:

The car always breaks down when I start for home.

There is a contrast between:

I always break the eggs first.
I'm always breaking the crockery.

The progressive often carries with it a hint of the speaker's disapproval, especially with adverbials such as *for ever* or *everlastingly*. Some more examples of this use, which is quite common, are:

I was continually falling ill.
They were for ever leaving the gate open.
He's always asking silly questions.
He's for ever losing his money.
They're always getting in the way.
You're continually making poor excuses.
She's been dropping things recently.
He'd been continually stealing from his friends.

In most of these examples there is no suggestion that the activity is continuous; the progressive is used because it is repeated and sporadic. But the activity may be both continuous (at every occasion) and repeated sporadically:

He's always grumbling.
She's for ever writing letters.

Indication of the speaker's disapproval of the activity may be carried by the intonation, by *eg*, a high fall on the adverbial.

4.4 Future

Although future uses of both progressive and non-progressive have normally to be marked by an adverbial, they differ in ways that cannot be accounted for in terms of the adverbial itself.

4.4.1 Progressive
The progressive is commonly used to refer to future activity:

I'm reading a paper at the conference tomorrow.

This use of the progressive is particularly common with verbs that indicate or imply motion:

I'm meeting him next week.
He's coming to see me soon.
They're taking the children to the theatre this evening.
He's joining the army next week.

But there is no restriction to such verbs:

I'm watching the play on television this evening.
We're having turkey for lunch tomorrow.

Deictic shift (3.2.3) marking the time at which the statement was
valid, *ie* at which the event was envisaged as future, is very
common with the progressive, especially with past tense:

I was reading a paper to the conference tomorrow.
I was meeting him next week.
He was coming to see me soon.

The combination of past tense and a future adverbial makes
clear here the two different times, one of the validity of the statement, the other of the proposed activity. Without the future time
adverbial the past validity meaning can be marked by accent and
the appropriate intonation, normally a fall-rise on the auxiliary:

I wás reading a paper.
I wás meeting him.
He wás coming to see me.

Similar sentences with the perfect (and here adverbial specification seems necessary) are (4.2.1):

I've been coming to see you for ages.
He's been going abroad for years.
I'd been coming to see him the next day   (but he died).
We'd been going to Paris for years   (but never went).

The third sentence here is an example of the past perfect used
for past-past (3.3.3). But all the others have perfect time
marking; the time at which the activity is or was proposed is the
period of time preceding and continuing up to the present or to
a point of time in the past.

4.4.2 Non-progressive

The non-progressives are also used with future reference. The
simple present is exemplified in:

I start work tomorrow.
He goes to Paris next week.
Exams begin on Monday.

As was noted in 3.2.4, the past tense form can be similarly used,
with the past tense itself indicating the time at which the statement was valid, but with future time (*ie* 'future in the past')
indicated by the adverbial:

At that time I didn't see him until tomorrow.

The progressive is used for 'simple' futurity to indicate a prediction or in the case of activity by the speaker an intention. The non-progressive, however, indicates that the activity is in some way scheduled, that there is a fixed decision or plan. This accounts for the difference between:

I'm starting work tomorrow.
I start work tommorow.

The first suggests that the speaker now expects or intends to start work; he may, perhaps, have been ill. The second indicates that tomorrow is the time fixed for him to start, *eg* by his firm or by the doctor. It is for such reasons that the first sentence below is more likely than the second:

Examinations start tomorrow.
Examinations are starting tomorrow.

The non-progressive future use is common with verbs such as START, BEGIN, FINISH, END, etc, simply because beginnings and ends of activities are often scheduled.

Still within the same meaning is the notion of total commitment by the speaker, refusal to accept any other possibility, a firm threat to act, as in:

Either shé leaves or I leave.
If he does that again, he goes to prison.

The second sentence could be said under two different sets of circumstances. It could be said where a prison sentence inevitably followed from an action (*eg* where it constituted contempt of court) or it could be said by a judge as a firm threat. These are not two distinct meanings: the essential point about both of them is the inevitability, the fixed nature of the course of events.

Not very different is the use of the simple present to confirm future arrangements:

You meet us at the station this evening.

There is hardly a plan or schedule here, merely an agreed arrangement. The present is also used to give directions:

You take the first on the left and then . . .

There is futurity, but not prediction. Rather there is just the one possible inevitable course of action, if you want to arrive at your destination.

4.4.3 Future and habitual

There are two ways in which future and habitual uses may be combined.

[i] The simple present is used with no habitual adverbial to refer to a future event that is part of a habitual pattern:

> *You get tea at five tonight.*
> *The baker calls on Saturday.*

This use is not very different from the one already considered except that there is reference not to a decision but to a regular pattern. In the second example *on Saturdays* (plural) would have indicated habitual activity. The singular *Saturday* may be taken to indicate the application of the habitual to a single future date.

[ii] The progressive may be used to refer to habitual intended activity. Examples in the present non-perfect are:

> *He's always coming to see me*   (but never does).
> *She's usually writing in a few days.*
> *He's always taking them on holiday*   (but hasn't yet).

The other progressive forms can be similarly used, though this usage is not common and the following examples are a little artificial:

> *Whenever I wanted to visit him, he was going away the next day.*
> *Whenever I've wanted to visit him, he's been going away the next day.*
> *Whenever I'd wanted to visit him, he'd been going away the next day.*

With the first of these two kinds of habitual-futures the adverbials used are of the type that refer to the future – *The baker calls tomorrow.*

It is even possible to say:

> *I've always read my paper tomorrow.*

This could be said at a conference where the speaker always read a paper on a certain day that (at the time of speaking) is 'tomorrow'. With the second kind, the adverbials are mainly of the type that indicates the habitual nature – *He's always coming to see us*, though adverbials that refer to the future, such as *the next day*, are also possible.

4.5 Progressive perfect

In the analysis of the perfect only non-progressive forms were fully considered. Although in general the same account can be given of the progressive perfect, there are some differences.

4.5.1 'Results'

The progressive perfect is often used for 'results' or more accurately current relevance. However, except in the complex use of it discussed in 4.5.2, it is not possible for the progressive to be used to indicate activity going on at a specific point of time (4.1.1) with the perfect. For that would create a conflict between the time marking of the perfect and of the progressive. Consider the present perfect progressive. The perfect indicates a period beginning in the past continuing up to the present, but also requires only present time adverbials. But a point of time within that period would be past and so marked as past requiring such impossible sentences as:

> *I have been working ten minutes ago/at ten o'clock.

The perfect progressive is used, however, to indicate incomplete action with current relevance:

> Someone's been moving my books.
> Who's been eating my porridge?

The implication here is that the books were not completely moved away, and that the porridge was not completely eaten, but that it is obvious that something has been done to the position of the books and that the porridge has been partly eaten. (In fact in the story from which this is taken, 'Goldilocks and the Three Bears', Father Bear and Mother Bear merely say 'Who's been eating my porridge?', while Baby Bear says 'Who's been eating my porridge and has eaten it all up?'. But that is intended to be amusing: Baby Bear uses the same expression, but then realises that his porridge has all gone.)

The progressive is also used to show that it is simply the continuing, durational aspect of the activity that has the current relevance:

> You've been working too hard. ('You need a rest' – to someone now in bed, certainly not still working)
> You've been playing with fire. (I can smell it)
> I've been drinking tea. (That's why I'm late)
> He's been talking about you. (I know something now)

The same kind of remarks are valid for the past perfect:

You'd been working too hard.
He'd been talking about you. etc.

Clearly, in these examples it is not the nature of the activity itself that is relevant, but the fact that it continued for some time.

4.5.2 A complex pattern
With more complex sentences phase marking becomes a little obscure. Consider:

Every time I've seen them, they've been swimming.

This is most likely to be interpreted to mean that they were swimming at the time at which I saw them – the perfect indicating that the period of time that includes my series of visits and of their swimming goes right up to the present time. But the sentence might also mean that at the time of each of my visits they had (previously) been swimming. The ambiguity arises from the fact that the perfect may be used to refer either to the overall period of time that we are talking about, or in addition about each repeated period. The overall period of time is clearly shown by *Every time I've seen them* to be one that began in the past and continues up to the present moment. But the successive periods of time that are to be related to the series of points of time – my seeing them – may either be periods that simply overlap these points of time (non-perfect type), or they may be periods that began before and continued up to the points of time. This may be shown diagrammatically:

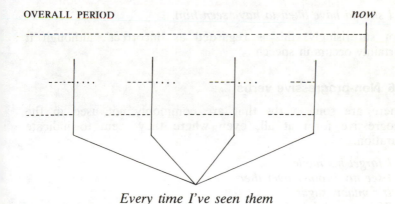

Every time I've seen them

The second interpretation is unlikely unless clearly marked. But there are situations in which the distinction is very clear:

Whenever I've tried carpentry, I've cut my finger.
Whenever I've had to go to the doctor, I've cut my finger.

Clearly in the first the finger-cutting and carpentry are simultaneous, in the second the finger-cutting is previous to the visit to the doctor (but related in terms of current relevance).

In the second interpretation the perfect form is 'doubly' perfect. We want to say the impossible:

*They have been having been swimming.
*I have been having cut my finger.

The past perfect is, also possible here (for this meaning only):

Whenever I've seen them, they'd been swimming.
Whenever I've had to go to the doctor, I'd cut my finger.

This is easily explained: each successive point of time in the past, indicated by *Whenever* . . . is taken as the point to which the past perfect relates, either in terms of activity going on throughout the period or of current relevance.

Related to these complex uses of the perfect is what might be called 'deictic phase' or 'sequence of phase' (see 3.2.4):

He's always said he's been willing.

The actual speaker shows his acceptance of the statement 'He's been willing'.

However, there are examples where the perfect seems redundant as in:

I should have liked to have seen him.

Not surprisingly, this is regarded as 'incorrect', although it certainly occurs in speech.

4.6 Non-progressive verbs

There are some verbs that are commonly not used in the progressive form at all, even where they seem to indicate duration:

I forget his name.
I see my brother over there.
It contains sugar.
They own a lot of property.

These verbs differ from the other verbs of English in that they usually, even in the present tense, occur with the non-progressive. The non-progressive is, in fact, the norm, and progressive forms are used only where there is specific reference to duration or one of the special features indicated by the progressive. This is illustrated by a sentence such as:

The man who's coming up the street looks like a boxer.

These non-progressive verbs fall into several types, but the most important distinction is between 'private' verbs and verbs of 'state'. It is possible to find reasons why these do not normally occur with the progressive, but the reasons are different for each type. Equally there are different explanations for more unusual occurrences with the progressive.

4.6.1 Verbs of state

There are many verbs which refer not to an activity but to a state or condition. The sense of duration is an integral part of the lexical meaning of the verb, and there is for this reason no need for a progressive form to indicate duration. Examples are:

CONTAIN	*It contains sugar.*
BELONG	*It belongs to me.*
MATTER	*It doesn't matter.*
DESERVE	*He deserves something better than that.*
CONSIST	*It consists of little but water and colouring.*
PLEASE	*It pleases me no end.*
DEPEND	*It depends on what you mean.*
OWN	*I own my own house.*

A special subgroup is that of the verbs which indicate the quality of creating sensations, those that may be treated as the intransitive forms of the verbs of sensation:

It smells sweet.
It tastes nice.
It feels soft.

The verbs of sensation SEE and HEAR have no similar intransitive forms, but are discussed further in 4.6.2.

Another subgroup is that of verbs of 'stance' (Quirk *et al.* 1985:205–6), notably LIVE, STAND and LIE:

We live in London.
The statue stands in the middle of the square.
Los Angeles lies on the west coast of the United States.

There are two notable uses of the verbs of state in the progressive. The first is for limited duration (see 4.3.2):

> *He's looking better since his operation.*
> *I'm feeling quite well now.*

With verbs of stance the distinction between progressive and non-progressive is even more specific, the former indicating a temporary, the latter a permanent, state:

> *We live in London.*
> *We're living in London.*
> *The statue stands in the middle of the square.*
> *The boy is standing in the middle of the room.*

With many of the verbs, however, the progressive is unlikely unless a change of state is indicated:

> *He's looking more and more like his father.*
> *It's mattering less and less now.*
> *It's tasting nastier and nastier.*

Conversely some potential verbs of state can be seen as a kind of conditional habitual of a non-progressive verb:

> *The bucket leaks.*   (It has a hole)
> *The bucket is leaking.*
>
> *The wood burns.*   (It is combustible)
> *The wood is burning.*

Here the state meaning is predictable on certain conditions: leaking takes place whenever water is poured in, combustion ensues whenever there is ignition. This may even be a plausible account of inductively known facts such as:

> *Oil floats on water.*
> *(The oil is floating on the water.)*

Clearly these are borderline cases that can either be handled lexically in terms of polysemy or grammatically in terms of the meanings of the simple and progressive forms.

4.6.2 Private verbs

Private verbs are those that refer to states or activities that the speaker alone is aware of. These are of two kinds, those that refer to mental activities and those that refer to sensations. Both commonly occur with non-progressive forms.

Examples of verbs referring to mental activities are:

THINK	*I think that's mine.*
IMAGINE	*I imagine he'll be there.*
HOPE	*I hope it's true.*
PLAN	*I plan to go to London tomorrow.*
FORGET	*I forget what you said.*
BELIEVE	*I believe that it's true.*

Examples of verbs referring to sensations are:

SEE	*I see my brother over there.*
SMELL	*I smell something burning.*
HEAR	*I hear music.*
TASTE	*I taste salt in this.*
FEEL	*I feel something hard.*

These verbs of sensation have two notable characteristics. First, they form part of an idiosyncratic lexical system that is discussed later in this section. Secondly, they often occur with CAN with no very obvious difference of meaning:

I can see my brother over there.
I can smell something burning.
I can hear music.
I can taste salt in this.
I can feel something hard.

In these examples CAN has no sense of ability. Indeed it is possible to contrast this use of CAN with its ability use with a verb of sensation:

I can see very small print.

This can mean either that I now see the small print or that I have the general ability to do so.

All the examples given so far of both types of verb have *I* as the subject. This is not only very common, but is, perhaps, the most basic use and explains why the verbs are most commonly found with the progressive. For, when these verbs are used, the speaker is in exactly the same position as the commentator; he is reporting something that is not perceived by the hearer. Just as the radio commentator uses the non-progressive because his main aim is merely to report, so too the person who reports on his own mental activities or sensations is simply reporting and so uses the non-progressive form. With most other verbs there is seldom need to report in the present because what is observable by the speaker is also observable by the hearer. But the private

verbs have the special characteristic that they refer to activities
available for perception by the speaker only. He alone can report
them and in so doing uses the appropriate form, the non-
progressive.

These verbs can be used with second or third person subjects,
but only to ask about the activity, or to report it at second hand
or by inference:

Do you imagine he'll be there?
Do you smell something burning?

She imagines he'll be there.
She smells something burning.

But the question forms are clearly asking for a report, while the
others report at second either the information that has been given
or is inferred. In neither case is there any need to indicate
duration.

There are some verbs of bodily sensation that are used with
both progressives and non-progressives with little difference of
meaning, if any, *eg* ACHE and ITCH:

My foot aches/is aching.
My arm itches/is itching.

The same appears to be true of FEEL in the sense of having a
physical sensation rather than merely a tactile sensation:

I feel/I'm feeling ill.

These, then, are optionally members of the class of private verbs.
SUFFER by contrast is not:

I'm suffering from a headache.

(*I suffer from headaches* would be interpreted as habitual.) The
reason may be that suffering is objectively observable in the way
that an ache or an itch is not, but there is also some arbitrariness
in the membership of the class.

The use of private verbs with the progressive is best seen in
three parts.

[i] In a few cases a private verb may occur in the progressive
where there is emphasis upon the duration:

I'm actually hearing your voice!

They also appear to be used in the progressive where there
are repetitions of the sensation, but usually only to imply
that these sensations are imaginary or hallucinatory:

He's seeing stars.
She's hearing voices.

[ii] In many cases, especially with verbs that refer to intellectual states, the progressive indicates mental activity, or the overt action that reflects it:

I plan to go tomorrow.
I'm planning my holidays.   (making arrangements)

I think he'll come.
I'm thinking about it.   (pondering)

I wish I were rich.
I'm wishing I were rich.   (making a wish)

The difference in meaning here is such that it ought perhaps to be treated lexically, *ie* as polysemy, but in other cases the progressive may indicate mere duration or limited duration:

I wonder whether he'll come.
I'm just wondering whether he'll come.

I remember what you said.
Now I'm rembering what you said.

There is obviously no clear line between what should be treated lexically in terms of polysemy and grammatically in terms of predictable meanings of the progressive.

[iii] It has already been seen that the verbs SMELL, FEEL and TASTE have two different uses, the one transitive with the sense of having the sensation, the other intransitive with the sense of having the quality to produce the sensation. The verbs are non-progressives in both their senses, but in one sense they belong to the private verbs, in the other to the verbs of state. There is yet a third use, with the meaning 'to act to achieve the sensation'. In this sense the verbs are not non-progressives. Examples of all three uses are:

I smell flowers.
The flowers smell lovely.
I'm smelling the flowers.

I taste salt in the soup.
The soup tastes salty.
The cook is tasting the soup.

I feel something rough.
The cloth feels rough.
I'm feeling the cloth.

The verbs SEE and HEAR are not similarly used in three senses. In comparable senses different verbs are used:

	I see my brother.
(LOOK)	*He looks well.*
(LOOK AT)	*I'm looking at my brother.*

	I hear music.
(SOUND)	*It sounds beautiful.*
(LISTEN TO)	*I'm listening to the music.*

Diagrammatically these can be displayed in three columns:

(1)	(2)	(3)
SMELL	SMELL	SMELL
TASTE	TASTE	TASTE
FEEL	FEEL	FEEL
SEE	LOOK	LOOK AT
HEAR	SOUND	LISTEN TO

(1) Lists private verbs with the sense of 'acquire the sensation', (2) verbs of state with the sense of 'produce the sensation', and (3) verbs that are not non-progressive and have the sense of 'act to acquire the sensation'.

In view of the differences in these functions and especially in view of the fact that SEE and HEAR are not used in all three senses, it is as well to treat them as different homonymous verbs rather than to account for them in terms of grammatical function.

Chapter 5

Voice

A complete chapter is devoted to voice, mainly because it is syntactically very different from the three other verbal categories. The first section will deal with voice proper – with the passive. The others consider some related structures that have close semantic and syntactic relations with the passive.

5.1 The passive

At the most formal level the passive is defined in terms of the last eight forms of the primary pattern. It should be recalled, however (3.1.1), that perfect progressive forms in the passive are rare and improbable. The form that corresponds to the active perfect progressive is the passive perfect non-progressive, progressive not being marked with this form.

The doctors have been examining him all morning.
He has been examined all morning by the doctors.
? He has been being examined all morning by the doctors.

5.1.1 Active–passive correspondence
Active and passive sentences can, for the most part, be shown to correspond as in:

A little boy played the piano.
The piano was played by a little boy.

Indeed, if the passive sentence is described as formed from the active, what is involved is that the second noun phrase, the grammatical object of the verb, is placed in subject position, while the first noun phrase, the subject, is placed after the verb with the preposition *by* as an 'agent'.

This was a basic fact for earlier forms of transformational-generative grammar with its notion of transformation (Chomsky 1957), permitting the simple formula:

$$NP_1 \ V_{act} \ NP_2 \rightarrow NP_2 \ V_{pass} \ by \ NP_1$$

The switching of the two noun phrases makes voice quite different from the categories of tense, phase and aspect. That voice does indeed require this transformation is clearly shown not only because of the meaning correspondence (voice neutrality – see 2.3.2) of active and passive, but also by the fact that without it the resultant sentence may be unacceptable:

A little boy was played by the piano.

The active–passive relationship is unaffected by the presence of tense, phase and aspect. Indeed, one of the arguments concerning the status of the auxiliaries depends upon the issue of voice neutrality with the primary auxiliaries:

A little boy has played the piano.
The piano has been played by a little boy.
A little boy was playing the piano.
The piano was being played by a little boy.

(But, as was noted above, there is possibly a restriction on the passivization of *A little boy has been playing the piano* into ?*The piano has been being played by a little boy*.)

Where modal auxiliaries are present it is not always the case that there is similar voice neutrality (see 2.3.2 and 6.1.3). On the other hand, voice neutrality is sometimes possible with catenatives (see 9.1.2).

5.1.2 Agentless passives

Although the active–passive relationship sees the subject of the active becoming the agent of the passive, passives often occur with no agents:

The boy was killed.
The thieves were caught.

There can be no corresponding active forms for the very simple reason that an English sentence always requires a grammatical subject.

Agentless passives are for this reason often used where no subject is available for the active sentence because the agent is irrelevant or unknown:

He was killed.

That work was soon completed.
The water was quickly boiled.

For this reason, it is very common in scientific writing, especially in reports on research, for the work may be described impersonally without indicating who did it (Svartvik 1966:70). Agentless passives are a most useful device for not providing irrelevant or undesirable information.

However, the agent may not be omitted if it provides an essential part of the information:

The ceremony was preceded by a minute's silence.
*The ceremony was preceded.

5.1.3 Passive and transitivity

The sentences considered in the previous sections all had objects, which were changed into subjects with passivization. This clearly implies that passivization is possible only with transitive verbs, *ie* those that have objects.

It is clear that not all noun phrases that follow the verb may become the subject of the passive:

The baker comes every day.
*Every day is come by the baker.

The reason is obvious: *every day* is an adverbial, not the object of *comes*. But there are other problems that are not so easily explained.

[i] A very common passive form is exemplified by:

The boy was given a present by the teacher.
We have been told lies.
The children were left a small fortune.

The corresponding active forms would be (with a blank indicating what would have been the subject with agentless passives):

The teacher gave the boy a present.
— told us lies.
— left the children a small fortune.

The transformational formula in terms of NP_1 and NP_2 is still valid for all these sentences: the second NP takes initial position when the sentence is passivized. But NP_2 (*the boy, us, the children*) is in traditional terms the indirect object while the third NP (*a present, lies, a small fortune*) is the direct object. This analysis seems to be supported by the fact that this direct object can also be the subject of the passive:

A present was given to the boy by the teacher.
Lies were told to us.
A small fortune was left to the children.

However, it can be argued that these are the passives of different active sentences, containing *to*:

The teacher gave a present to the boy.
— told lies to us.
— left a small fortune to the children.

It is not only *to* that may ·be involved in this syntactic pattern. *For* also occurs with the same type of sentence:

He bought John a book.
John was bought a book.
He bought a book for John.
A book was bought for John.

The simplest way of handling these sentences is to say that GIVE, TELL, LEAVE, BRING are di-transitive verbs that take two objects as well as a single object plus *to/for* and noun phrase. With passivization an object still becomes the subject of the passive, but it is the first object where there are two. The two active constructions thus account for two different passives.

[ii] There are many sequences of verb and preposition that may be passivized even though the second NP is clearly not the object of the verb but part of the prepositional phrase:

He looked after the old man.
The old man was looked after by him.
They had sat in the chair.
The chair had been sat in.

Many, but not all, of these are prepositional verbs, which are discussed in detail in 10.3. There is a similar situation with the phrasal prepositional verbs (10.4):

This noise cannot be put up with.
She was done away with.

It is true also of similar constructions of the type:

The matter was taken care of.

The house was set fire to.
The rubbish was soon got rid of.

In all these examples it is clear that the verb plus the following element is treated, for the purposes of passivization, as a single unit; there are semantic reasons for this (see Ch. 10).

[iii] There are several catenatives which, when followed by a *to*-infinitive, form a verbal sequence that is voice neutral, *ie* can be passivized with no change of meaning. One is SEEM:

John seemed to understand the situation.
The situation seemed to be understood by John.

Others are APPEAR, HAPPEN, COME, CHANCE (9.2.9).

Other verbs such as BEGIN, START, STOP may also be voice neutral, but only if there is no suggestion of agency by the subject:

The rain began to spoil the flowers.
The flowers began to be spoilt by the rain.

But

John began to read the book.
*The book began to be read by John.

5.1.4 Restrictions on the passive

There are cases where the active–passive relationship is not maintained. Most common are those where there is an active, but passivization is not possible.

[i] There are verbs that seem to be transitive and to have objects that nevertheless never, or rarely, occur in the passive, *eg* RESEMBLE, LACK:

John resembles his father.
*His father is resembled by John.
The car lacks a mirror.
*A mirror is lacked by the car.

With some verbs the passive is possible with one meaning where there is activity, but not in another where there is indication only of a state:

The jar holds oil.
*Oil is held by the jar.
The thief was held by the police.
The king possessed great wealth.

> *Great wealth was possessed by the king.*
> *The city was soon possessed by the enemy.*

Other such verbs are CONTAIN and HAVE (8.2.1). More idio-syncratic are the different meanings of MARRY and EQUAL:

> *Jack married Jill.*
> **Jill was married by Jack.*
> *They were married by the priest.*
> *Two and two equals four.*
> **Four is equalled by two and two.*
> *He is equalled in strength by no one.*

[ii]   There is a slight problem with noun phrases indicating quan-tity ('How much?'). These will not normally occur as the subject of the passive, as illustrated by:

> *The book weighs a pound.*
> **A pound was weighed by the book.*
> *The boy grew six inches.*
> **Six inches were grown by the boy.*

These verbs are intransitive, though they can also be tran-sitive. When transitive they passivize:

> *The greengrocer weighed the plums.*
> *The plums were weighed by the greengrocer.*
> *The gardener grew the beans.*
> *The beans were grown by the gardener.*

If this is the correct interpretation, *a pound* and *six inches* are not the objects of the verb while *the plums* and *the beans* are. Notice *what?* with WEIGH, but not with GROW (in the first sense):

> *What did it weigh?*
> *!What did he grow?*

With verbs that explicitly indicate measurement, WEIGH, MEASURE, TOTAL, COST, etc, *what* may be used; with others a form that indicates the kind of measurement is needed:

> *What does it measure?*
> *How long did the session take?*
> *How far does it stretch?*

Although *what* might seem to indicate that these are tran-sitive verbs with objects (as opposed to *how far* which is clearly adverbial), that does not correlate with the possi-bility of passivization.

Slightly different is the contrast illustrated by:

He ran a mile to work.
*A mile to work was run by him.
Bannister first ran a mile in four minutes.
A mile was first run in four minutes by Bannister.

Only in the sense of running on the race track is passivization possible, presumably because running a mile is a specific sporting event and *a mile* or *the mile* refers to a particular kind of race that can be run.

Conversely, there are some verbs that appear only in the passive, *eg* RUMOUR:

It was rumoured that . . . .

There is no active form *X rumoured that . . . .*
Somewhat similarly, SAY and REPUTE are found only in the passive when followed by the *to-* infinitive:

John is said to be rich.
He is reputed to be a good scholar.

A little less obvious is *be drowned*, where the agent is not merely irrelevant or unknown, but non-existent when it means 'died by drowning':

He fell into the river and was drowned.

5.1.5 The functions of the passive

One function of the passive has already been noted, that it allows the agent to be omitted, if it is irrelevant or unknown (5.1.1).

Another, but more problematic, function is that of thematization, *ie* the placing of a certain noun phrase in subject position for the purpose of prominence. This is particularly useful in narrative to retain the same subject in successive sentences (or in a sentence with coordinate clauses):

John came in. He was immediately welcomed by the committee.
John came in and was immediately welcomed by the committee.

In many cases, however, it is difficult to establish unequivocally why a certain noun phrase is placed in subject position, except to say that it is treated as the theme, *ie* what is being talked about.

There is some connection between theme, subjectivization and animacy. It has already been noted (5.1.3) that a verb such as BEGIN is voice neutral only when an animate agent is not present.

A reasonable explanation of the unlikeliness of *The book began to be read by John* is that since an animate agent is present, it must be in subject position. Similarly the rules for 'case relations' (below 5.4.1) require that if an (animate) agent is present it must function as the grammatical subject. It is, for this reason, that the first of the following pairs of sentences is rather more likely to occur:

The birds have eaten all the strawberries.
All the strawberries have been eaten by the birds.

A child was killed by the runaway car.
The runaway car killed a child.

In terms purely of theme or what is being talked about *the strawberries* and *the runaway car* might seem to be the more likely candidates for subjects, but the animates are chosen.

There appear to be other more formal explanations for the use of the passive.

[i] It is rarer with the progressive than with the perfect or the modals (and this may account for the near-impossibility of the passive perfect progressive).

[ii] It is common where the agent is long (in terms of number of words, and especially when the agent is coordinate (two or more noun phrases joined by *and*)) (Svartvik 1966:71). The passive is to some degree a device for placing long (and 'weighty') agents in final position.

It should be noted that although in general the meaning of active and passive sentences is the same except in terms of thematization, other factors may affect the meaning, notably the presence of 'logical' words such as quantifiers and negatives, *eg*:

Every student read one book.
One book was read by every student.

The most natural interpretation of the first is that each student read a book (not necessarily the same book) and of the second that a particular book was read by all the students. But this is a matter of the scope of the quantifiers. The sequence of *every* and *one* indicates that the first says what is true of every student, the second what is true of one book. There is a similar situation with:

Many students didn't read the book.
The book wasn't read by many students.

The first says that a lot of students failed to read the book, the second that the book was read by only a few students.

More subtly, there is a difference between:

Beavers build dams.
Dams are built by beavers.

Sentences of this type are usually to be interpreted as having generic subjects, 'beavers in general' or 'beavers typically'. Clearly if beavers typically build dams it does not follow that dams are typically built by beavers.

Finally, it should be noted that there are other devices for thematization, notably the use of HAVE (8.2.2).

5.2 Passive gradience

There are combinations of BE plus *-en* forms (the 'past participle') that are clearly not true passives (Quirk *et al.* 1985:167, Granger 1983:104–15):

This problem is complicated.
I'm damned if I will.
He was interested in linguistics.
John was married but Bill was still single.

There are two respects in which these may differ from true passives:
(i)   the *-en* forms function in some or all respects like adjectives;
(ii) there are no corresponding active sentences, and the *-en* forms are lexically restricted.

These two features are somewhat independent of each other and are also matters of degree rather than absolute criteria.

There are, therefore, potentially many different classes of forms, but for simplicity, only three will be recognized here.

5.2.1 Pseudo-passives

The term 'pseudo-passive' is used here where (i) there is no plausible corresponding active, (ii) the *-en* forms seem to be wholly adjectival, and are lexically restricted. (This use of the term differs completely from the use found in Palmer 1974.)

The essential test of adjectival function is that they occur:
(a)   in attributive position (in a noun phrase before a noun);
(b)   in predicative position after verbs other than BE, *eg* SEEM, BECOME;

(c) with intensifiers such as *very, rather* and comparative/ superlative *more/most*;
(d) coordinated with a true adjective.

[i] Some of the *-en* forms are wholly adjectival as shown by:

> *A complicated problem.*
> *The problem seems complicated.*
> *The problem is very complicated.*
> *The problem is difficult and complicated.*
> (*A very complicated problem*)
> (*The problem seems very complicated.*)

Other examples are illustrated by:

> *The room is very crowded.*
> *His resources seem limited.*
> *She is a devoted mother.*
> *She is young and sophisticated.*

Other forms that function similarly are *celebrated* and *organized*.

With all of these there are no obvious active forms. At one extreme *sophisticated* would not be associated by most people with the rather rare verb SOPHISTICATE; at the other, *complicated* seems to be connected with the verb COMPLI-CATE, but *the problem was complicated* cannot be extended by *by John* and is not related to *John complicated the problem*.

Some forms do not occur attributively, but have the other characteristics of adjectives:

> *John seems prepared to help.*
> *He is very engrossed in his work.*
> *They are closely connected with his family.*

But it is obvious that with these examples the *-en* form is closely associated with the following infinitive or pre-positional phrase, and that this blocks attributive use.

[ii] Some forms show no adjectival function though there are no corresponding actives:

> *The house was situated in the country.*
> *This article is concerned with phonetics.*
> *You aren't supposed to do that.*

There is no possibility of **very situated*, **a situated house*, **The house seems situated*. (*Concerned by/at*, in a rather different sense, has adjectival features – see 5.2.2).

There are numerous dubious cases where a corresponding
active form might be thought possible:

The library is intended to be used.
Your trust was misplaced.
We are faced with great difficulties.
The wall was lined with books.

The first is probably best taken as an agentless passive, and
a similar analysis would be possible for *forbidden,
permitted*, etc, but not *supposed* (above), since there is no
active *X supposes you to . . . .* The second is more difficult:
could it be argued that the trust was misplaced by you? The
third might be seen as the passive of *Great difficulties face
us*, but that is not wholly convincing. Similarly the fourth
might be seen as the passive of *Books lined the wall.*

5.2.2 Semi-passives
There are some *-en* forms that appear to have corresponding
actives, yet exhibit adjectival features:

He was embarrassed by her actions.
Her actions embarrassed him.
He was very embarrassed by her actions.
He seemed embarrassed by her actions.
He was embarrassed by and angry with her actions.

Other examples are:

I felt rather let down by his absence.
He was very elated by his success.
She was very concerned by her failure.

Other forms are *encouraged, shocked*.
Many such *-en* forms, however, can occur not only with *by* but
also with other prepositions:

They were all worried about the accident.
The accident worried them all.
They were all worried and nervous about the accident.

I was surprised at her behaviour.
Her behaviour surprised me.
I was very surprised at her behaviour.

They are satisfied with his actions.
His actions satisfy them.
A satisfied customer.

He is disappointed in you.
You disappoint him.
He seems disappointed in you.

Other forms are *impressed* (*with, by*), *concerned* (*at, by*), *delighted* (*with, by*). All relate to some kind of emotional condition.

With *interested* only *in* (not *by*) is possible:

John is interested in linguistics.
Linguistics interests John.
John is very interested in linguistics.

Some of the forms even have derived negatives:

He was unconcerned by the events.
I was unimpressed with his friend.
John is uninterested in linguistics.

5.2.3 Statal passives

There is a distinction between the function of *were married* in:

They were married at the church.
They were married for many years.

The first is an example of a passive (but see 5.1.3). In the second the form *married* has some adjectival functions:

A married man.
They are married and happy.

The *-en* forms that function in this way are essentially perfect in meaning and refer to a resultant present state as shown by the close similarity of:

The glass has been broken.
The glass is broken.

My bags have been packed.
My bags are packed.

They have been divorced.
They are divorced.

Moreover, they occur with *already* which normally requires the perfect:

My bags are already packed.
They are already divorced.

*I pack my bags already.
*He divorces her already.

I have already packed my bags.
He has already divorced her.

Although these appear to have something in common with the pseudo-passives there is a big difference. The pseudo-passives are lexically restricted, *ie* cannot be freely formed from any verb. But there are no such restrictions on these (the 'statal' passives). Any verb that has a passive may also have a statal passive:

The boy is hurt.
The trees are cut down.
The exams are finished.
The garden is dug.

Yet even with these statal passives there are degrees of 'adjectiveness', as may be seen by comparing *defeated* with *killed*:

The troops were defeated and miserable.
The animals were killed and ready to sell.
The troops looked defeated.
?The animals looked killed.
The defeated troops.
?The killed animals.

But this is more a matter of difficulty in contextualizing these forms than of any absolute grammatical restriction.

5.3 GET

GET is handled among the catenatives (9.2.2), but it also appears to be used in a way similar to BE for the formation of the passive as in:

The child got killed by a car.
The child was killed by a car.

However, GET cannot freely replace BE as shown by the unlikeliness of:

*The lesson got read by a choirboy.
*The letter got written by a poet.
(The lesson was read by a choirboy.)
(The letter was written by a poet.)

The reason appears to be that GET carries with it the meaning of 'arrive at a resultant state' and very often GET + *-en* forms can be treated in terms of a statal passive:

The picture got broken.

Yet GET can appear with an agent which indicates a corresponding active, though this would not be possible with a statal passive:

The picture got broken by the children.
The children got punished by the teacher.

It seems, then, that the function of GET is related to both the ordinary passive and the statal passive. It is, however, more common in colloquial than in formal language and sometimes carries with it a hint of disapproval:

Why did the children get punished?
How did the plate get broken?

Many GET + *-en* forms, however, can be treated as pseudo-passives since GET can also be used, like BECOME with adjectives:

He got/became angry.
He got/became confused.
He got/became angry and confused.

5.4 Lexical passive

There are several types of active sentences that are both semantically and syntactically like the passive.

5.4.1 'Case' relations
It has long been known that many verbs in English function both as transitives and intransitives, *eg* RING and BREAK in:

He rang the bell.
The bell rang.
The wind broke the window.
The window broke.

The significant point is that the object of the transitive verb is the subject of the intransitive. Syntactically, and to some degree semantically, the intransitive is like the passive:

The bell rang.
The bell was rung.
The window broke.
The window was broken.

There is more than this, however. Consider OPEN:

The door opened.

The boy opened the door.
The key opened the door.
The boy opened the door with the key.

The last sentence illustrates the maximum number of noun phrases that appear to be directly associated with the verb. In semantic (and fairly traditional) terms we may refer to *the boy* as the 'agent' (or 'actor'), *the door* as the 'goal' and *the key* as the 'instrument', or describe them in terms of three 'cases', (Fillmore 1968) 'agentive', 'objective' and 'instrumental'. The sentences considered show that agent, goal and instrument may all function as the grammatical subject. But there are some severe restrictions. First, the goal must always be present, it is not possible to say:

*The key opened.
*The boy opened.

Secondly, priority for subject place is given to agent, instrument and goal in that order *ie* (*a*) the goal can be subject only if the other two are absent, (*b*) the instrument can be subject only if the agent is absent as shown by the impossible:

*The door opened with a key.
*The door opened by the boy.
*The key opened the door by the boy.

(For *The door opens with a key* see 5.4.2). The goal can, of course, occur as subject if the verb is passive:

The door was opened with a key.
The door was opened by the boy.

It is clear from this that the transitive/intransitive functions of verbs like OPEN must be handled together with voice.

The semantic relations between the transitive and intransitive are of a variety of kinds. The examples considered are close to that of active and passive, the intransitive like the agentless passive merely leaving the 'agent' unstated. But this is not enough for:

The soldiers marched.
The sergeant marched the soldiers.

In the first *the soldiers* is the agent since marching is a voluntary action. *The sergeant* semantically represents a further 'causative' element, the one who caused someone else to act. As a result the passive is semantically very different from the intransitive:

The soldiers were marched.

There is, however, little or no causation in:

He walked the children across the road.
I'll run you to the station.

Both have rather the same sense of accompaniment. The first means 'walked with the children'. The second is semantically more complex; it relates presumably to running a car, *ie* to mean 'run the car with you in it'. But the syntax is clear enough, and it is syntactically that these intransitive/transitive forms resemble voice.

5.4.2 'Adverbial' passives
Many verbs can be used in a 'passive' sense in such sentences as:

These shirts wash well.
The meat cuts easily.

There is a clear distinction between these and the intransitives that were discussed in the previous subsection. This is illustrated by the ambiguity of:

The door doesn't open in wet weather.

This can either mean that it stays shut or that it cannot be opened. There is, however, no ambiguity in:

The door opens with a key.

This cannot be treated in the same way as *The door opened*; since an instrument is mentioned, it must be placed in subject position according to the 'case' rules, permitting only *The key opens the door*. It must be interpreted, therefore, as an adverbial passive, with the meaning 'The door can be opened with a key'. These uses of the active in the 'passive' sense are 'adverbial' in that they normally occur with adverbs and indicate how the items are or are being washed, cut, sold, etc. *The shirts wash well* means that they can be or are washed successfully.

There is a little doubt about the status of SELL in:

Oranges are selling cheaply today.

A contrastive pair of sentences that has often been quoted is:

They're selling like experts.
They're selling like hot cakes.

The first means that they are selling something, the second that something is being sold. These are probably best treated in terms of transitive and intransitive and of case relations, particularly because the progressive indicates activity, not a quality or characteristic, but it may be relevant that the intransitive form usually requires some kind of adverbial expression. What is indicated is not just an activity, but also a quality or characteristic.

Chapter 6

The modals of possibility and necessity

The discussion of the modal verbs is divided into two chapters. The first begins with quite a long, but very necessary, discussion of some general issues, and then deals individually with the modals of possibility and necessity – MAY, CAN, MUST, NEED and OUGHT TO. The second deals with WILL and SHALL and the related issues of future time reference and conditionals.

In these chapters there will also be an account of the 'semi-modals', BE BOUND TO, BE ABLE TO, HAVE (GOT) TO, BE GOING TO and BE WILLING TO. These are formally not even auxiliaries, let alone modals (see 6.1.7), but are semantically related to the modals and partially suppletive for them. They are most suitably treated in these chapters. For a more detailed discussion see Palmer 1979.

6.1 Characteristics of the modals

The modals share a number of syntactic and semantic features in addition to the morphological features discussed in 2.2.9.

6.1.1 The paradigms
The paradigms of the modal system again (see 3.1.1) have sixteen forms, as can be shown for WILL:

(1)	*will*	*take*	
(2)	*would*	*take*	
(3)	*will*	*be*	*taking*
(4)	*would*	*be*	*taking*
(5)	*will*	*have*	*taken*
(6)	*would*	*have*	*taken*

(7)	will	have	been	taking	
(8)	would	have	been	taking	
(9)	will	be			taken
(10)	would	be			taken
(11)	will	be		being	taken
(12)	would	be		being	taken
(13)	will	have	been		taken
(14)	would	have	been		taken
(15)	will	have	been	being	taken (?)
(16)	would	have	been	being	taken (?)

This is essentially an extension of the primary paradigms, with the addition of the forms of WILL, *will* and *would*. The finite forms of the primary auxiliaries are replaced by the corresponding infinitive (second column). The infinitive does not, of course, mark tense; this is marked instead by the forms of WILL. As with the primary paradigms, therefore, the first form is finite and marks tense; all the other categories are marked in exactly the same way as before.

There is only one paradigm for each modal; there are no participials, infinitival or imperatival phrases, since the modals have no participles, infinitives or imperatives.

SHALL, CAN and MAY have a similar set of sixteen possible forms. MUST, OUGHT, DARE and NEED make no distinction of tense and, therefore, have paradigms of only eight which are in most respects present rather than past tense. OUGHT is idiosyncratic in that it alone of the modals is followed by the *to*-infinitive rather than the bare infinitive. The close association of *to* with the preceding auxiliary is shown by the fact that there is, in normal speech, a single not a double [t]: [ɒːtə] rather than [ɒːt tə] (see 11.5).

Numbers 15 and 16 are again marked with a question mark. They are even more unlikely to occur than the corresponding forms of the primary paradigms. Numbers 11 and 12 are also marginal and are marked as 'wanting' in one grammar (Palmer and Blandford 1939:131). Where the meaning of duration might seem to require such progressive forms, the corresponding non-progressive forms are quite normal as in:

He'll be examined, while we are there.

It would not be impossible, but most unusual, to say:

?He'll be being examined, while we are there.

There are, however, some issues about the relationship

between these morphologically distinct present and past tense forms. First, all of them are found in the sequence of tenses or deitic shift relations of reported speech:

> *I will come.*
> *He said he would come.*
> *You shall have it.*
> *He said she should have it.*
> *He can speak Japanese.*
> *She said he could speak Japanese.*
> *He may come tomorrow.*
> *I said he might come tomorrow.*

Secondly, and in contrast with the first point, not all of them are regularly used to refer to past time: only *could* (6.3.1) and, less commonly, *would* (7.1.3) have simple past time reference. Thirdly *would*, *could*, and *might* often function as the tentative (see 3.2.5) forms corresponding to *will, can, may* (7.1.2, 6.3.2):

> *Will you help me?*
> *Would you help me?*
> *I can do that for you.*
> *I could do that for you.*
> *He may come tomorrow.*
> *He might come tomorrow.*

But *should* is not the tentative form corresponding to *shall*. Rather, it belongs with OUGHT TO being often very close in meaning to it. In this function it is best treated simply as a distinct modal verb and so shown in small capitals SHOULD. There are, moreover, problems concerning the relation of SHOULD/OUGHT TO to MUST. Fourthly, there is a major issue concerning the use of the forms in conditional sentences (7.4.3).

Because there are considerable differences in the uses of the past and present tense forms of the modals, some of the discussion that follows will be in terms of the forms, rather than the lexemes, of *will* and *would, can* and *could* rather than WILL and CAN etc. Often, however, it will not matter much whether reference is to form or lexeme, *eg* in the case of *must*/MUST, since there is only one form. In such cases reference will be to the lexeme; where there is reference to the form, there is a clear implication that other forms of the same lexeme are being handled separately.

6.1.2 Types of modality

The modal verbs have three main functions, which will be called 'epistemic', 'deontic' and 'dynamic'. These can be illustrated with *may* and *can* by:

    John may be in his office.   (Epistemic)
    John may/can come in now.   (Deontic)
    John can run ten miles with ease.   (Dynamic)

Roughly, the difference in meaning between these three is that the first (epistemic) makes the judgment that it is possible that John is in his office, the second (deontic) gives permission for John to come in, the third (dynamic) states that John has the ability to run ten miles with ease.

There is, however, another dimension along which the modal verbs may be distinguished. The examples above with *may* and *can* can be interpreted in terms of some kind of possibility, whereas *must* seems to express some kind of necessity:

    John must be in his office.   (Epistemic)
    John must come in now.   (Deontic)

The first of these makes a judgment that John is bound to be in his office, the second lays an obligation upon him to come in. (Deontic *must* is more problematic – see 6.5.3.)

For this reason, a distinction will be made between 'kinds' of modality (epistemic, deontic and dynamic) and 'degrees' of modality (possibility and necessity).

In addition, however, to possibility and necessity, it is essential to recognize a third degree of modality. For *will* as well as *may* and *must* can make a judgment, and is thus also an epistemic modal:

    John will be in his office.

There are, therefore, (at least) three degrees of epistemic modality. But *will* also provides a further degree of dynamic modality in addition to that of *can*. It expresses the subject's willingness whereas *can* expresses his ability:

    John will always help his friends.

Not surprisingly, *can* and *will* can easily be conjoined, if both are dynamic:

    John can and will help his friends.

Further, *shall* is used to give an undertaking on the part of the speaker to make a promise or a threat:

    You shall have your reward tomorrow.

Although this is rather different from the uses of deontic *may/can* and *must*, it is to be treated as deontic because giving an undertaking, like giving permission and laying an obligation, involves the speaker in some kind of active relationship with others (see below).

There would seem to be a basic pattern:

	Epistemic	Deontic	Dynamic
Possibility	may	may/can	can
Necessity	must	must	
?	will	shall	will

(There are, however, other modal verbs to be considered.)

The three kinds of modality can be distinguished in terms of both form and meaning. The most obvious formal point relates to the distribution of *may* and *can*: only *may* is epistemic, only *can* is dynamic, though both may be deontic, though with stylistic differences. (It is obviously convenient to talk about *may* 'being epistemic', *can* 'being dynamic', etc, and to refer to 'epistemic, deontic and dynamic modals' rather than, more accurately, to 'modals with epistemic, deontic and dynamic functions'.) Further formal criteria will be discussed later (6.1.3).

The semantic differences are no less clear. An epistemic modal is used to express a judgment by the speaker about the truth of the proposition he is presenting ('what he is talking about'). A deontic modal actually does something; it is performative (see Austin 1962:4) in that the speaker gives permission, lays an obligation or in some way influences or directs the behaviour of his addressee (or, with *shall*, of himself). This was called 'discourse oriented' in the previous edition of this book (Palmer 1974). A dynamic modal predicates something ('says something about') the subject of the sentence. This was called 'speaker oriented' in the previous edition. Although 'discourse oriented' and 'speaker oriented' are no longer used to identify the two kinds of modality, they will often be referred to to emphasize their essential characteristics.

6.1.3 Tense, negation, voice

In the discussion of auxiliary and full verb (2.3.2) it was suggested that the TNP (Tense Negation Passive) test could be used to decide whether, in fact, auxiliaries could be treated as if they were full verbs. The argument becomes more crucial for the modals, because it is convenient to draw a semantic and partly formal distinction between the 'modality' and the 'proposition' (see above). In general, it can be said that the modality is what is expressed by the modal verb and the proposition what is expressed by all that follows, including the main verb. It must be admitted, however, that the term 'proposition' is less appropriate for deontic and dynamic modality than for epistemic; with the latter there is indeed a judgment on what is said, but with the others the modality relates to some kind of activity or events that can, must, etc, be performed. But a single term is convenient and 'proposition' will be used.

It is important to add that the modality/proposition distinction is not wholly in a one-to-one relationship with the distinction between the modal auxiliary and the main verb. This is especially true where there is negation, as exemplified by:

You mustn't come.

Here it is the modal verb that is negated by the ending *-n't*, but semantically it is the proposition, not the modality, that is negated, since this means 'It is necessary for you not to come', *ie* 'You must-n't come' not 'It is not necessary for you to come'.

With this distinction of modality and proposition it is now possible to consider the issues of tense, negation and voice, though attention will, for simplicity, be confined here to the possibility and necessity modals.

Tense
With epistemic modals only the proposition may be marked for past time, by the use of *have*:

John may/must have been in his office yesterday.

The modality, however, cannot normally be marked as past and there is a simple reason for this: by using an epistemic modal the speaker actually makes a (performative and so present time) judgment. As was noted in 3.3.3, non-finite *have*, including *have* with modals as here, can be interpreted as past as well as perfect (although this is not possible for finite forms of HAVE). In fact, it can, with a modal, also be interpreted as 'past-past' as well as past perfect (with a pattern similar to that of the reported speech forms of 3.2.3). This can be shown by a comparison of modal forms with corresponding simple declaratives:

(past)	*John was in his office yesterday.*
	John may have been in his office yesterday.
(present perfect)	*John has already been in his office.*
	John may already have been in his office.
('past past')	*John had been in his office before she came.*
	John may have been in his office before she came.

(past perfect)   *John had been in his office for two hours.*
                        John may have been in his office for two
                        hours.

With deontic modals, neither modality nor proposition can be marked for past time. There is again a simple reason: a deontic modal is performative – it gives permission, for example, at the time of utterance and, obviously, cannot give permission for actions that have already taken place.

With dynamic modals only the modality can be marked for past tense/time:

John could run ten miles with ease   (when he was younger).

All that has been said so far concerns the use of tense to mark past time. But, as was noted in 6.1.1, the past tense forms of the modals are also used to mark unreality or tentativeness. Since the epistemic and deontic modals have no past tense forms used for past time (except in reported speech), it follows that their past tense forms can only be unreal or tentative (epistemic and deontic *might*, epistemic *would*, deontic *could*). But the past tense forms of the dynamic modals (*could* and *would*) can be either past time markers or unreal/tentative. Further ambiguity can arise with all types of modality in reported speech, where *might, could* and *would* are used to report not only *may, can* and *will*, but also *might, could* and *would*:

May I come in?
Might I come in?
I asked if I might come in.
John can speak French.
John could speak French.
He said John could speak French.
John will be there now.
John would be there now.
He said John would be there now.

Negation
There are two problems in an analysis of the negative forms. The first is that different modals may be used for the same kind of modality. The second is that not all theoretically possible negative forms exist, though alternative and semantically close forms are often available.

With epistemic modality either the modality or the proposition may be negated:

John can't be in his office.
John may not be in his office.

The first indicates 'not possible that', *ie* it negates the modality. Here the modal verb is changed – *can't* is used instead of *may*. The second negates the proposition and indicates 'possible that . . . not'. Paraphrases are 'It is not possible that he is in his office' and 'It is possible that he is not in his office'. There are, however, no forms of the necessity modals that are used for the negation of either the modality or the proposition (see 6.5.1).

With deontic modals only the modality is normally negated for possibility, but both are negated for necessity:

John can't/may not come in now.
John needn't leave now.
John mustn't leave now.

The first of these denies permission and so can be seen as indicating no possibility, *ie* as negating the modality. (There is no obvious way of negating the proposition – see 6.2.2.) The second denies obligation and so indicates no necessity, *ie* it negates the modality. Once again the modal form is changed – *needn't* for *must*. The third asserts obligation not to act and so indicates 'necessity not', negating the proposition.

With dynamic modality, only the modality may be negated:

John can't run ten miles with ease.

This indicates lack of ability, *ie* it negates the modality, not the proposition. Presumably we seldom, if ever, need to state that someone has the ability not to perform an action.

Voice
The epistemic and deontic modals are voice neutral. Not surprisingly, perhaps, if someone makes a judgment about, or indicates a deontic attitude towards, a proposition expressed in the active, he makes the same judgment, indicates the same attitude, if the same proposition is expressed in the passive:

John may meet Mary on the train.
Mary may be met by John on the train.
John may/can meet Mary, (I don't mind).
Mary may/can be met by John, (I don't mind).

With dynamic modality, however, there is no voice neutrality, since the modality relates to the subject (is 'subject oriented') and that is changed with passivization:

John can speak French.
!French can be spoken by John.

(But the situation is a little more complex than this – see 6.2.3). In diagram form the overall position is, then:

		Modality	*Proposition*
Epistemic	tense	No	Yes
	negation	Yes	Yes
	voice	Yes	
Deontic	tense	No	No
	negation	Yes	Yes
	voice	Yes	
Dynamic	tense	Yes	No
	negation	Yes	No
	voice	No	

Two conclusions can be drawn from this discussion. First, it confirms on formal grounds the distinction of epistemic, deontic and dynamic modality. Secondly, in some respects the modals are like main verbs, in that they do not pass the TNP tests as successfully as the primary auxiliaries. Nevertheless, there are still restriction upon them in terms of TNP and they are fully auxiliaries in terms of the NICE properties and of the paradigm.

6.1.4 Neutral modality

A problem arises from the fact that *can* and *must* may be used to express possibility and necessity that is 'neutral' or 'circumstantial' in that it does not emanate from the speaker and so is not strictly deontic (yet is not epistemic or dynamic either). This is clearly illustrated where the modality depends only on a stated condition:

If you want a screwdriver, you can get it at Woolworths.
If you want a screwdriver, you must go to an ironmonger's.

There are three possible ways of accounting for this. One is to say that there is a fourth type of modality, 'neutral' modality. However, this potential fourth type is often difficult to distinguish. *Can* seems to be indeterminately dynamic and neutral; indeed in the example given it might seem to refer to the subject's ability. *Must* seems often indeterminately deontic and neutral; it is often unclear whether the speaker imposes the obligation or simply says that it exists.

A second solution is to say that there are only two types of modality, epistemic, which is formally and semantically quite distinct, and 'root' modality, which comprises all the rest. (This distinction is widely used, but appears to have originated in Hofmann 1976.) This is too drastic; the distinction between deontic and dynamic modality is quite clearly shown in the distribution of *may* and *can* and in the TNP tests, especially in the fact that deontic modals cannot have past tense forms.

A third solution is to recognize that there is neutral modality, but to acknowledge that it is not wholly distinct from one of the others, *ie* that there is indeterminacy. Thus neutral *can* shades into dynamic *can* and neutral *must* into deontic *must*.

In practice, there is no justification for treating neutral modality separately from the other kinds. Neutral possibility will be considered with dynamic and neutral necessity with deontic. But the distinction between neutral and deontic necessity becomes of some importance when MUST is compared with HAVE GOT TO. For HAVE GOT TO quite specifically excludes the involvement of the speaker: the necessity does not come from his laying of an obligation. But *must* sometimes seems equivalent to HAVE GOT TO, sometimes in contrast with it. It is thus possible to distinguish the deontic uses of MUST when it contrasts and the neutral use when it does not (see 6.6.2).

6.1.5 Possibility/necessity and negation
Although they will be discussed in detail later, it may be convenient to set out here, in summary form, the modal verbs that are used in terms of (i) kind of modality (epistemic and deontic only), (ii) negation of either modality or proposition, (iii) possibility and necessity.

For possibility the basic table is:

	Positive	Neg. modality	Neg. proposition
Epistemic	may	can't	may not
Deontic	may/can	may not/can't	—

For necessity the basic table is:

	Positive	Neg. modality	Neg. proposition
Epistemic	must	—	—
Deontic	must	needn't	mustn't

Two points are obvious from these tables. The first is that in two places different verbs are used for negation of the modality.

The second is that there are gaps. However, most of these gaps can be filled by making use of the relations between possibility and necessity in terms of negation. The point is that 'not possible' is equivalent to 'necessary . . . not' and 'not necessary' to 'possible . . . not', and vice versa. If, for instance, it is not necessary to do something, it is possible not to do it. These equivalences can be shown as:

Not possible   ≡   Necessary not
Not necessary   ≡   Possible not

It follows from this that the missing negative forms of *must* can be supplied by those of *may/can*, though in the reverse order: *may not* for negation of the modality and *can't* for negation of the proposition. Similarly, instead of negating the proposition for deontic *may/can* it is possible to negate the modality of deontic *must – needn't*. The amended table is, then:

	Positive	Neg. modality	Neg. proposition
Epistemic	may	can't	may not
Deontic	may/can	may not/can't	(needn't)
Epistemic	must	(may not)	(can't)
Deontic	must	needn't	mustn't

It should not, however, be assumed that the alternative forms are wholly identical in meaning or in distribution, particularly in the case of *must* and *need*.

6.1.6 Non-assertion
As was noted in 2.2.7, negation and interrogation can be handled along with other features under the single heading of non-assertion.

The relevance of this to the modals is that the forms used with negation are also used with other types of non-assertion, *eg* with a semi-negative:

John may be in his office.
John can't be in his office.
John can hardly be in his office.

The same point is true, though less obviously, for:

All you need do is go to London.
All you must do is go to London.

All you must do here provides a non-assertive context, for that alone would explain the occurrence of *need* in the first sentence. The difference between *need* and *must* is that the modality is non-assertive with the first, the proposition with the second, as the paraphrases show:

> *There is no necessity to do anything but go to London.*
> *There is necessity not to do anything but go to London.*

There are some specific points concerning the modals and interrogation. First, it is obvious that epistemic and deontic modality are not strictly performative when used with interrogation. No judgment is made by an epistemic modal, no permission given or obligation laid by a deontic modal. Rather, and quite naturally, the speaker asks the addressee whether he makes the judgment, gives permission or lays obligation. Secondly, and as a corollary, only the modality is questioned – it is not possible to question the proposition.

The forms used for negation are, quite naturally, also used for interrogation:

> *John can't be in his office.*
> *Can John be in his office?*
> *John needn't go now.*
> *Need John go now?*

The situation is, however, complicated by the fact that there is no absolute requirement to use the non-assertive forms in interrogation:

> *Does he have some money?*   (any)
> *Must John go now?*   (need)
> *May John be in his office?*   (can)

Here the speaker expresses a rather more positive attitude towards the statement being questioned (see below for details). Of particular importance in this respect is the pattern formed with tag questions. With a positive sentence a negative tag is normally required and vice versa:

> *He's coming, isn't he?*
> *He's not coming, is he?*

With modals the form of the modal does not change with tag questions:

> *He must come, mustn't he?*
> *He must come, needn't he?*

He mustn't come, must he?
**He mustn't come, need he?*

Negative interrogatives (see 2.2.7) raise particular problems for
the modals. They are best dealt with in the appropriate sections.

6.1.7 Other forms

For the most part this section has been discussing just the present
tense forms *may, can, must* and *will*, though the past tense forms
might, could and *would* have been mentioned. These past tense
forms are closely related to the present tense forms, but there
are sufficient problems with *might* and *could* to justify a separate
section (6.3), though *would* will be handled with *will* (7.1, 7.2).

NEED is discussed with MUST as a necessity modal, but there is
no obvious place for DARE. It has to be handled here because it
is clearly a modal in some of its functions, and, in particular, is
very like NEED. But it does not easily fit into the general scheme
(see 6.8).

OUGHT TO and near synonymous SHOULD also raise problems,
but clearly have some kind of relationship with MUST and are
dealt with soon after the sub-section on *must*.

Of considerable relevance to the study of modality are the
semi-modals, BE BOUND TO, BE ABLE TO, HAVE TO/HAVE GOT TO, BE
GOING TO and BE WILLING TO. These are clearly not modals. In
particular they do not pass the paradigm test, but may actually
co-occur, as can be seen by the contrast of:

He's going to have to come.
**He'll must come.*

Yet they appear to have the NICE properties because they are
composed of BE or HAVE plus a following verb. They are closely
related to the modals, moreover, sometimes seeming to have the
same meanings, sometimes indicating specific contrasts. They
will, therefore, be handled in the same chapters as the modals
to which they are related.

There is one final point on the arrangement of the next two
chapters. Since there are two dimensions along which the modals
may be classified, there are two ways of organising the discussion.
In *Modality and the English modals* (Palmer 1979) the chapter
divisions were based upon kinds of modality, beginning with a
chapter on epistemic modality. In this more practical book it
seems more sensible to proceed, as far as possible, along the
other dimension, which allows for individual forms (or closely
related pairs) to be discussed separately, beginning with *may* and
can.

6.2 *May* and *can*

It is essential to handle *can* and *may* in a single section (and similarly *could* and *might* – in 6.3), not only because both indicate possibility, but also because there are important syntactic relations between them, though these differ according to the kind of modality involved.

6.2.1 Epistemic

May alone expresses epistemic modality, except with non-assertion (see below). It can be paraphrased 'possible that . . .', but with the suggestion that the speaker makes a judgment about what 'may' be. It can occur with various types of proposition, *eg* those indicating actions (simple form), activities (progressive form) or states. There is thus a correspondence between the following trios:

John goes to London.
John is working.
John is there.
John may go to London.
John may be working.
John may be there.

All of the modal examples given above can be interpreted in terms of habitual or future time reference and so may be collocated with *eg every day* or *tomorrow*. But only the last two of them may refer to a simple present action and so be collocated with *eg at this moment*. That would not be possible with the example *John may go to London*. That is, however, not surprising since it is also unlikely that the non-modal form *John goes to London* could be interpreted in that way (but see 4.2.2). Moreover, even when the reference is to future time, the progressive is often used in preference to the simple form even though no duration is involved:

John may be coming tomorrow.

The reason appears to be the ambiguity of *may* with the simple form: it is possible for it to be interpreted as deontic, as giving permission:

John may come tomorrow.

(There is a similar situation with *must* (6.5.1) and *will* (7.1.1)).

May often occurs with adverbs. With *perhaps* and *possibly* the adverb does little more than reinforce the notion of possibility.

But *well* considerably strengthens the possibility, and implies something close to probability:

> *He may well be surprised by your suggestion.*
> *He may well have gone by now.*

There is one slightly different use of *may*. It is often used to indicate simply that the speaker entertains a proposition: he merely accepts it for consideration. This is the so-called 'concessive' use as in:

> *Whatever he may think, he'll still come.*
> *We may not like it, but we'll come.*

Typically, *may* occurs here with *whatever* or a following *but*. It seems reasonable to treat this as a variety of epistemic possibility.

Non-assertion

With negation, either the modality or the proposition may be negated. The modality is negated by *can't* ('It is not possible that . . .'), the proposition by *may not* ('It is possible that . . . not . . .'):

> *John can't go to London.*
> *John may not go to London.*
> *John can't be working.*
> *John may not be working.*
> *John can't be there.*
> *John may not be there.*

Examples with *have* (see below) are:

> *You can't have met her.*
> *You may not have met her.*

Can is also used with a semi-negative or in other non-assertive contexts:

> *John can hardly be still in his office.*

With interrogation, only the modality can, of course, be questioned and again *can* is used:

> *Can John be in his office?*

But *may* is possible too, thought *might* (6.3.2) is more likely:

> *May (might) John be in his office?*

Similarly, both *can't* and *may not* are possible with negative interrogation, though again *might not* is more likely:

Can't/may not/might not John be in his office?

This would mean 'Isn't it possible that John is in his office?'. The same meaning would be possible with *not* after the subject:

Can/may John not be in his office?

This could, however, also be taken to be a question about the negative proposition, especially with stress on *not* ('Is it the case that John may not be in his office?', 'John may not be in his office, may he?'). But there is no way, except with a tag, of expressing questions about the negation of the modality ('Is the case that John can't be in his office?', 'John can't be in his office, can he?').

As with assertive *may*, so with non-assertive *can*, the progressive is used to refer to simple future events (and is, indeed, the normal form):

John can't be coming tomorrow.
Can John be coming tomorrow?

The reason is similar. A simple form would be interpreted as either deontic or dynamic (permission or ability):

John can't come tomorrow.
Can John come tomorrow?

Tense
Like all epistemic modals, *may* and its related forms mark the proposition as past with *have*:

John may/may not/can't have been here yesterday.

Voice
Like all epistemic modals, *may* is voice neutral:

John may have seen Mary.
Mary may have been seen by John.

6.2.2 Deontic
Both *may* and *can* are used for deontic possibility (giving permission) but *may* is mostly literary, formal or old-fashioned. In speech *can* is more common (see Palmer 1979:60, Ehrmann 1966:12):

You may be seated – the meeting will commence.
You can come in now – we're ready.

The first might be uttered by the president of a society, the second by participants in a guessing game.

May and *can* are also used in somewhat stylized utterances as:

You can (may) take it from us.
You can (may) rest assured.

Here the speaker wishes to reassure the addressee of the truth of what has been said or the satisfactory nature of the situation. This can easily be interpreted as an extension of the notion of permission. The speaker allows the addressee to be reassured by his own participation in saying that matters are all right.

Can, however (and to a lesser extent *may*), is also used where it seems rather to give an instruction often of a brusque or impolite kind:

You can leave me out of your plans.
You can forget all about that.

Here the speaker signals that he wishes to be left out, that the addressee should forget the issue. Yet *can* is by no means equivalent, or even similar, to *must* here. It would be possible to treat this as another degree of deontic modality, but the simplest solution is to treat it as deontic possibility, the giving of permission being sarcastically to be interpreted as an expectation. The speaker assumes the authority to permit, and implies that what he permits will be done.

Very similar to this is the idiomatic:

You can say that again.

This is a colloquial expression to agree with what has been said.

Non-assertion
Either the modality or the proposition may be negated, but the forms are not identical with those used for epistemic modality. There is, moreover, some curious idiosyncrasy in that *may not* and *cannot* negate the modality (refuse permission) although *mustn't* and *shan't* negate the proposition (lay an obligation, give a guarantee that the event will not take place – see 6.5.3, 7.1.4).

For possibility, the modality is negated by *may not* and *cannot*:

You may not leave now.
You cannot leave now.

There is no regular way of negating the proposition; this is best expressed by using the logically equivalent form of necessity expressed by *needn't* (It is possible . . . not . . . ≡ It is not necessary . . .):

You needn't leave now.

However, if the context makes it clear, and particularly if there is a contrast, the accent on *not*, with *may nót* or *cannót*, can be used to give permission not to act:

You can (may) come, or you can (may) nót come, as you wish.

Here the context would imply that the proposition was negated, that there was permission not to come. But in other contexts the emphatic *not* would be interpreted as an emphatic negation of the modality, as an emphatic denial of permission:

You can (may) nót come: you must stay here.

May and *can* are quite often used in interrogation to convey a polite request:

May I get you a drink?
Can I phone you back?

In this context *may* is quite common; the reason is, perhaps, obvious. The speaker asks permission because he wishes to be polite, and, if he wishes to be polite, he will also use a formal expression. *May* then becomes appropriate.

With negative interrogation the position is similar (but not quite identical) to that of epistemic *may/can*. The usual interpretation is 'Isn't it permissible . . .?' or 'I can/may . . . can't I/may I not?':

May not I get you a drink?
Can't I phone you back?

It is also possible to place *not* after the subject:

May I not phone you back?
Can I not phone you back?

This can also be interpreted in the same way, but in the right context and with stress on *not* could negate the proposition ('Do I have permission not to phone you back?'). But again there is no way, except with a tag, of expressing an interrogative with the modality negated:

I can't phone you back, can I?

May is also commonly used in the expression *if I may:*

I'll come tomorrow, if I may.
That is foolish, if I may say so.

The reason is the same as that for interrogative *may*. In the first example the speaker is actually asking for permission. *If I may* has the same function as *May I?* In the second he is being apolo-

getic for what he is saying – and the apology takes the form of
a polite request, *ie* 'please allow me to say so'.

Tense
There are no past tense forms: deontic modals cannot be marked
for tense in either modality or proposition (6.1.3).

Voice
There is some degree of voice neutrality:

> *John can/may help Henry.*
> *Henry can/may be helped by John.*

Here the speaker may be giving permission for John to help
Henry or Henry to be helped by John, but often permission is
clearly given to the person indicated by the subject of the verb.
If the speaker specifically gives John permission, the passive loses
that particular sense. It may be significant that very commonly,
where there is a passive, it is agentless:

> *This proposal can/may be accepted.*

The permission is not overtly granted to anyone in particular.

6.2.3 Dynamic
All the clear cases of dynamic possibility, which predicate the
possibility to the subject of the sentence and are thus subject-
oriented, have *can*, never *may*.

[i]   *Can* is often used to indicate ability on the part of the
      subject:

> *John can run three miles with ease.*
> *They can speak French.*
> *My destiny's in my control – I can make or break my life.*

In this sense *can* is very close to BE ABLE TO and often
interchangeable with it. But there are important differences
(see 6.4, but compare also 6.3.1).
   'Ability' is, however, too narrow a description of dynamic *can*. For it is often used to indicate what inanimate
objects 'can' achieve, *eg* (Ehrmann 1966:13):

> *Religion can summate, epitomize, relate and conserve the
> highest ideals and values.*

[ii] *Can* often seems to have a neutral sense, to say that some-
      thing is possible without suggesting that this depends on
      anyone's ability. Or, perhaps, it is 'circumstantial' in that

the circumstances make it possible. This is particularly true
where there is a passive:

> *It can easily be rubbed out.*
> *I'll see what can be done.*

Often, though, the circumstances are indicated:

> *You can get the job only if you don't want it.*
> *The only way you can succeed is to work hard.*

It is, however, often very difficult to distinguish this from
the ability sense. It may be that the circumstances include,
in part, the subject's own characteristics, as these examples
show.

[iii]   *Can* is also used to indicate characteristic behaviour of
people, often in a derogatory sense:

> *He can tell awful lies.*
> *She can be very unkind at times.*

This is clearly dynamic in that it is subject-oriented, but
may have something in common with the existential use
discussed in 6.2.4[ii]. But one important difference
between this and the ability use is that here *can* cannot be
replaced by BE ABLE TO.

[iv]   *Can* is very commonly used with private verbs, especially
verbs of sensation:

> *I can smell something burning.*
> *I can see the moon.*

Here there is very little sense of ability, but this use of *can*
is subject-oriented in that the subject alone is involved. But
it indicates that he does, in fact, experience the sensation
rather than that he is able to experience it. But *can* may
equally still have the ability sense with a private verb:

> *He has marvellous eyes – he can see the tiniest detail.*

There is then potential, but rarely actual, ambiguity. *Can*
is also used with other types of private verbs, *eg* those of
a conceptual kind, REMEMBER, UNDERSTAND, with minimal
sense of ability:

> *I can't remember a thing.*
> *I can't understand what he is saying.*

These differ little, if at all, from:

> *I don't remember a thing.*
> *I don't understand what he is saying.*

Can also occurs with a number of verbs in a semi-idiomatic sense but only in non-assertive contexts with AFFORD, BEAR, BE BOTHERED, STAND:

> *I can't afford a new car.*
> *He can't be bothered to help.*
> *Can you stand all that noise?*

There is some sense of ability here, but in none of the cases considered is *can* replaceable by BE ABLE TO.

[v]   *Can* is often used to make suggestions, *ie* to suggest what is dynamically possible and so to imply that it might or should be done:

> *I can do that for you.*
> *We can send you a map if you wish.*
> *You can say you won't go.*
> *If you get the sack, you can always work for me.*

With first person pronouns the speaker makes an offer. With other persons he invites action; often *can* occurs with *always* in this sense, even though only one occasion is envisaged:

> *You can always say 'No' to the proposal.*

It might be thought that this is a deontic use of *can* similar to that of *You can forget about that* (6.2.2). But *may* is quite impossible here and certainly never occurs in this sense with *always*. The conclusion must be that this is dynamic.

Non-assertion

The negative form *can't* is used with all the different senses of *can* to negate the modality only. But with this negative form the ability and neutral senses are even more difficult to distinguish. After all, if there is no possibility it makes little difference whether that possibility depends on the subject or the circumstances, *eg*:

> *The people who cannot very easily raise their wages.*

On the other hand, the following example indicates (negative) ability:

> *They can't speak a word of English.*

Can and *can't* are used in interrogations with all the senses, but there is one special use of *can* in polite requests such as:

Can you pass the salt?
Can you remind me what you said?

This is best seen in terms of *can* being used for suggestion ([v] above), the interrogative form being required for politeness. *You can pass the salt* would be far too peremptory in most circumstances. Similarly the negative interrogative is used as a plea, a very earnest request:

Can't you let me have it?
Can't you help him?

BE ABLE TO would not be appropriate with these requests and pleas. *Are you able to pass the salt?* would be interpreted as a very sarcastic remark, implying 'What's the matter with you? Can't you perform a simple service?'

Tense
With dynamic modality only the modality can be past. For this, *could* is available (discussed in 6.3.1), though there are some restrictions on past tense/past time.

Voice
The issue of passivation is far from clear and simple. Where there is neutral possibility, there is voice neutrality:

Hard work can cure depression.
Depression can be cured by hard work.

Indeed the possibility of the passive usually suggests neutral possibility as in:

It can't be done.

If, however, *can* is clearly subject-oriented, to indicate either ability or characteristic, that subject orientation would not be maintained in the passive, and there would be no voice neutrality:

They can speak French.
!French can be spoken by them.
She can waste money.
!Money can be wasted by her.

However, a person's ability to do something often depends on the characteristics of other persons and things as in:

Really strong men can lift cars.

It is equally possible to say:

Cars can be lifted by really strong men.

It is debatable whether there is voice neutrality here. Does the second sentence refer to the ability of strong men? Or does it merely follow that, if the one sentence is true, so is the other, because of the dependence of the ability on the characteristics of both subject and object.

6.2.4 Problem types

[i] It is a little difficult to account for *may* (and more commonly *might* – see 6.3.1) with *as well*:

We may as well go.

This is a rather reluctant suggestion. It says 'There is no point in staying, it would be just as sensible to go'. Although at first this might seem deontic in that it suggests action, it is significant that only *may*, not *can*, is used. This rather suggests that it is epistemic with the paraphrase 'It may be the best thing to do in the circumstances'. *May have* is possible but less likely than *might have*:

We may as well have gone.

[ii] There is a use of *can* to express 'some' or 'sometimes'. This may be called the 'existential' use:

Lions can be dangerous.

This may mean that some lions are dangerous or that lions are sometimes dangerous. Other examples with distinct 'some' and 'sometimes' meanings are:

Speech days can be revealing.   (some)
This can mean, but it doesn't always
mean that . . .   (sometimes)

In written and especially in scientific language *may* is also used (Huddleston 1971:297–8):

The lamellae may arise de novo from the middle of the cell and migrate to the periphery.

However, where there is a clear sense of characteristic, *may* is unlikely to be used, especially in speech. There is a contrast between (Leech 1969:223):

> *Lions can be dangerous.*
> *Lions may be dangerous.*

The latter would almost certainly be interpreted epistemically ('It may be that lions are . . .'). But here *can* has much in common with the characteristic use discussed in 6.2.3[iii].

6.3 *Might* and *could*

Formally *might* and *could* are the past tense forms of *may* and *can* and a great deal that can be said about them could conveniently have been said earlier.But there are some differences and some problems.

6.3.1 Past tense

[i] *Might* and *could* are found in reported speech, where there is deictic shift, to report *may* and *can*. This is true of all kinds of modality:

John may be in his office.	(Epistemic)
John may/can come in.	(Deontic)
John can run ten miles with ease.	(Dynamic)
She said John might be in his office.	
John might/could come in.	
John could run ten miles with ease.	

Their functions exactly mirror those of *may* and *can* and it is through this relationship that they can be formally identified as their past tense forms.

[ii] Where reported speech is not involved, there can be no past tense for the modality with epistemic or deontic modals (see 6.1.3, 6.2.1, 6.2.2) – possible counter-examples might seem to be:

> *For all I knew, he might have done it.*

It might seem that this means 'It was possible that . . .' ie past time epistemic modality. But the context clearly shows that the speaker is indicating what he thought or believed at the time. This then still involves deictic shift of 'He may have done it' (see 3.2.4 for similar examples).

With dynamic possibility, however, *could* is regularly used to indicate past time:

> *He could run ten miles with ease, when he was younger.*

There is, however, an important restriction. In the ability sense the positive form *could* is not used if there is an implication of 'actuality' (see Palmer 1977), *ie* if it is implied that the relevant event took place. This contrasts with the negative *couldn't*, which has no such restriction:

*I ran fast, and could catch the bus.
I ran fast, but couldn't catch the bus.

The alternative form for the first uses BE ABLE TO (see 6.4):

I ran fast and was able to catch the bus.

However, this is not simply a matter of the actual forms *could* and *couldn't* but more generally of assertion and non-assertion. In a non-assertive environment *could* (as well as *couldn't*) is possible:

All he could think of was this child.
He was laughing so much he could hardly speak.
There was little they could think of.
No-one could get a mortgage.

Could is also possible if there is an implication of success, but limited success, or success with difficulty:

I could almost reach the branch.
I could just reach the branch.

There is (see above) no restriction if the reference is to general ability in the past. Nor is there any if there is reference to a sequence of action or a habitual action:

I could get up and go to the kitchen whenever I wanted to.
My father could usually get what he wanted.

This restriction does not apply to the characteristic use of *could*, because that does not imply the actuality of any single action:

She could be very unkind at times.

More surprisingly, it does not apply to the use of *could* with private verbs, even though there might seem to be actuality:

I could see the moon.
I could understand all he was saying.

These imply that I did see the moon and that I did understand.

There is no use of *could* to correspond to the 'suggestion' use of *can*. The reason is that although this was treated as dynamic, it has what is essentially a deontic sense: the suggestion is made or implied by the utterance itself.

6.3.2 Tentative

Might and *could* are used as tentative forms of epistemic *may* in all its possible environments, to express a lower degree of possibility:

> *John might/could go to London.*
> *John might/could be working.*
> *John might/could be there.*

Similarly the non-assertive forms *might*(*n't*) and *could*(*n't*) occur in the same kinds of environment as *may*(*not*) and *can*(*'t*):

> *John mightn't be there.*
> *Could John be in his office?*

However, as was noted in 6.2.1, *might* and *mightn't* are more natural than *may* and *may not* in interrogation, and *could* is, perhaps, a little more likely than *can*.

Surprisingly, perhaps, although *might* is the tentative form of *may*, when it is used with *well* it strengthens the possibility, so that *might well* is stronger than *may*:

> *He might well be in his office.*

Conversely with *just* the possibility is weakened:

> *He might just agree to your suggestion.*

Might is also used in the concessive sense:

> *Whatever he might say, he'll come.*
> *We might not agree, but we'll come.*

Might and *could* are less commonly used deontically as the counterparts of *may* and *can*. They are, in fact, almost entirely restricted to the use of the interrogative for a polite request:

> *Might I ask you a question?*
> *Could I get you another drink?*

Here, like *may* and *can*, both forms are used, but *might* is more formal.

With dynamic modality a tentative use of *could* is used for suggestions and requests:

> *I could do that for you.*
> *You could always say 'No' to his suggestion.*
> *Could you pass the salt?*

These again are merely more polite than corresponding sentences with *can*.

6.3.3 Problem types
There are three problem types of *might* and *could*.

[i] *Might* is used like *may* (see 6.2.4) with *as well*:

> We might as well go.

Might have is also used:

> We might as well have gone.

However, this is not to be interpreted as 'It might be the best thing in the circumstances if we went' with *have* indicating past time for the proposition. Rather it means 'It would have been the best thing if we had gone'. This raises the rather complex issue of unreal conditionals and the modals (see 7.4.3[iii]).

[ii] *Might* is also used to make a suggestion:

> You might try the Abbey National.
> We might go and visit your mother.

Might have is used as a reproach:

> You might have told me.

In both cases *could* can be used, with little change of meaning:

> You could try the Abbey National.
> You could have told me.

There is no problem here with the interpretation of *could*. It can be seen as dynamic like the dynamic use of *can* for a suggestion (6.2.3[v]), stating what is tentatively possible and so implying that it should be done. That, however, leaves *might* unexplained, for *may* is never dynamic, but alternates with *can* only in the deontic sense. It is probably not worth while to argue that, since *might* and *could* are both used here, they must be deontic. For they are different. Like *may*, *might* would not be used with *always*:

> You can (*may) always say 'No'.
> You could (*might) always say 'No'.

Moreover, *could have* is open to the interpretation 'would have been possible', but *might have* is not. *Might* and *might have* are therefore different from *could* and *could have* and are best seen as having idiosyncratic idiomatic uses here.

[iii] *Might* is also used, though mostly in literary contexts, to refer to habitual activity:

> *In those days we might go for a walk in the woods.*

Again *could* is possible here, and is to be explained as the habitual past tense/past time form of *can*: 'we were able to (and did)'. But again this would suggest a special dynamic use of *might*, unless it can in some way be interpreted in terms of existential 'sometimes' (6.2.4[ii]).

6.4 BE ABLE TO

The main problem with BE ABLE TO is to explain how it differs from CAN (*can* and *could*).

It certainly often expresses ability, as might be expected from its form, as in:

> *You are able to look at the future in this very objective way.*

Just as *can* is sometimes found co-ordinated with *will*, so BE ABLE TO is linked with BE WILLING TO:

> *. . . hard and long thought, which few of us are able or willing to give.*

But again ability must be taken to include the 'ability' of inanimate objects:

> *These small rooms aren't able to contain all who wish to come.*

BE ABLE TO also sometimes appears to express neutral possibility:

> *By applying these disciplines they are able to become better communicators.*

There are, however, a number of conditions under which BE ABLE TO and CAN are not interchangeable.

[i]   BE ABLE TO is used only in the ability and neutral senses of CAN, not in any of its other senses, *eg* to indicate characteristics, with private verbs or to make suggestions.

[ii] Because it is not a modal, BE ABLE TO, unlike CAN, may co-occur with other modals or other verbs:

> *He might be able to come.*
> *He wants to be able to speak French.*

[iii] The past tense forms of BE ABLE TO are available where *could* is not because actuality is indicated (see 6.3.1[ii]).

I ran fast, and could catch the bus.
I ran fast, and was able to catch the bus.

[iv]   There is a preference for BE ABLE TO rather than CAN if there
is actuality even in the present:

By this means they are able to cut their prices.

This means 'can and do cut their prices'. *Can*, however, is
not ruled out here.

[v]   BE ABLE TO is rather more formal than CAN. It is found
especially in written texts:

You may make arrangements elsewhere if you are able to.

CAN would be more usual here in speech.

Since BE ABLE TO is not a modal, there are no problems about
negation or tense. The modality can be negated or made past by
the regular processes (*isn't able to, was able to*, etc). But it seems
less voice neutral than *can*:

This can't be done.
?This isn't able to be done.

6.5 MUST and NEED

MUST is the modal used for necessity (though with some suppletion
from *need* and possibly *ought* – see 6.7).

6.5.1 Epistemic

Although *may* as the marker of epistemic possibility may be
paraphrased as 'It is possible that . . .', it is not strictly possible
to parapharase *must*, the marker of epistemic necessity, as 'It is
necessary that . . .'. This, however, results only from the fact that
the word *possible*, but not the word *necessary*, can itself be used
in an epistemic sense. That does not, however, invalidate the
technical distinction between epistemic possibility and necessity.

The best paraphrase is 'The only conclusion is that . . .' (with
may being similarly paraphrased 'A possible conclusion is that
. . .'). The notion of conclusion is important. *Must* cannot be
paraphrased 'It is certain that . . .', which merely indicates the
strength of the speaker's belief. It essentially makes a conclusive
judgment, usually from evidence of some kind. Nor is it sensible
to debate whether *must* is stronger or weaker than a factual statement (which is normally assumed to be true). For it does not
simply present a proposition as true; it specifically indicates a

judgment by the speaker. In that sense it is clearly epistemic and modal.

Like *may*, *must* may refer to various types of proposition, *eg* to those relating to single actions, to activities (with the progressive) or to states (see 6.2.1):

John must go to London.
John must be working.
John must be there.

However, as with *may*, the simple form (*John must go to London*) would almost always be interpreted as deontic, if it refers to a single action. Similarly, where there is reference to a future action, the progressive is used, although no duration is involved:

John must be coming tomorrow.

There is, however, an alternative way of avoiding this ambiguity (or misinterpretation), by the use of BE BOUND TO. This is almost always to be interpreted epistemically:

John is bound to come tomorrow.

There is also some danger of ambiguity where there is reference to future states as in:

John must be there tomorrow.

This might well be interpreted as deontic, but there is no ambiguity with:

John is bound to be there tomorrow.

Non-assertion
There are no forms of the epistemic necessity modals that are regularly used for non-assertion. Although the negative forms *must't* and *needn't* are used for deontic necessity, they are rarely used for epistemic necessity. Instead, equivalent forms of the possibility modals are used:

John must be in his office.
John can't be in his office.
John may not be in his office.

This is possible because of the logical equivalences (see 6.1.5):

Not possible ≡ Necessary not
Possible not ≡ Not necessary

Mustn't, however, is used epistemically in interrogation, in tag questions and with negative interrogatives:

> *He must be there, mustn't he?*
> *Mustn't he be there?*

It is also possible if there is specific contrast with (*eg* denial of) *must*:

> A. *He must be there.*
> B. *No he mustn't!*

The fact that the *can* and *may* forms are usually used suppletively supports the suggestion by Lyons (1977:801) that for epistemic modality in English possibility is more basic than necessity.

Tense

With epistemic modals past tense can be marked only in reported speech, where there would appear to be deictic shift. However, *must* has no corresponding past tense form (*as may* has *might*); as a result the same form can be used even where deictic shift is expected:

> *He must be in his office.*
> *She said he must be in his office.*

Have is again used to mark the proposition as past:

> *John must have been in his office.*
> *He must have been flying too low.*

Voice

Like *may*, epistemic *must* is voice neutral:

> *John must have noticed Mary.*
> *Mary must have been noticed by John.*

6.5.2 BE BOUND TO

It was noted in the last section that because of potential ambiguity *must* is seldom used epistemically with future time reference. Instead the semi-modal BE BOUND TO is used:

> *John is bound to be there tomorrow.*
> *John is bound to come tomorrow.*

These are unambiguously epistemic (at least in colloquial English). BE BOUND TO is not, however, restricted to future reference. It could be used instead of *must* elsewhere:

John's bound to be there.   (now)
John's bound to be working.   (now, tomorrow)
John's bound to go to London. (every day)

However, BE BOUND TO is not wholly equivalent to MUST. It expresses greater certainty with less implication of conclusion. It can be modified by *almost*, whereas *must* cannot:

John's almost bound to be in his office.
*John almost must be in his office.

It sometimes has the sense of inevitability in a combined deontic (neutral) and epistemic sense as in:

The government is bound to act.

Here the speaker both concludes that the government will act and sees it as incumbent on it to do so.

6.5.3 Deontic
MUST is very commonly used for deontic necessity, though in many cases it seems to be quite neutral in its involvement of the speaker, or indeterminate. Nevertheless there are many examples of *must* being used by a speaker to impose the necessity:

You must go now.
You must get a permanent job.

One very striking use of MUST is in issuing invitations or making offers in a host/guest situation:

You must come and visit us sometime.
You must have another piece of cake.

Here clearly the speaker is not laying an obligation in the sense that he is trying to force the addressee to act. Rather it appears at first that he is merely giving permission (and this would seem to reverse the situation with *can* discussed in the last section). But in the situation it is polite for the speaker to insist, because the addressee might be hesitant. To give explicit permission (with MAY or CAN) might, in fact, be quite rude. Although then this use of *must* is associated with a social convention, it can still be treated as deontic necessity.

A rather more idiomatic use of *must* is with the first person *I* as in:

I must say . . .
I must confess . . .

I must admit . . .
I must agree . . . etc.

Here the speaker actually says, confesses, admits, agrees, etc; the utterances are performative in a rather different sense. But they can best be seen as rather specialized uses of deontic necessity: the speaker imposes upon himself the necessity to say, confess, admit, agree, etc.

However, is must be noted that there are plenty of examples of *must* that do not seem to involve the speaker, and as such are not strictly deontic, but neutral:

If you want to be rich, you must work hard.

Here the obligation to work hard does not emanate from the speaker, but is dependent on the condition that the addressee wants to be rich. But although there is no clear line between strictly deontic and non-deontic MUST, the distinction remains important for the status of HAVE (GOT) TO and its relationship with MUST. This is discussed in the next section (6.6).

Non-assertion
With negation the situation is quite simply that *mustn't* negates the proposition, but *needn't* the modality:

You mustn't go now.
You needn't go now.

The first says that you must not-go, *ie* that you must stay, the second that there is no obligation to go.

It would be unwise, however, to see NEED and MUST as semantically equivalent. This becomes clear in the interrogative forms where there are two possibilities:

Must I go?
Need I go?

It is not enough to say that NEED supplies the non-assertive form for MUST. It is, rather, that MUST expresses obligation, usually (though not always) associated with the speaker, but NEED expresses a need or requirement. *Needn't* becomes available as the negative because the absence of requirement excludes obligation, including obligation imposed by the speaker. But in the interrogative there is a potential contrast between 'Do you oblige me to go?' and 'Is there any need for me to go?' and this is essentially the contrast made by *Must I?* and *Need I?*

There are also negative interrogative forms:

Mustn't I go?
Needn't I go?

The most obvious interpretation of *mustn't* is in terms of a negative interrogative, the counterpart of a positive assertion of the obligation – 'Isn't it the case that I must go?'. Although native speaker intuition is uncertain here, it seems that *Mustn't I go?* could also mean 'Is it the case that I mustn't go?' and that *Needn't I go* is to be interpreted as a positive question about negated modality 'Is it the case that I needn't go?'. (See Palmer 1979:97.)

There is, however, an important point about NEED. The modal forms are available only with the NICE properties that are associated with non-assertion, negation and interrogation. In all other cases the full verb NEED is used. The modal and the full verb are clearly distinguished in that the modal has no -s form and is followed by the bare infinitive. In addition, of course, the full verb requires DO with negation and interrogation (see 2.2.8):

*He need to come.	He needs to come.
He needn't come.	He doesn't need to come.
Need he come?	Does he need to come?

Tense

Once again (see 6.5.1) there is no way of marking the modality as past. For strictly deontic MUST, this follows from the performative nature of the modality, but where MUST is not strictly deontic, that explanation is not valid. There is no semantic reason why we cannot say:

If you wanted to be rich, you must(ed) work hard.

But MUST has no past tense form, and this is, therefore, impossible. Equally, however, English has no need of such a form, since when MUST is not strictly deontic, it can be replaced by HAVE (GOT) TO (see 6.6. for further discussion):

If you wanted to be rich, you have to work hard.

However, as with epistemic *must*, deontic *must* can appear in reported speech where there is deictic shift:

He must come tomorrow.
She said he must come the next day.

Although there is no past tense form for MUST, there is a form for NEED – *needn't have*:

I needn't have gone.

This means simply that there was no need or necessity for me to go. This suggests quite strongly that NEED, unlike MUST, is never strictly deontic. It just indicates 'necessity' (or 'need') without in any way suggesting that it implies obligation imposed by the speaker. For strictly deontic modals have, by definition, no past tense forms.

6.6 HAVE (GOT) TO

Although HAVE (GOT) TO is not a modal, it is treated here because of its close relationship with MUST and NEED. Indeed there will be some further discussion here of these two modals.

It is necessary to anticipate a discussion found in 8.2.1 concerning the full verb HAVE and its auxiliary-like qualities. The point is that even as a full verb HAVE may have the NICE properties and does not require DO for negation, inversion, etc. This is equally true of the semi-modal HAVE TO:

He has to go.
He hasn't to go yet.
Has he to go?
He has to go and so has she.
He hás to go.

However, forms with DO are also possible and preferable in negation and inversion:

He doesn't have to go.
Does he have to go?
He has to go and so does she.
He dóes have to go.

Forms of HAVE GOT TO are also available (but they cannot occur with DO, because they are formally perfect forms of GET):

He hasn't got to go.
Has he got to go?

This does not suggest that, after all, HAVE TO is a modal. It is merely a reflection of the fact that the full verbs BE and HAVE share these features with the auxiliaries (as discussed in 8.1 and 8.2).

It should also be noted that HAVE TO is often phonetically [hæf tə/tuː] with devoicing of the consonant. This would not be possible with *have* in other uses (*eg have two*, which must be [hæv tuː]).

6.6.1 Epistemic

HAVE TO and HAVE GOT TO are rarely used epistemically in British English, although they are more common in American speech especially in such expressions as:

You've got to be joking.

This is now found in Britain, but the more likely form is:

You must be joking.

Moreover, an epistemic/neutral contrast can be seen in:

You must be mad to risk your life like that.
You've got to be mad to risk your life like that.

There is a very curious use of HAVE TO in sentences such as:

The book had to be there – I'd looked everywhere else.

This indicates that the speaker was, after all, right in his conclusion and is roughly equivalent to 'The only place it could possibly have been was there and it was there!' What is curious is that this appears to be epistemic (to relate to a conclusion that was, after all, correct), but is clearly in the past. For it was suggested earlier that epistemic judgments are always in the present. However, the verb being used is not the modal MUST, but the semi-modal, and semi-modals do not have the same restrictions. It is, therefore, possible to argue that this is, unusually, an objective epistemic judgment in the past, *ie* 'It was necessary to conclude . . .' (but without the implication that it is the speaker who is drawing the conclusion).

6.6.2 Neutral

By far the commonest use of HAVE (GOT) TO is to express obligation that is independent of the speaker (with HAVE GOT TO more usual colloquially):

He's got to go to hospital.
I've got to be at the airport at four.
If you want to succeed, you have to work hard.

In many cases, however, MUST can be used instead of HAVE (GOT) TO. This is certainly true of two of the examples above:

I have to go into hospital next week.
I must be at the airport at four.
If you want to succeed you must work hard.

It is less likely in the first example, almost certainly because the speaker wants to make it clear that he does not approve of the obligation to go into hospital, whereas he is not against going to the airport or getting his addressee to work hard. HAVE (GOT) TO can thus quite specifically deny the speaker's involvement in the obligation.

Two very good attested examples (Palmer 1979:93) show that MUST and HAVE (GOT) TO are often completely synonymous:

> *I must have an immigrant's visa. Otherwise they're liable to kick me out.*
> *I've really got to know when completion date is likely. Otherwise I might well find myself on the streets.*

In both cases the fact that there is only one alternative (shown by *otherwise*) indicates the reason for the necessity.

By contrast MUST could not be used in:

> *It's a slow walk. He's got to fight his way through the crowds.*

The necessity here is not imposed on the subject (a boxer trying to get to the ring) by the speaker. Moreover, it seems that MUST is not used to refer to actions already taking place: we do not oblige people to do things they are already doing. By contrast HAVE (GOT) TO is used even if action is taking place, *ie* like BE ABLE TO (6.4), it is used where there is actuality.

As a semi-modal HAVE TO (but not HAVE GOT TO, which is formally the perfect of GET) may be preceded by other verbs as in:

> *He's going to have to come tomorrow.*

MUST is impossible here because it is a modal.

Non-assertion

In general, the negative forms of HAVE (GOT) TO negate the verb itself (*ie* the modality):

> *I haven't got (don't have) to go to the airport.*
> *If you don't want to succeed, you haven't got (don't have) to work hard.*

Needn't would also be possible here, but with a slightly different meaning, denying a need rather than an obligation.

Less commonly the negative forms negate the proposition:

> *You haven't got (don't have) to play around in here.*

This might well mean 'you mustn't' rather than 'you needn't'.

Tense
Since HAVE (GOT) TO is not a modal, it has normal past tense forms. But past tense *had to* is more common than present tense *have/has to*:

I have (got) to go now.
I had to go yesterday.
He said he had to go.

It is rarely, if ever, used with past tentative forms, but that is generally true of all verbs except modals.

If MUST is so often not different in meaning from HAVE (GOT) TO, why does it not equally have past tense forms? The answer must be that this 'neutral' use is peripheral. In its basic function it is deontic (when it is not epistemic) and as such in contrast with HAVE (GOT) TO; in that function (where HAVE (GOT) TO cannot be used) it has no past tense form, because it does not need one. Even when it appears to be neutral, then, MUST is still formally a deontic modal. (This in itself is a good reason for not being too concerned with whether there is a distinct neutral kind of modality: 'neutral' MUST is just a variation of deontic MUST.)

Voice
HAVE (GOT) TO seems generally to be voice neutral, but not common in the passive (Palmer 1979:77):

John's got to meet Mary.
Mary's got to be met by John.

6.7 OUGHT TO and SHOULD

OUGHT TO and SHOULD are handled together in this section because in their most important function (deontic) there is little difference between them. But *should* is formally the past tense of SHALL and can function as such, though only in reported speech (see 7.1.4, 7.2.3[iii]). There are, moreover, two other functions of *should* (epistemic and 'evaluative') that must be considered.

6.7.1 Deontic
There is very little difference in meaning, if any, between OUGHT TO and SHOULD when used deontically:

You ought to come tomorrow.
You should come tomorrow.

They are even interchangeable in tag questions:

He ought to come tomorrow, shouldn't he?

SHOULD, however, is more common in colloquial speech (and the above sentence would be must less natural with the forms switched).

There are, however, problems with their status and interpretation. In Palmer 1974 (120–2) it was suggested that MUST is always discourse oriented and SHOULD and OUGHT always subject oriented. I now would argue that they are alike in being deontic or neutral.

One difference between MUST and SHOULD/OUGHT TO is that MUST does not allow that the event will not take place:

*He must come, but he won't.
He ought to come, but he won't.

MUST seems to lay an absolute obligation, not envisaging non-compliance. SHOULD and OUGHT TO express less absolute obligation and do not exclude non-compliance. Indeed, often they imply that the event will not take place:

I ought to be ashamed, but I'm not.
You should read more – you don't read enough.

However, there is no necessary implication that the event does not or will not take place. In the following sentence what is 'necessary', is also true:

It ought to be nice, at that price!

A simple treatment of SHOULD/OUGHT TO (or *should/ought to*) is to see them as the tentative or unreal form of *must*, related to *must* rather as *could* and *might* are related to *can* and *may* (see 6.3.2). Compare:

You could ask him.
You should ask him.

Both suggest action, one by saying that it is tentatively possible, the other that it is tentatively necessary. However, if these forms are treated as the tentative forms of *must*, it must be said that they do not have the other functions of past tense forms of a modal (such as *could* for *can*) – to refer to past time or in reported speech. Moreover, it is possible to interpret *could* in the example above as a conditional form of *can* ('You would be able to, if you wanted to'), but *should/ought to* cannot similarly be shown to be conditional forms of *must*. The tentative relationship between them and *must* is, then, purely semantic and not formal.

Non-assertion
Like *mustn't*, the negative forms *shouldn't* and *oughtn't to* negate
the proposition, not the modality. There is a tentative obligation
not to act:

> *You shouldn't/oughtn't to come tomorrow.*
> *He shouldn't/oughtn't to have done it.*

By contrast (but also like *must*), the interrogative forms question
the modality:

> *Should I come?*
> *Ought he to know?*

These ask whether there is a tentative obligation.
There is no way of negating the modality with *should* and
ought. But there is no need to negate tentative obligation. The
absence of tentative obligation is covered by the absence of
obligation in general and *needn't* is therefore available:

> *You needn't come tomorrow.*
> *He needn't have done it.*

Tense
Past time is indicated by *should/ought to* followed by *have*:

> *You should/ought to have come.*
> *I should/ought to have been ashamed.*

Even more than the present tense forms, these usually imply that
the event did not take place. Yet it is not impossible to say:

> *He should have been there – and he was.*

These forms require two comments. First, if they are the past
time forms, then SHOULD and OUGHT TO cannot be deontic,
though they could be neutral (and are not strictly parallel to
must). The same point was made of *needn't have* (6.5.3).
Secondly, they are even more closely parallel to *could have* in:

> *I could have done it.*
> *I ought to have done it.*

One seems to imply failure to commit a possible action, the other
failure to commit a necessary one, because they refer to what
would have been possible and what would have been necessary.
However (see above), while *could have* can be treated as a
conditional form of *can*, *should/ought to have* are not conditional
forms of *must*. Yet the two sets of forms are very similar in their
use (see 7.4.3).

Voice
OUGHT TO and SHOULD appear to be voice neutral:

> *John ought to/should meet Mary.*
> *Mary ought to/should be met by John.*

6.7.2 Epistemic
SHOULD can be used epistemically:

> *You should be meeting him this afternoon.*
> *They should be on holiday now.*

The meaning of SHOULD here is roughly 'It is likely or probable that . . .'.

Epistemic SHOULD shares with deontic SHOULD the feature that it allows for the non-event. It too, therefore, can be treated as conditionally or tentatively necessary, and thus related to epistemic MUST. It is quite certainly not equivalent to epistemic WILL which expresses a fairly confident expectation (see 7.1.1).

Often it is not easy, or even possible, to distinguish epistemic and deontic SHOULD, *eg*:

> *The work should take about three days.*
> *The books should fit on to that shelf.*

There is little real difference, in effect, between an epistemic and a deontic sense here. The tentative necessity may be seen as belonging either to the speaker's judgment or to the actual situation.

It is theoretically possible to imagine OUGHT TO being used epistemically but that seems very rarely to occur. In general OUGHT TO is interpreted deontically (see Palmer 1979:49).

6.7.3 'Evaluative' *should*
Should is often used in subordinate clauses after expressions of surprise and similar feelings:

> *It is surprising that he should say that.*
> *It is ridiculous that I should not be allowed to work.*
> *I am sorry that you should have been disturbed.*

Here there is no sense of necessity and in all cases a simple, non-modal, form of the verb could have been used, *eg It is surprising that he said that.*

The sense of surprise can be carried by *should* even without a verb or other expression of the emotion:

> *That he should do such a thing to me!*

This is not easy to explain, though it may seem to have something in common with the use of the subjunctive in other languages, particularly Romance, in similar circumstances.

Quite often *should* occurs after the word reason:

There is no reason why it should be surprising.
I see no reason why that should be so.

Here, however, it could be argued that the use of *should* is epistemic because *reason* suggests that a judgment is being made. However, the notion of a reasonable judgment is more naturally expressed by *will*; it is probably more satisfactory to see this too as a use of this 'evaluative' *should*.

6.8 DARE

The formal status of DARE has already been considered (2.2.8). DARE does not fit easily into the semantic framework of the modals. It has roughly the meaning 'have the courage to . . .':

I daren't ask him to come.
Dare I ask him?

But the modal verb (as opposed to the full verb DARE with TO) has some characteristics of the modals. It is often (as in the first example), conditional or tentative with a sense of 'would(n't) dare to'.

On the other hand even modal DARE can be used with past time reference though it cannot have any past tense marking:

I wanted to go, but I daren't.

There is also a past tense form with *have*:

I daren't have gone, although I wanted to.

However, this is not normally to be treated as a simple past, equivalent to *didn't dare*, but as conditional, like *wouldn't have dared*. (For the conditional uses of DARE see 7.4.3[i].)

Surprisingly, DARE can be voice neutral. Two examples are to be found in works on the modals:

These two aspects of death cannot be successfully separated, but they dare not be confused or identified.
Inflation is a problem that dare not be neglected.
(Ehrman 1966:71; Pullum and Wilson 1977:785).

This is curious because the sense of DARE suggests that it is subject oriented, and subject oriented modals are not expected to be voice neutral (see 6.1.3 and *will* in 7.1.2).

Chapter 7

The modals WILL and SHALL

This chapter is mainly concerned with WILL and SHALL in both their modal and their future uses. It will also deal with the related issue of future time marking by other forms and with conditionals, in which the modals play an important role.

7.1 Modal WILL and SHALL

In their purely modal functions WILL and SHALL are unrelated: WILL can be epistemic or dynamic, SHALL deontic only.

7.1.1. Epistemic WILL
Will can be used epistemically in a way similar to *may* and *must*:

John'll be there now.
John'll be working.

There are even greater restrictions on reference to the future than with epistemic *may* and *must* (6.2.1, 6.5.1). In general, *will* is used epistemically only with reference to present states and activities, as in the examples above. Where there is future time reference it is difficult, if not impossible, to identify an epistemic use as distinct from a simple future use of *will* (and, indeed, it has been argued that the future use of *will* is essentially part of its epistemic use):

John'll be there tomorrow.
John'll come tomorrow.

With reference to habitual actions, *will* is likely to be interpreted not as future, but as dynamic (6.1.2), in a habitual sense:

John'll go to London every day.

This would normally be taken to refer to the customary, characteristic action of John. However, with the progressive an epistemic sense with reference to the future is again (see 6.2.1, 6.5.1) possible:

John'll be going to London tomorrow.

It is tempting to refer to the meaning of *will* as probability, alongside possibility and necessity for *may* and *must*. But the word 'probable' does not provide a good paraphrase. A better paraphrase is again in terms of conclusion: 'A reasonable conclusion is that . . .'. Other examples are:

The French'll be on holiday this week.
No doubt, you'll remember John.

Unlike *must*, *will* does not draw its inference from evidence. There is a contrast between:

John will be in his office.
John must be in his office.

A possible reason for uttering the first sentence might be that he usually is there or that he is there when he is not at home. A reason for the second might be that the lights are on in the office or that he cannot be found anywhere else.

Non-assertion
Won't appears to negate the proposition:

He won't be in his office.

This seems to mean 'It is reasonable to infer that he is not in his office'. However, that does not differ very much in its meaning from 'It is not reasonable to infer that he is in his office', which negates the modality. Possibly no distinction can be drawn between negation of the modality and negation of the proposition. But only the modality can be questioned:

Will he be in his office?

Tense
With epistemic modals, only the proposition can be past, marked with *have*:

They'll have been on holiday all last week.

However, *would* is used as the tentative form:

They'd be on holiday this week.

Would may also be used in reported speech to report *will* (or *would*):

> *He said they'd be on holiday this week.*
> (*They'll be on holiday this week.*
> *They'd be on holiday this week.*)

Voice
All epistemic modals are voice neutral.

7.1.2 Dynamic WILL

[i]   *Will* is used to express volition or willingness on the part
       of the subject. It is thus clearly 'subject-oriented' and
       dynamic, *eg*:

> *We can't find a publisher who will take it.*
> *John will help you to find a job.*

This volition use, however, always carries with it the
meaning of futurity (or actuality – see 6.3.1) as can be seen
by comparing:

> *John's willing to do it, but he's not going to.*
> **John'll do it, but he's not going to.*

The second sentence is distinctly odd, because *will* not only
expresses willingness, but also indicates the action will take
place. As a result, it is often very difficult to distinguish this
will of volition from the *will* of futurity, though the distinction is necessary (see especially on conditionals – 7.4.2[iv]).
       The distinction is, moreover, much clearer if *will* is
accented or negated (*won't*) where there is a meaning of
insistence or refusal:

> *If you will play with fire, you'll get burnt.*
> *She loves him, so she won't leave him.*

Like the *can* of 'ability', the *will* of 'volition' can apply
to inanimate objects. This Jespersen (1909–49 IV.239)
distinguishes as 'power', *eg*:

> *Some drugs will improve the condition.*
> *The books will easily fit into this corner.*

This use explains what I earlier (Palmer 1974:112) called
the 'inference' use of *will*:

> *Oil will float on water.*

[ii]   Very close to this use (and again like *can*) *will* is often used
       to make suggestions:

> *I'll do that for you.*
> *We'll do anything you ask.*
> *We'll keep in touch, then.*
> *Perhaps you'll let me know.*

The meaning varies according to the subject. In the first the speaker offers to act, and similarly in the second, though in cooperation with someone else. In the third he is agreeing with his addressee; *we* here means 'you and I'. In the fourth sentence he is suggesting, *ie* politely reqesting action by his addressee.

[iii]   *Will* is also used for what Jespersen calls 'habit':

> *She'll sit for hours watching television.*
> *So one kid will say to another . . . .*

This indicates typical as well as habitual behaviour. It may be compared with the 'characteristic' use of *can*, which indicates potential rather than habitual behaviour.

Non-assertion
The negative form *won't* negates the modality only. As an example above shows this often carries the sense of refusal.
   The interrogative is (again like *can*) used to make requests:

> *Will you pass the salt?*
> *Will you make sure the water's hot?*

This is, obviously, close to the use of *will* to make suggestions. The negative, again, is more of a plea, though more direct than *can't*:

> *Won't you help me please?*

Alternatively, it is used as a very polite suggestion especially where it is the addressee rather than the speaker who benefits:

> *Won't you come in?*
> *Won't you have some more coffee?*

Tense
Would is used as a past tense form of *will* for volition, not only in reported speech, but also for past time reference. As with *could*, however, there is a restriction on its use if there is an implication of actuality (see 6.3.1 [ii]):

> **I invited him to the party and he would come.*

But there is no objection to the negative (or any other non-assertive):

> *I invited him to the party, but he wouldn't come.*
> *All he would do, was say he was sorry.*
> *Would he help us, do you think?*

Similarly, *would* is possible if there is reference to habitual actions:

> *He would come to the party whenever he was invited.*

(This last use however is difficult to distinguish from a purely habitual use, corresponding to the habitual *will*.)

Would is used as the tentative form of *will* when used for suggestions, and in the interrogative form is used for requests:

> *I would do that for you.*
> *Perhaps you'd let me know.*
> *Would you pass the salt?*

Would is also used, though in a formal style, to indicate habitual activity in the past, and is then almost equivalent to *used to* (8.4):

> *We would go for long walks in the park.*
> *We used to go for long walks in the park.*

There is no exactly parallel form of *will*. The nearest is obviously that of habit, but *would* does not necessarily suggest, as *will* does, that the habitual activity is typical of the speaker.

Voice
Dynamic WILL is not voice neutral since it always indicates some characteristic of the subject. There is a clear difference between:

> *John won't meet Mary.*
> *Mary won't be met by John.*

If these are interpreted in terms of refusal it is John who refuses in the first, Mary in the second.

7.1.3 BE WILLING TO
It is convenient to deal with BE WILLING TO here, because its chief interest is its contrast with the *will* of volition.

The basic difference is that it simply indicates willingness with no indication of actuality (see 6.3.1). It is for this reason that we may contrast:

> *John's willing to come, but he's not going to.*
> **John will come, but he's not going to.*

I invited him to the party and he was willing to come.
*I invited him to the party and he would come.

In addition, of course, BE WILLING TO can occur with other verbs where *will* cannot:

He would be willing to come.
He may be willing to come.
He seems to be willing to come.

7.1.4 Deontic SHALL

With *shall* the speaker gives an undertaking, guarantees that an action will take place. It can thus be described as making a promise or a threat:

You shall have it tomorrow.
He shall be told.

With first person subjects, however, it is not always easy to decide whether the speaker undertakes to act or merely indicates that he will do so in the future. Indeed, it could always be argued that if a speaker indicates that he will (in the futurity sense) do something, he is often giving an undertaking that he will, *eg*:

I shall apologize for my rudeness.
We shall take care of the poor.

Shall is, however, different from deontic *may* and *must* in that it does not permit or oblige someone else, usually the addressee, to act, but guarantees that the speaker will act. But it is deontic in the essential characteristic that it influences or directs behaviour and that it is performative.

Shall is used in archaic and formal style for commands as in *Thou shalt* . . . of the Ten Commandments, and is often found in legal language which imposes a law or regulation:

The 1947 law shall have effect . . . .

It is also commonly used, in fairly formal language, after verbs of insisting, etc., where the speaker's involvement is made quite explicit:

I intend to see that . . . the maximum penalty shall be imposed.

Non- assertion
The negative *shan't* negates the proposition – it guarantees that the action will not take place:

You shan't have it.

He shan't be told.

There is no way of negating the modality ('I don't guarantee').

The interrogative with the first person is used to make a suggestion or offer:

> *Shall I open a window?*
> *Shall we go now?*

This is not entirely predictable from the use of assertive *shall*: it does not ask if the addressee guarantees the action will take place, but only if he wants it to take place. But it is still clearly deontic and, like all interrogatives, questions the modality.

Tense
The form *should* is used as an analogue of *shall* only in reported speech:

> *You shall have it tomorrow.*
> *He said I should have it tomorrow.*

In other cases *should* is close to OUGHT TO (6.7): it is too different in meaning to be interpreted as the tentative form of SHALL.

Voice
Like other deontic modals *shall* is normally voice neutral.

7.2 Future WILL/SHALL

There is a traditional view of *will* and *shall* as markers of the future tense in English, *shall* being used with first person forms (*I, we*) and *will* with all others. There is no doubt that there is a use of *will* (and much less commonly of *shall*) to refer to the future, but the claim that *will* and *shall* alternate with person has long been known to be false (see Fries 1925, 1927). Even in the future use, *will* often occurs with *I* and *we*, while *shall* (with *I* and *we* only) is restricted to a formal style, and is not used at all in some dialects, especially in Scotland and the USA (Wekker 1976:47). In what follows the discussion will be almost entirely about *will*, but it should be remembered that *shall* may also occur (with *I* and *we*).

Whether English has a future tense has been a matter of some debate and will be discussed later (7.2.3).

7.2.1 Conditionality
Will (and less commonly *shall*) is the verb that is commonly used in the apodosis (the main clause) of conditional sentences referring to the future (see 7.4.1):

If John comes, Mary will leave.
If John comes, I'll/I shall leave.

This pattern provides a quite neutral or unmarked conditional: if one event occurs, the other will. The use of any form other than *will* would carry with it some further meaning, *eg*:

If John comes, Mary is going to leave.

This might suggest, perhaps, that Mary had already stated what she intends to do.

Will may also occur where there is clearly a condition implied in a previous sentence or where it is introduced by a temporal conjunction:

You put it under your pillow and a fairy will come.
When the demand for labour exceeds its supply, wages will rise.
The trade gap will not improve until something is done about inflation.

In other cases, however, there is a sense of conditionality, with no very clear condition either stated or implied:

That will give us time to acclimatize.
Bridget will tell you she was at the lecture.
The nurseryman will sell you the right seeds.

In none of these examples does *will* simply indicate a future event, but merely that something will turn out to be true under certain conditions (*eg* 'if we stay a few weeks', 'if you ask her', 'if you go to the shop'). In a very large number of cases, *will* has this conditional sense and may be contrasted with BE GOING TO (7.3.2).

7.2.2 'Modal' future
Will is often used to refer to the future where there is clear reference to a future that is envisaged, planned, etc, and not simply in future time. In this sense there is a modal rather than a real (tense) future. At least five types of examples may be noted:

[i]   The future events are envisaged and a relevant verb used to indicate that:

Is it ever envisaged that the College will hive itself off from the University?
I suspect the Abbey National will say 'No'.

[ii]   The future event is hoped or prayed for:

We pray that God will look upon the hearty desires of his humble servants.
I hope the students will be interested in this.

[iii] The future scene is already set by some other future markers (*eg* BE GOING TO, IS TO):

There's going to be a National Enterprise Board which will be expected to do things in Scotland.
The TUC is to launch a publicity campaign . . . posters will go up all over the country.

[iv]   The event is part of a plan, as in the Queen's Speech to Parliament:

My Government will make it their duty to protect the freedom of the individual.

[v]   *Will* is used to give instructions or guidance:

Mrs Dodgson will walk on my right.
Private Jones will report at 0800 hours.

As with conditional *will*, none of these examples indicates events that are simply future in time at the moment of speaking.

7.2.3 Future tense

The traditional idea that *will* and *shall* are auxiliaries for future tense is still held by some scholars. The issue is not a particularly important one, but it is well worth while to consider the ways in which forms with future *will* and *shall* function rather like tense forms and the way in which they do not.

[i]   WILL and SHALL are modal verbs. Formally they belong quite clearly to the modal system, not the tense system of English.

[ii]   In spite of the talk of future tense, forms with *will/shall* rarely seem to refer to a plain future, but carry connotations of conditionality, envisaging, etc. On the whole BE GOING TO is semantically closer to future tense, though it too has other connotations. Admittedly, there are occasions where *will/shall* is used to refer simply to the future:

The year two thousand and fifteen when I shall be ninety.
Most areas will have rain or thundery showers.

However, the first example is explained by the total inappropriateness, in the context, of BE GOING TO (see 7.3.2). The second comes from a weather forecast and is to be explained as being formal and part of a semi-technical language. It is also true that BE GOING TO is far more common in speech than in writing. At most a better case for *will/shall* as markers of future tense could be made for written language than for speech (see 7.3).

[iii] In terms of negation and voice, the forms are indeed like tense markers. For there is no independent semantic marking of auxiliary and main verb in terms of negation and all forms are voice neutral.

The situation with tense is more complex. To begin with, *would* is sometimes used, though mostly in formal, written English to indicate events that are future in the past (Leech 1971:48):

Twenty years later Dick Whittington would be the richest man in London.

Unlike *was going to* (see 7.3.2) *would* necessarily implies that he did in fact become the richest man. But such forms are rare and literary.

However, *would/should* regularly occur in reported speech:

It will be dark soon.
He said it would be dark soon.
I shall be better tomorrow.
He said he would be better tomorrow.

In the second pair of examples, there is an alternation of WILL/SHALL: *would* is used to report *shall*, because *should*, like *shall*, it not used with other than first person.

There is also the fact that *will/shall*, like other modals, occurs with *have*:

I shall have finished it soon.
You'll have seen him when I arrive.

These are usually called 'future perfects', though semantically they may be either perfect or past in the future.

These facts do not strongly argue against the notion of future tense, since there are other quite complex tense/time relations (especially that of 'past-past'). But equally they lend no support to it. (But see Wekker 1976.)

There is one final factual point. The progressive form is often used to avoid ambiguity with the *will* of volition:

John won't be coming tomorrow.
(*John won't come tomorrow*)
Will you be coming to the party?
(*Will you come to the party?*)

In each case the second sentence is likely to be interpreted in terms of the WILL of volition ('John refuses', 'Would you like to come?'). This is especially characteristic of non-assertive forms, but not confined to them.

There were similar examples of the progressive with epistemic modals (6.2.1, 6.5.1). Indeed, it has been argued, though not entirely convincingly, that future *will* is essentially epistemic (see Palmer 1979:118–19).

7.3 BE GOING TO

BE GOING TO is important because it too relates to the future and is often either in contrast or in free variation with WILL. It is, of course, one of the semi-modals. It is not identical in form with the progressive form of GO (although it is clearly historically related to it and still contains a sense of going – see below). This is clear if the following are compared:

I'm going to tell you a story.
I'm going to London tomorrow.

In slow formal speech there will be no difference, but in a more rapid conversational style the semi-modal, like many auxiliaries, has weak forms. It may be reduced to no more than [gənə], but this cannot be used as the progressive form of GO.

7.3.1 Current orientation

In most cases BE GOING TO can be interpreted in terms of current orientation (see McIntosh 1966:105 who speaks of 'present orientation') in that it relates to the future from the standpoint of the present or, if the verb is past, of the past. It is thus a 'future in the present' or a 'future in the past', and similar in some ways to the perfect with its current relevance (which indicates, so to speak, 'past in the present' or 'past in the past'). Three types of example may be noted.

[i]   There clearly is current activity that is leading to an event in the future:

> *Free kick given Scullion's way; its going to be taken by Trevor Hockey.*

This is taken from a commentary: the commentator can actually see the player moving to take the kick. He is 'going to' a future event.

[ii]   There is a decision or intention:

> *At the moment they're decorating their house and they're going to alter parts of it.*

At the moment here provides the time indicated for both verbs. Not only is the action of decorating present; so too in that of 'going to' make alterations.

[iii]   There is reference to the immediate future:

> *I'm going to play that same chord as loudly as possible.*
> *I'm just going to tell him all about it.*

This is like (though in reverse) the use of the perfect with *just*. The future is so close to the present that it can almost be seen as part of it.

[iv]   There is a sense of inevitability:

> *Concorde is going to be a gigantic financial disaster.*
> *Inevitably, the Government is going to look silly.*

In all these cases the future event can be seen as coming from the present, or alternatively events in the present can be seen as proceeding ('going') towards the future.

7.3.2 Contrast with WILL/SHALL

Obviously, the best way of showing the difference between WILL/SHALL and BE GOING TO is to consider examples where they are, or could be, in contrast.

[i]   The use of BE GOING TO explicitly shows that there is no conditionality:

> *I'm buying an awful lot of books here. It's going to cost me a fortune to get them home.*

Here it is clear that the speaker intends to take the books home. The use of *will* would merely say that it would cost him a fortune *if* he took them home.

There is a contrast then between:

> *The paint'll be dry in an hour.*
> *The paint is going to be dry in an hour.*

The first is conditional ('if you leave it', 'if you are patient');

the second indicates what will inevitably happen (and could be a warning to act before it does). Similarly consider:

I'll be at home all day.

This is more appropriate than a form with BE GOING TO when there is an implication of 'if you need me'.

[ii]   By contrast BE GOING TO will not be used if there can be no sense of current orientation, no reference at all to the present. *Will/shall* therefore occurs where only the future is involved:

My babe-in-arms will be fifty nine on my eighty ninth birthday . . . the year two thousand when I shall be ninety.

This may seem to be a clear case of *will/shall* used for pure futurity. But the relevant prior is that BE GOING TO would be quite inappropriate, and *will/shall* is the only form available.

Inevitably, there are plenty of contexts in which either *will/shall* or BE GOING TO is equally appropriate. In such contexts it may just be possible to suggest that there is a sense of conditionality or of inevitability, but it must not be assumed that the choice of one form or the other can always be explained. It is easy enough to determine the situations in which *will/shall* is appropriate and BE GOING TO inappropriate, and vice versa, and to distinguish them in terms of 'conditional' or 'modal' future contrasted with a future with current orientation. But although they may be seen to be semantically different, it does not follow that there are no situations in which either is equally appropriate, so that in a particular context there is no explanation why one is used rather than the other.

Finally there are, of course, syntactic differences between the semi-modal and the modal. Most obviously the semi-modal may be used after other verbs:

He seems to be going to make a statement.
*He seem to will make a statement.

Non-assertion

With negation, rather strikingly, *won't* is more common than the negative forms of BE GOING TO. It appears to be the case that if the occurrence of the event is denied, the distinctions between *will* and BE GOING TO are irrelevant. (If there is no event there is often no current orientation.) The distinction is largely neutralized and *won't* is the preferred form, *eg:*

I won't be back tonight.
He won't leave until October.

However, BE GOING TO is often used not to contrast with futurity WILL, but to avoid a possible interpretation in terms of volition:

He's not going to come.
He won't come.

The first, unlike the second, cannot be interpreted as 'he refuses to come'. Another example of a device to avoid the ambiguity was noted in 7.2.3.

Tense
BE GOING TO has regular past tense forms to refer to future in the past, often to imply that, although there was 'past orientation', *ie* intention, the future event may not have materialized:

He was going to come the next day.

Here the speaker suggests that he does not know whether in fact he came or not. In the rare occasions where *would* is used for future in the past (7.2.3), the implication is that the event took place.

Voice
BE GOING TO is voice neutral. A clear example was given in 7.3.1[i].

7.4 Conditionals

Conditionals are dealt with in this chapter because they involve certain specific functions of WILL and SHALL.

7.4.1 The basic pattern
The grammar of conditional sentences in English is, in reality, very simple, though dependent on several quite specific rules. Unfortunately, accounts of it often confuse the basic pattern by introducing distinctions that are not independent parameters, but are simple consequences of characteristics, especially those of tense, of the conditionals themselves (see below).

A conditional sentence consists of two parts, the *if*-clause or protasis and the main clause or apodosis. Its function is to indicate that the truth of one proposition is dependent upon another.

All conditional sentences (except where there is ellipsis, 'something left out', see below) are of the semantic form 'If *p*, the, *q*'.

There is no restriction on the kind of proposition that may be represented in the two parts of a conditional sentence. In particular, there is no restriction on the tense, though relations between the tenses will determine how the conditional is to be interpreted (see below). Thus, although the first sentence below may seem far more natural and common than the second, both are possible and both indicate that the one proposition is dependent upon the other:

> *If John comes, Mary will leave.*
> *If John comes, Mary left.*

In both cases Mary's leaving is seen as dependent upon John's coming, but whereas in the first the speaker predicts that one event will follow the other, in the second he infers that, if the one event takes place, the other must have taken place too.

There are, however, in English and many other languages two kinds of conditional, real and unreal. In real conditionals the speaker merely presents the propositions that are linked, without indicating any views about them. In unreal conditionals he indicates that he has doubts about the propositions, or, in particular about the proposition expressed in the protasis. Unreality is expressed, as elsewhere in English (see 3.2.5), by the use of the past tense. It is that that distinguishes the real and unreal conditionals:

> *If John comes, Mary will leave.*
> *If John came, Mary would leave.*

The real/unreal distinction is indicated by the contrast *comes/came*, *will/would*.

These two sentences represent an important and common class of conditionals that may be called predictive or causal. They suggest that one event will or would follow another event. The two events are thus related in time (the event in the protasis precedes the event in the apodosis) and have some kind of causal link between them. Moreover, both events are in the future and, as such, both hypothetical.

There is, however, another important kind of predictive/causal conditional relating to the past as in:

> *If John had come, Mary would have left.*

Very often, but not always, these are counter-factual in that they relate two propositions that are contrary to the factual situation.

With this example there would generally be an implication that John did not come. However, this is not necessarily so. It would be possible to continue:

> . . . *and since John came, Mary must have left.*

Formally, this conditional is unreal. For unreality is again expressed by tense marking, but in a more complex way. Since it is both past and unreal, tense needs to be marked twice: a 'past-past' form is required. In the protasis the form *had come* is used. This is found elsewhere in English to express past-past (see 3.3.3): *had come* is the 'past-past' of past *came*, present *come*. In the apodosis there is again double marking, once with *would*, and once with *have*. This follows from the fact that there can be no form such as **had will*, because of the rules about the modal paradigm, but the marking of the (second) tense with a following *have* is exactly like that of *needn't have* (6.5.3), *ought to have* (6.7.1) and *daren't have* (6.8).

Predictive conditionals in the past are generally unreal (but see 7.4.2). There is a simple reason for this. The past, unlike the future, is known and any such conditional in the past must at least suspend judgment on the facts, or indicate some degree of doubt or disbelief. There are then three important types, all predictive. A further set of examples is:

If it rains, the match will be cancelled.	(real)
If it rained, the match would be cancelled.	(unreal)
If it had rained, the match would have been cancelled.	(unreal)

Apart from these rules concerning tense marking for unreality, there are two other rules for conditionals. First, for conditionals referring to the future, WILL (or SHALL) is not used in the protasis. This is true of both real and unreal conditionals. It is not possible in English to say (except with a quite different meaning – see 7.4.3):

> *!If John will come, Mary will leave.*
> *!If John would come, Mary would leave.*

The plain future conditionals require *comes* and *came* here.

Secondly, the apodosis in unreal conditions must contain a modal verb (in its past tense form). Thus the first of each pair below may be unreal, but the second must be real:

> *If John came, Mary would leave.*
> *If John came, Mary left.*

If John had come, Mary would have left.
If John had come, Mary had left.

The second of each pair have to be interpreted as 'If John came, it follows that Mary left', and 'If John had come, it follows that Mary had left'. The past tense form of the apodosis alone cannot indicate unreality, but only time. (For the interpretation of these see 7.4.2.)

The absolute need for a modal in the apodosis is shown by considering:

If John comes, Mary is going to leave.
If John came, Mary was going to leave.

Here BE GOING TO is used instead of *will*; this is less common but possible. The first example can still be regarded as predictive and is a real conditional, but the second cannot be treated as its unreal counterpart. It must be treated as real and past, in contrast with a sentence containing *would* which would be unreal and future.

Although WILL is the modal most associated with conditionals other modals can be used. But they involve both semantic and formal problems and will be discussed in detail later (7.4.3).

Finally in this section, it is to be noted that there are conditionals in which the condition is not explicitly stated. The remaining sentence is, then, essentially an apodosis with no protasis. The rules are the same. The conditional nature of *will* has already been discussed, but there are also plenty of examples of (unreal) *would* and *would have*. There are various possibilities, *eg*:

[i]   The condition is implicit in the linguistic context (but not marked with *if*):

      You would be unwise to do that.
      No one would want to publish a book as difficult as that.

[ii] The condition is simply contained in a pronoun such as *it* or *that* meaning 'if it were so', 'if you did that', etc:

      That wouldn't be sensible.
      It would be very nice.

[iii] There is an implied 'if I were you' (giving advice):

      I shouldn't be in too much of a hurry.
      I wouldn't risk it.

[iv]   The implicit condition is vague, but simply relates to a
       possible or different state of affairs:

> *I would encourage people not to smoke.*
> *You wouldn't want to harm him, would you?*

7.4.2 Other types

The conclusion of the last section was that all conditional
sentences are basically the same, but that there are three
common types that generally indicate some kind of causal
connection between two possible events. But there are other
possibilities.

[i]   *If* seems to have the sense of 'whenever' in:

> *If John comes, Mary leaves.*
> *If it rained, I went by car.*

This interpretation is possible, of course, only because the
simple forms of the verb are treated as habitual; the 'whenever' sense is not, then, strictly a feature of *if*, but of the
verb.

These can be seen, however, as real conditionals with a
causal implication, and, if so, provide examples of real
conditionals in the past. But they are restricted to habitual
actions, and, provided there is no modal in the apodosis,
distinct from unreal future conditionals.

[ii]   There is no causal connection in:

> *If John came, Mary left.*
> *If John comes tomorrow, Mary left yesterday.*

Indeed, a causal connection is impossible in the second
example, because the events referred to in the protasis are
subsequent to those referred to in the apodosis. In both
cases the interpretation is in terms of the speaker's inference. He infers that the one event took place because of
the evidence of the other. But although there can be no
causal connection between the events, the two propositions
are conditionally linked, the truth of one implying the truth
of the other.

Within this type of conditional may be included such
sentences as:

> *If he's Prime Minister, I'm a Dutchman.*

The conditional relation between the two propositions here
is wholly in accordance with the rules of formal logic!

Sentences of this type are sometimes described as 'hypo-theticals', rather than conditionals (*eg.* Dudman 1983:3*ff*). But they are not truly very different. The absence of a causal connection and, therefore, the implication of infer-ence is a result of the time relation between the two prop-ositions. The general pattern of 'If *p* then *q*' still holds. In fact drawing a distinction between hypotheticals and conditionals creates a problem concerning the status of conditionals involving simultaneity of the propositions as in:

If John's here, Mary is too.
If John's working, he's happy.

Because these propositions do not refer to momentary actions, but to continuous states, these can be seen in terms of cause and effect, or equally in terms of inference. It is, therefore, open to debate whether they are 'hypotheticals', or 'true conditionals' (and whether the true conditionals can be present as well as past or future).

There are unreal counterparts to these, but the rule that a modal must be present applies, and *would* has to be supplied:

If John were here, Mary would be too.
If John was working, he would be happy.

These, however, are indistinguishable in form from future conditions. The distinction of hypothetical and conditional seems then to create more problems than it solves.

[iii] There is some kind of ellipsis ('something left out') in sentences such as:

If you want to know, I haven't seen him.
If you're going out, it's raining.

These have to be interpreted as something like:

If you want to know, I'll tell you that I haven't seen him.
If you're going out, you ought to know that it's raining.

In other words, it is the giving of the information or the relevance of the information, not the proposition, that is dependent on the proposition in the protasis.

This is not a phenomenon confined to conditionals. There is something similar in:

He works hard, because he wants to be rich.
He works hard, because he's at the office every morning at nine.

The first gives a reason for what is stated in the *becuase* clause ('he works hard'), the second gives a reason for stating it.

7.4.3 Conditionals and modals
There are some problems concerning the use of modal verbs within conditional sentences.

[i]   As was stated in the last section, an unreal conditional must contain a modal. This does not necessarily have to be *would* and *would have*; *could* and *could have* are equally possible:

> *If John came, Mary could leave.*
> *If John had come, Mary could have left.*

Some modal verbs, however, do not have the appropriate past tense form. There is thus no unreal conditional corresponding to:

> *If John comes, Mary must leave.*

MUST has no past tense forms; the nearest equivalent are forms of HAVE TO:

> *If John came, Mary would have to leave.*
> *If John had come, Mary would have had to leave.*

However, *ought to/should* may function as past (unreal forms) and permit the trio:

> *If John comes, Mary ought to/should leave.*
> *If John came, Mary ought to/should leave.*
> *If John had come, Mary ought to/should have left.*

With NEED (*needn't*) similar forms are possible, though the full verb is also available:

> *If John comes, Mary needn't leave.*
> *If John came, Mary needn't leave/wouldn't need to leave.*
> *If John had come, Mary needn't have left/wouldn't have needed to leave.*

The same is true of DARE, although the full verb forms may be more common:

> *If John comes, Mary daren't leave.*
> *If John came, Mary daren't leave/wouldn't dare to leave.*
> *If John had come, Mary daren't have left/wouldn't have dared to leave.*

[ii] Purely conditional *would* has a very different function from

other conditional forms, particularly *could* and volitional *would*. For *would* carries no meaning of its own other than to indicate conditionality. But *could* seems to have the sense of 'would be able to' or '*would can', and volitional *would* the sense of 'would be willing to' or '*would will'. With *could* and volitional *would*, therefore, it would seem that it is the modality, the ability or volition, that is unreal, whereas with conditional *would* it is the event itself. But, in fact, with *could* and volitional *would* semantically either the modality or the event can be conditional. Compare:

> *If he worked hard, he could pass the exam.*
> *If he so desired, he could pass the exam.*

In the first it is the ability to pass the exam that is dependent on working hard, but in the second there is no question of the ability – it is the passing of the exam that is dependent on the desire to do so. The first is paraphrase-able 'would be able to', the second 'can and would'. Consider similarly:

> *There is just one thing I would say . . . .*
> *No one could have guessed that it would take so long.*

These do not mean 'I would be willing' 'No one would have been able to guess', but 'I am willing and would (if you permit) say', and 'No one was able to and would have guessed'.

[iii] Where there is a deontic or epistemic modal in the apodosis, it is best interpreted as 'outside' the whole sentence. It relates to both parts, not just to the apodosis. Consider:

> *If John comes, I might leave.*
> *If John comes, you must leave.*

These are best seen as 'It is possible that if John comes I shall leave', 'I oblige you to leave if John comes'. The judgment, and the laying of obligation do not depend on John coming. It is leaving that depends on John's coming, and the judgment or obligation relates to the whole sentence. This type of interpretation is clearly necessary for a sentence such as:

> *I might have walked out.*

This (an implicit condition) does not mean 'It would be possible that I walked out' but 'It is possible that I would have walked out'. Even more striking is:

If he had stayed in the army, he must/might have become a colonel.

The meaning of this is 'It must/might be that if he had stayed in the army he would have become a colonel'. In all these cases there is nothing conditional about the epistemic modality, but only about the proposition on which it makes a judgment. (See Huddleston 1977, Palmer 1978.)

[iv] There is nothing to prevent a modal from occurring in the protasis, though an epistemic modal may often be difficult to interpret, *eg*:

If John may come tomorrow, Mary will leave.

This probably means that Mary will leave (now), if there is a possibility that John will come tomorrow.

There is, however, a particular problem with *will/shall*. It was noted earlier that future *will/shall* are not used in simple predictive (causal) future conditionals. This does not, however, apply to volitional *will*. There is, therefore, a contrast between:

If John comes, Mary will leave.
If John'll come, Mary will leave.

The second has to be interpreted 'If John is willing to come'. Similary consider:

If medicine will save him, he'll be safe.

This is clearly the 'power' use of *will* (7.1.2[i]).

However *will/shall* can occur in a future sense in protases in sentences such as:

If the play will be cancelled, let's not go.
If he'll be left destitute, I'll change my will.

The essential characteristic of such sentences is that the events in the protasis are subsequent to those of the apodosis. The meanings are 'If, if we go, the play will be cancelled (when we arrive) let's not go' and 'If, if I change my will, he'll be left destitute, I'll change my will'. The futurity of *will* is not simple futurity as seen from the time of speaking, but futurity from the time of the conditional event, and this is marked by *will/shall*. (See Palmer 1983.)

Chapter 8

Marginal verbs

There are several verbs that are marginally auxiliaries, particularly the non-auxiliary forms of BE, HAVE and DO.

8.1 BE

BE is used in English as a full verb, though with the formal characteristics of an auxiliary (the NICE properties), and in IS TO.

8.1.1 Full verb

BE is a full verb in:

> *He is very sad.*
> *He was in the garden.*

In function the verbal forms are exactly paralleled by the forms in:

> *He seems very sad.*
> *He sat in the garden.*

Unless there is a completely new definition of 'auxiliary', BE is a full verb in these sentences. It is not followed by any other verb, and has no place at all in the tables that have already been set up. The full verb has the following characteristics of an auxiliary:

(a) it has all the finite and non-finite positive forms – *am, is, are, was, were, been* and *being*, all with the same function with regard to number and person as the auxiliary BE (11.1.1);

(b) it has all the weak forms (11.1.3):

I'm sad. [aɪm sæd]
He's sad. [hiːz sæd]
We were sad. [wiː wə sæd] etc

(c) it occurs in negation, inversion, code and emphatic affirmation without DO:

He isn't sad.
Is he sad?
I am sad and so is he.
He is sad.

Not only do these forms occur without DO, but, with certain exceptions (see below), they cannot occur with DO:

*He doesn't be sad.
*Does he be sad?
*I am sad and so does he.
*He dóes be sad.

It is because of these characteristics of BE, even when a full verb, that Palmer and Blandford (1939:122) talk of the 'anomalous finites', to include these as well as the auxiliary verbs proper.

Like the auxiliaries, then, full verb BE does not usually occur with DO. However, DO may occur with auxiliary BE in the imperative form, and is obligatory in the negative imperative, because there is no form **ben't* (3.1.2):

Do be reading when I come in!
Don't be reading when I come in!
(Be reading when I come in!)

The same is true of the full verb:

Do be at home when I arrive!
Don't be at home when I arrive!
(Be at home when I arrive!)

However, the full verb also occurs with DO where the auxiliary cannot:

Why don't you be more careful?
(*Why don't you be reading?)
If you don't be good, I shall punish you.
(*If you don't be reading, I shall punish you.)

Here the forms with DO suggest single occasions (perhaps to complain about a careless action, to rebuke a naughty child). By contrast, the forms without DO might refer to a permanent characteristic (though they could also be used in the other sense too):

> *Why aren't you more careful?*
> *If you aren't good, you'll never succeed.*

DO seems a little less likely if there is no negation:

> *Why do you be so foolish?*
> *(Why are you so foolish?)*

But it could be argued that these forms with DO involve a formally different verb BE, which has only one finite form *be* (instead of *am, is, are*) in view of:

> *?If you be good, I'll reward you.*

This verb also occurs (I have attested it in children's speech at least) with the meaning 'act the part of':

> *If you be the Queen, I can be the King.*

8.1.2 IS TO

There is a set of forms *am to, is to, are to, was to* and *were to*, which functions rather like modal verbs:

> *He's to come tomorrow.*
> *You're to be congratulated.*

The set does not, however, contain any non-finite forms: there is no *be to, *being to or *been to. It is, therefore, inappropriate to refer to the verb BE TO; instead it will be referred to as IS TO. It has all the characteristics of an auxiliary (as indeed do all forms involving BE), but in addition, like the modals, has no finite forms and cannot be preceded by any other verb. But unlike the modals, it has different forms for number and person.

There are four basic uses, the first two essentially temporal, the other two modal in character:

[i]   Present tense forms refer to future events that are planned or part of an arrangement:

> *Certain colleges are to be designated for special development.*
> *There's to be a new leader.*

Futurity can be indicated by an infinitive form of a verb without *to*:

> *The batsmen still to come are . . . .*

[ii] Past tense forms usually refer simply to events that, in the

event, took place later than the time being referred to; they mark a future in the past:

Worse was to follow.
He was to make amends later.

But they may also be used to refer to planned events, as in [i], which may or may not have taken place:

The cocktail party which was to precede the dinner party was a disaster/did not take place.

[iii]   Past and present forms refer to what is reasonable, or possible:

I cannot see how this is to be avoided.
Mistakes were to be expected, if not condoned.

[iv]   The present tense forms are used to give or relay a command or instruction:

You are to come tomorrow.
He is to work here all day.

Tense has already been discussed with the examples above. Negation is a little more complex. With the first two uses, the future event is simply denied. With the two modal uses, however, there is a difference. In the 'reasonable' sense, it seems to be the modality that is negated to mean 'it cannot reasonably be':

Genuine progress is not to be found in all those twentieth-century inventions.

This means 'It cannot be found', 'It is not reasonable to suppose that it will be found'. By contrast, in the command/instruction use it is the proposition that is negated. There is a requirement not to act:

You are not to come tomorrow.
He is not to work here all day.

There are idiomatic forms closely related to these:

John is to blame.
The house is to let.

These have to be interpreted in the passive: 'John is to be blamed', 'The house is to be let' (the first in a modal, the second in a temporal sense). But this is not a freely formed construction. There are no similar sentences:

*John is to praise.
*The house is to sell.

8.2 HAVE

HAVE is a most versatile verb with at least six different uses. (It is preferable to talk of one verb with different uses than of six different homonymous verbs, since the dividing line between them is not clear and they have, in varying degrees, semantic and formal features in common.)

Two of the uses, those of the marker of perfect in phase (3.3) and of the semi-modal (6.6), have already been discussed. It is also used as a full verb in both a stative and a dynamic use (8.2.1) and in a set of constructions which indicate 'affected' subject (8.2.2).

8.2.1 Full verb

Like BE, HAVE is a full verb. There is a close formal (and semantic) similarity in the pairs:

He has three houses.
He owns three houses.
We had great difficulty.
We experienced great difficulty.

It is necessary, however, to distinguish two uses here, one 'stative' and indicating possession in the general sense, the other 'dynamic' and indicating experience, achievement, etc. Semantically the difference can be seen in the two possible interpretations of each of the following:

We had sandwiches.
She had a son.

In the stative use these mean 'We took sandwiches with us' and 'She was the mother of a boy'. In the dynamic use they mean 'We ate sandwiches' and 'She gave birth to a son'.

There are at least four formal distinctions between the two uses:

[i]   In the stative use, HAVE commonly has the weak form found in the auxiliary:

> *He's no friends.*   ([hiːz])
> *They'd plenty of money.*   ([ðeɪd])
> *I've plenty of time.*   ([aɪv])

However, the use of weak forms is not as regular here as with the auxiliary in colloquial speech.

[ii] Stative HAVE is often replaced in colloquial speech by HAVE GOT, which is morphologically, but not semantically, the perfect of GET:

I have three pounds.
I've got three pounds.
She has four brothers.
She's got four brothers.
Mary had a pretty face.
Mary'd got a pretty face.

The HAVE forms of HAVE GOT almost always occur as weak forms (apostrophe -'ve, -'s, '-d in writing).

[iii]   Stative HAVE commonly occurs with the NICE properties:

I haven't any money.
Have you a pencil?
I have a pencil and so has he.
He hás some money.

Yet forms with DO also occur:

I don't have any money.
Do you have a pencil?
I have a pencil and so does he.
He dóes have some money.

These are often associated with American speech, but they are by no means confined to it. It must also be allowed that in colloquial British speech the HAVE GOT forms are more likely than the forms of HAVE without DO.

[iv]   Stative HAVE never occurs in the passive. It is not possible to say:

*Three pounds are had by me.
*A pretty face was had by Mary.

But passives are rare with the dynamic use (see below).

As can be seen from the examples, the stative use of HAVE has the notion of possession in the wide sense, to include ownership, family and social relationships, whole/part relations, etc. In all cases there is some sense of existence combined with some close 'having' relationship with the subject.

Dynamic HAVE occurs in a variety of senses, referring to experience, achievement, receiving, plus some types of action:

Have a holiday.	
Have a good time.	
Have a child.	('give birth')
Have sandwiches.	('eat')
Have difficulty.	('experience')
Have a walk.	('go for a walk')

Have a sleep.
Have a breakfast.

There is some idiomatic restriction on the possible objects, since one can *have a drink* but not *have an eat (Wierzbicka 1982). Dynamic HAVE does not usually occur in the weak forms. It would be very curious to say:

We've a walk every day.
We'd a good holiday.

More strikingly, dynamic HAVE does not normally occur with the NICE properties:

**We hadn't a holiday.*
**Had you a good time?*
**We had a walk and so had you.*
**We hád breakfast.*

In all cases a form with DO is required.

One interesting contrast is provided by the fact that HAVE may be used in the sense of 'stock' for a shop. There can therefore be a distinction between:

The supermarket hasn't any icecream
The supermarket doesn't have icecream.

The first can only mean that there is none there, the second that it doesn't stock it (though this is also indicated by the absence and presence of *any*). There is nothing odd therefore about:

The supermarket hasn't any icecream, but it dóes have icecream.
A. *Does the supermarket have icecream?*
B. *Yes, but it doesn't have any now.*

In a very few cases, a passive is possible:

A good time was had by all.
Breakfast can be had at eight.

But it is not possible to say:

**A sleep was had by me.*
**A child was had by the woman.*

8.2.2 'Affected' subject
There is potentially triple ambiguity in (Chomsky 1965:21–2):

I had a book stolen.

This is shown by glossing:

(a) *from my car when I stupidly left the window open*;
(b) *from his library by a professional thief who I hired to do the job*;
(c) *almost . . . but they caught me leaving the library with it.*

Only the first type will be discussed in detail here. The second type represents a causative use of HAVE which is dealt with in the chapter on catenatives (9.2.2). The third type is a little problematic and will be briefly considered at the end of the section.

The function of the first type is, essentially, to place in subject position the noun phrase that represents the person (or item) indirectly affected by the action. Thus in the example given the subject suffered the loss of a book. In this respect it is somewhat similar to the passive in which, in relation to the active, a noun phrase is moved into subject position. This is shown in the comparison between:

I had a watch given to me.
A watch was given to me.

In the active *a watch* is the object and *me* the prepositional object:

X gave a watch to me.

If compared with an active sentence the passive can be seen to place *a watch* in subject position and the HAVE construction to place *me* (*I*) in that position.

In fact, it is also possible to use the passive to place *me* (*I*) in subject position:

I was given a watch.

This, however, is best seen as the passive of (5.1.3):

X gave me a watch.

This is not, therefore, directly relevant to the issue.

The HAVE construction is best seen as derived not directly from the active, but from the passive:

(*X stole a book from me*)
A book was stolen from me.
I had a book stolen from me.

In the most easily explained form of the construction the

subject of the sentence has a coreferential pronoun later in the sentence either after a preposition or in the possessive form. This is shown by:

> *She had the child taken from her.*
> *I had my house burgled last night.*

In theory the passive and the HAVE construction taken together can move into subject position any noun phrase in the active sentence. This is illustrated in the artificial paradigm:

> *Arthur took Bill's book from Claude to Dennis.*
> *Bill's book was taken from Claude to Dennis* (*by Arthur*). [Passive]
> Bill *had* his *book taken from Claude to Dennis* (*by Arthur*)
> Claude *had Bill's book taken from* him *to Dennis* (*by Arthur*).
> Dennis *had Bill's book taken from Claude to* him (*by Arthur*).

However, in the example considered at the beginning of the section there is no coreferential pronoun; it has *a book*, not *my book*, and does not include *from me*. In this sentence the indefinite article can be interpreted to mean 'one of my', and indeed it is possible to say *I had one of my books stolen*. The reason for this appears to be as follows. English does not distinguish between an indefinite ('a my') and a definite ('the my') use of *my* and the other possessive pronouns. A possessive pronoun in this construction is always to be interpreted as definite. An indefinite article will however be interpreted here as indicating possession by the subject, because the use of the construction itself indicates that the subject is directly affected by the action. It would follow that if I was affected by the theft of a book, it is likely that the book was mine.

There is a parallel structure with an *-ing* form instead of an *-en* form in the complement of HAVE:

> *John has men working for him.*
> *He had his wife working in the shop.*

These are essentially the active counterparts of the basically passive forms that have just been discussed. They can be derived from the active:

> *Men work for him.*
> *His wife works in the shop.*

Once again there is a coreferential pronoun either after the preposition or in the possessive form.

Rather different, however, is a sentence such as:

He has a sister living in Bristol.

This does not mean that he is affected by the fact that his sister lives in Bristol, but rather that he has a sister and that she lives in Bristol. There is even a potential formal difference in that the weak form is much more natural here than in the previous examples:

He's a sister living in Bristol.

This supports the suggestion that this is the stative HAVE of possession, not the HAVE of affected subject.

There are also sentences such as:

He has twenty men under him.
Bill has his arm in a sling.

The nearest sentence without HAVE would be:

Twenty men are under him. (or *There are twenty men under him.*)
Bill's arm is in a sling.

This Quirk *et al.* (1985:1411) call '*have* existential', but it clearly has the same function of indicating the affected subject.

Once again there is a different sense in:

He has a brother in the army.

This means 'He has a brother, and he is in the army'. It would, for that reason, be less easy to contextualize:

He has his brother in the army.

This cannot mean 'He has his brother and he is in the army' and must therefore be interpreted in terms of an affected subject. A possible interpretation might be that he has arranged for the brother to be in the army or that he cannot agree to support a peace movement because his brother is in the army.

Also possible are constructions such as:

The car had its roof open.

This is the 'affected NP' construction related to:

The roof of the car was open.

Because of this there is ambiguity in:

The car has its roof damaged.

This relates to the ambiguous:

The roof of the car was damaged.

Since this can be treated either as a regular passive or as a statal passive (5.2.3), the HAVE sentence can mean either that the car suffered damage to its roof or that its roof was in a damaged state.

The third interpretation of the example quoted at the beginning of the section is more difficult to account for. It has, or is supposed to have, the meaning 'I almost succeeded in stealing the book'. Most people would find it difficult to arrive at this interpretation, but it is much clearer in other contexts with other verbs:

We had them beaten, and then they scored.
We scored and then we had them beaten.

These two examples show that the meaning can be interpreted in terms of either 'almost' or 'at last'. The common notion is, perhaps, that of temporary success. It is debatable whether this is similar to the use that has been discussed in this section. It could be argued that the subject is affected by the temporary success. But it remains a little idiosyncratic and idiomatic in that it is more natural with a verb such as BEAT, which carries a lexical meaning related to success and failure.

8.2.3 Summary
This is a good place to summarize the uses of HAVE. Six may be recognised:

    [i]   The auxiliary, the marker of perfect phase. (3.3)
    [ii] The semi-modal HAVE TO. (6.6)
    [iii] The stative full verb. (8.2.1)
    [iv] The dynamic full verb. (8.2.1)
    [v] The verb of affected subject. (8.2.2)
    [vi] The catenative of causation. (9.2.2)

These fall into three main types in terms of their auxiliary-like qualities, notably the NICE properties and the weak forms:
(a) The marker of perfect phase is a true auxiliary and has all the NICE properties (and does not occur with DO) and regularly occurs in weak forms.
(b) The semi-modal and the stative full verb may have the NICE properties, but also occur with DO and have the alternative forms of HAVE GOT. Weak forms are possible, but not regular.
(c) The dynamic full verb, the verb of affected subject and the catenative do not have the NICE properties and do not normally occur in weak forms.

8.3 DO

There are three uses of DO. One, the use of DO as the 'empty' auxiliary, has already been discussed (2.2.6).

DO is also a full verb as in:

He does a lot of work.
I'll do my duty.
He did nothing about it.

The full verb, unlike BE and HAVE, does not have the NICE properties. In negation, inversion, etc, the auxiliary DO is required:

He doesn't do a lot of work.
Does he do a lot of work?
He does a lot of work and so do I.
He dóes do a lot of work.

It is not possible to say:

*He doesn't a lot of work.
*Does he a lot of work?

(In the other two it is not possible to make a formal distinction. DO in the code example above, for instance, has nothing to show that it is the auxiliary not the main verb, but patterning with the others shows that it is.)

Similarly, the full verb has no weak forms, though its *-s* form *does* is the same as that of the auxiliary, (which is morphologically irregular in speech [dʌz], not *[duːz]).

Thirdly, there is an 'empty' full verb as seen in:

What does he hope to do?
What do you like doing?
What do you want done?
It would be very foolish to do so.

Do is used here to mean no more than 'to act', standing for any dynamic verb. Although this is very like the empty auxiliary it is clearly different from it. In particular, the auxiliaries cannot occur in the position it occupies here. (The modals are ruled out by their lack of non-finite forms but BE and HAVE are not):

What does he hope to be/have?
What do you like being/having?
*What do you want been/had?
It would be foolish to be so.

BE and HAVE here are either impossible or else cannot be interpreted as auxiliaries, for it would not be reasonable to reply to the first 'He hopes to be playing' or 'He hopes to have finished', but only 'He hopes to be a policeman' 'He hopes to have a car' (where BE and HAVE are full verbs). By comparison with these, the DO forms above are to be identified as forms of a full verb, not of auxiliary DO.

8.4 USED TO

USED TO is a very marginal member of the primary auxiliaries. In terms of the NICE properties its status is very dubious since some forms are much more acceptable than others:

> *He usedn't to act like that.*
> *? Used he to act like that?*
> **I used to act like that and so used he.*
> *He úsed to act like that.*

The verb, however, also occurs with DO:

> *He didn't use to act like that.*
> *Did he use to act like that?*
> *I used to act like that and so did he.*
> *He did use to act like that.*

Some speakers of English might feel uncomfortable with some of these – that they are slightly substandard. But with code *did* is the only possible form.

The commonest negation form is with *not* [nɒt]:

> *He used not to act like that.*

If the negative is interpreted as negating *used* then it is here an auxiliary, but it could be argued that *not* negates the following verb, and that USED is a full verb like PREFER in:

> *He prefers not to act like that.*

The semantics give no answer. It is impossible to distinguish not being in the habit of doing something and being in the habit of not doing something.

The verb looks orthographically like the full verb USE, but it has little in common with it semantically. Moreover, it is distinct morphologically in that the normal form is [juːst] and not [juːzd], which is the past tense of USE only (compare the similar form of *have* [hæf] 6.6 and *cf* 11.5).

8.5 BETTER, RATHER, LET'S

It was once, half jokingly, suggested that English has three auxiliaries [betə], [ɔːtə] and [gɒtə] (*better, ought to* and *got to*). For the 'weakening' of the *to* see 8.5. The first is to be treated as *had better* as shown by:

You hadn't better go.

In the positive form, however, there is often no indication in speech of the *had* form even though it is written:

You'd better go.

But although interpretation in terms of *had better* is the traditional one, it results in a completely idiosyncratic form since HAVE does not otherwise occur with the bare infinitive:

**You had go.*

Closely associated with *had better* is *would rather*. In normal conversation the distinction of *had* and *would* is lost since both are merely [d]. It could be plausibly argued that these are related in terms of discourse and subject orientation, *had better* indicating what the speaker (or hearer), *would rather* what the subject, regards as desirable. There are no obvious past time forms to support this formally, but it is supported to some degree by the passivization test:

He'd better meet her.
She'd better be met by him.
He'd rather meet her.
! She'd rather be met by him.

Let's is what grammarians would call the 'first person imperative' as in:

Let's go.

It is quite distinct now from the verb LET (= PERMIT) as in:

Let us go.

The *let's* form can have the strong form (*let us*) as well as the weak (*let's*), but the full verb LET can occur only with the 'strong' form. It occurs with the tag *shall we*:

Let's go, shall we?

This relates it to the imperative where the normal tag is *Won't you*:

Go, won't you?

Chapter 9

The catenatives

The catenatives and the complex phrase in which they function
are illustrated by sentences such as:

He kept talking.
I want to go to London.
I saw John come up the street.

In these sentences there are two full verbs, the first a catenative.
But there is no limit upon the number of verbs that may co-occur
in this way, provided that all except the last are catenatives.
Examples of sentences with more than two are:

I got him to persuade her to ask him to change his mind.
He kept on asking her to help him get it finished.
*I don't want to have to be forced to begin to try to make more
money.*

The term 'complex phrase' is, as was seen in the first chapter, a
little misleading in that there are two or more verb phrases;
indeed, that there are two or more clauses involving subordination. But these complex phrases are grammatical units of a kind
that other sequences involving verb forms are not. They are
merely one step further in terms of freedom of association from
the verb phrases involving first the primary auxiliaries and then
the modals. They are quite different, in this way, from sequences
such as (see 9.3.1):

I bought the boat to sail the world.
He walked away thinking about the disaster.

In these there is no close relationship either semantically or
syntactically between *bought* and *to sail*, *walked* and *thinking*.
The link is entirely one of the syntax of clauses within the

sentences. But there is a much tighter syntactic and semantic relationship between the catenative and its following verb; there is a great deal to be said about the restrictions of occurrence. It is impossible, for instance, to say:

*He kept to talk.
*I want going to London.

These are as ungrammatical as:

*He has talking.
*He can to go to London.

This suggests that the catenatives share some grammatical characteristics with the auxiliary verbs (in varying degrees – some are very like the modals – see 9.2.9), and justifies talking about 'complex phrases' as distinct from sequences of verb phrases in successive clauses.

For simplicity only complex phrases with two verb forms (one catenative) will be discussed; this makes it possible to identify the main and the subordinate clause. In practice, as shown above, there may be much longer complex phrases, but the relationship between each successive verb form remains largely the same. (For a detailed listing see Van Ek 1966.)

9.1 Classification

This section considers the main criteria that are relevant for the classification of catenatives and complex clauses. Some more theoretical issues are left until 9.3.

9.1.1 Basic structures

There are two obvious sets of criteria for the classification of the catenatives in terms of the constructions with which they occur.

First, there are the four types of verb forms with which they may be followed (the four that were first noted in 2.1.1):

bare infinitive	He helped wash up.
to-infinitive	He wants to go to London.
-ing form	He keeps talking about it.
-en form	He got shot in the riot.

For the majority of the catenatives, however, only the second and third are relevant.

Secondly, a noun phrase may or may not occur between the catenative and the following verb. The sentences above may be compared with (though not in every case with the same verb):

bare infinitive	*He helped them wash up.*
to-infinitive	*He wants them to go to London.*
-ing form	*He kept them talking a long time.*
-en form	*He had the rioters shot.*

The precise syntactic status of the noun phrase is a topic for later discussion (9.1.3). But a distinction will be made between complex phrases 'with' or 'without NP'.

9.1.2 Aspect, phase, tense and voice

As was seen in 5.1.1, the paradigms of the modal auxiliaries consist of a modal followed by all the possible infinitival forms – eight in all, marking aspect, phase and voice (tense being marked by the auxiliary itself). A similar basic paradigm might seem appropriate for the catenative + verb sequence, *eg*:

(1) *I expect to take.*
(3) *I expect to be taking.*
(5) *I expect to have taken.*
(7) *I expect to have been taking.*
(9) *I expect to be taken.*
(11) *I expect to be being taken.*
(13) *I expect to have been taken.*
(15) *I expect to have been being taken.*

This, however, is unhelpful because the catenatives can also be independently marked for all the categories (*expected*, *am expecting*, *have expected*, *have been expecting*, *am expected*, etc) with the same meanings as all other verbs. What is of relevance here is the marking of these categories in the subordinate clause (by the infinitives, *-ing* form and *-en* form).

One restriction is determined by the forms themselves. There is no distinction in form between phase and tense since with the non-finite forms both perfect and past are marked with HAVE (see 3.3.3). But there are other restrictions too. A full paradigm (of eight forms, not sixteen, since phase and tense are not distinct) is found only with the *to*-infinitive, and even there (11) and (15) are rare. The bare infinitive and *-en* form have a very limited set of distinctions.

[i] Of the three categories, voice is the easiest to deal with. The *-en* form is always to be interpreted as passive and often corresponds to a bare infinitive in the active:

He saw them eat.
He saw them eaten.

He had them beat the carpet.
He had them beaten.

With other verbs the *-en* form is the passive of the *to*-infinitive, though the passive infinitival is also possible with little difference in meaning:

I want them to beat the carpet.
I want them beaten.
I want them to be beaten.

Apart from these forms the passive is regularly found with both infinitivals and participals. The infinitival forms have been illustrated in the paradigm above; examples of participials are:

They stopped punishing him.
They stopped being punished.
They stopped them punishing them.
They stopped them being punished.

However, there are some verbs where the passive is unlikely, especially with the *-ing* form, when there is an intervening noun phrase:

They kept them working.
?They kept them being taught.
I want them working.
?I want them being taught.

The restriction is almost certainly semantic. One usually 'keeps' or 'wants' others taking action, not being acted on. Yet for the last sentence a passive is possible with a *to*-infinitive instead of the *-ing* form:

I want them to be taught.

[ii] Aspect is a little more difficult. With some verbs the bare infinitive and the *-ing* form are quite clearly related in terms of aspect:

I saw the boys cross the road.
I saw the boys crossing the road.
He had them beat the carpet.
He had them beating the carpet.

These function like:

The boys crossed the road.
The boys were crossing the road.

They beat the carpet.
They were beating the carpet.

But this contrast is not always possible:

I made him talk to me.
*I made him talking to me.

There are some verbs in which a difference of aspect might be seen in the contrast of *to*-infinitive with *-ing* form:

He started to speak, but was soon interrupted.
He started speaking, and kept on for hours.

But the semantic distinction is less clear here than with SEE. It is even less clear in:

I like swimming.
I like to swim.

Nor is there an obvious difference between:

I intend going tomorrow.
I intend to go tomorrow.

In many cases, however, the *-ing* form appears to be intrinsically progressive, even where there is no contrast with a (non-progressive) infinitive *eg*:

He kept talking.
He kept them talking.

But with some verbs, notably the verbs of attitude (9.2.7), the *-ing* form carries no progressive meaning with it:

I don't like them reading comics.
(They read comics.)

Yet there are no forms of the type *being talking* with two successive *-ing* forms, whether the progressive is indicated or not. Such forms are as unlikely with LIKE as with KEEP:

*He kept being talking.
*He kept them being talking.
*I don't like them being reading when he comes.
(They are reading now.)

In fact, there is a more general restriction on sequences of *-ing* forms. If the catenative itself is in the *-ing* form, a following *-ing* form is, at best, most unlikely:

?He's keeping talking.
?He's just starting speaking.

It would appear that there is simply a restriction on two successive *-ing* forms in English.

The occurrence of *-ing* forms followed by *-en* forms has already been discussed in the consideration of voice above. There appear to be some restrictions on this construction.

With the *to*-infinitive form, aspect may be marked by the presence or absence of a following *-ing* form:

I intend to work when he comes.
I intend to be working when he comes.
I don't like them to read comics.
I don't like them to be reading comics.

But with some verbs a *to*-infinitive plus *-ing* form is not possible.

*He started to be speaking.

[iii] Phase and tense are not distinguished, both being marked by HAVE (see above). Tense/phase may be marked in the subordinate clause, but there are considerable restrictions. In particular it does not occur with the bare infinitive, though there are no obvious grammatical reasons for this:

*I saw him have crossed the road.
*I made him have talked to me.

There is one set of verbs with which *have* plus the *to*-infinitive commonly occurs, that of 'reporting' (9.2.3):

I believe John to have gone.
I believe John to have been tricked.

These occur commonly with passivization of the main clause:

John is believed to have gone.
John is believed to have been tricked.

That both past and perfect may be so marked is clear:

John is believed to have gone yesterday.
John is believed to have gone already.
(John went yesterday.)
(John has already gone.)

Phase/tense is also marked with *-ing* forms:

I remember going.
I remember having gone.
I remember being beaten.
I remember having been beaten.

But REMEMBER, along with a few other verbs (9.2.6), is
idiosyncratic in this respect because *-ing* forms with and
without HAVE refer to past time, with no apparent difference of meaning. With most other verbs HAVE is unlikely
to occur either with *-ing* forms or the infinitives:

He decided to have gone.
He strives to have finished.
?I enjoyed having seen him.*
I finished having talked.
Can you justify them having done that?

9.1.3 Identity relations
This section is concerned with the identity of the subject of the
main clause and, in particular, whether it can be identified with
the subject or object of the main cause, or neither. This involves
also the status of any intervening noun phrase. The problem is
easily illustrated in:

John wanted to talk.
John kept talking.
John wanted the men to talk.
John kept the men talking.

Here it is clear intuitively that the subject of *to talk* and *talking*
in the first two sentences is *John*, whereas in the second two it
is the intervening noun phrase *the men*. These intuitions are
supported by a comparison of the possible and impossible (or
most unlikely) sentences:

The hens lay eggs.
The hens want to lay eggs.
The farmers want the hens to lay eggs.
The farmers lay eggs.
The farmers want to lay eggs.
The hens want the farmers to lay eggs.

The sentences show that the subject of the subordinate clause is
identical with the subject of the main clause if there is no intervening noun phrase, but identical with the noun phrase, if there
is one. The last two sentences would incorrectly identify *the
farmers* as the subject of LAY.

These relationships may be shown formally by using subscript
indices to indicate identity with the unstated ('missing') subjects
of subordinate clauses in round brackets, with square brackets
showing the subordinate clause:

(1) NP$_1$ V [(NP$_1$) V]
(2) NP$_1$ V [NP$_2$ V]

But this simple picture needs some modification.

[i] There are some verbs for which it may be argued that the intervening noun phrase is both the object of the verb of the main clause and the subject of the subordinate. A further formula is needed:

(3) NP$_1$ V NP$_2$ [(NP$_2$) V]

This will distinguish between such sentences as:

I wanted the doctor to examine the boy.
I persuaded the doctor to examine the boy.

Here there are three noun phrases, the third being the object of the verb of the subordinate clause. The question at issue is whether or not the second NP, *the doctor*, is the object of *wanted* and *persuaded*, *ie* which of the following formulae is appropriate:

NP$_1$ V[NP$_2$ V NP$_3$]
NP$_1$ V NP$_2$ [(NP$_2$) V NP$_3$]

There are two arguments that clearly establish the first formula as appropriate for WANT and the second for PERSUADE.

First, passivization of the main clause gives:

The doctor was persuaded to examine the boy.
*The doctor was wanted to examine the boy.

The possibility of the first sentence indicates clearly that *the doctor* is the object of *persuaded*, for it is now the subject of the passive; the impossibility of the second shows that it is not the object of *wanted*.

Secondly, there are two possible sentences with the subordinate clause in the passive:

I wanted the boy to be examined by the doctor.
I persuaded the boy to be examined by the doctor.

But they are very different. The first is clearly directly related to the original sentence with passivization of the subordinate clause. The second is not, for there is now a difference of meaning in that it is the boy and not the doctor who is persuaded. Compare also:

I wanted John to play the piano.
I wanted the piano to be played by John.
I persuaded John to play the piano.
*I persuaded the piano to be played by John.

The contrast can be explained by saying that *the doctor* is not the object of *wanted* in the original sentence, but that it is the object of *persuaded*, where the object of the main clause is identical with the subject of the subordinate clause. This becomes clear if the formulae are spelled out with words:

I wanted [the doctor to examine the boy].
I persuaded the doctor [the doctor to examine the boy].

Passivization of the subordinate clause of the first sentence produces the sentence required, but passivization of the second would lead to:

I persuaded the doctor [the boy to be examined by the doctor].

The object of the main clause is now no longer the subject of the subordinate. What is needed is that *the doctor* is replaced by *the boy* in the main clause:

I persuaded the boy [the boy to be examined by the doctor].

This argument no less than the first shows that *the doctor* is the object of *persuaded* but not of *wanted*. It also establishes the identity of the object of the main clause and the subject of the subordinate.

There are, then, three basic constructions that will account for the majority of the catenatives:

(1) NP_1 V [(NP_1) V]
(2) NP_1 V [NP_2 V]
(3) NP_1 V NP_2 [(NP_2) V]

[ii] There are other verbs with NPs that do not exactly fit either the PERSUADE or the WANT pattern. ORDER would seem at first sight to be like PERSUADE:

I ordered the chauffeur to fetch the car.
The chauffeur was ordered to fetch the car.

Main clause passivization clearly establishes *the chauffeur* as the object of *ordered*, and PERSUADE, but not WANT, would be possible in the two sentences. Yet ORDER seems to function like WANT:

I ordered the chauffeur to fetch the car.
I ordered the car to be fetched by the chauffeur.

Here the passivization of the subordinate clause suggests that *the chauffeur* is not the object of *ordered*, and WANT could be substituted for ORDER in both sentences.

Semantically, too, ORDER seems to function in two ways. Either orders are given to someone to do something or they are given that certain things shall be done. These two meanings accord well with the two possible constructions. It could be argued that there are two verbs ORDER, one like WANT the other like PERSUADE, with structures such as:

I ordered [the chauffeur to fetch the car].
I ordered the chauffeur [the chauffeur to fetch the car].

Yet it seems rather to be the case that ORDER is not unambiguously either of the one type or the other. For it is not possible to establish which of the two constructions is an appropriate analysis for a sentence like:

I ordered the chauffeur to fetch the car.

In order to establish whether ORDER is like WANT or PERSUADE we need to appeal to the meaning – to ask whether orders were given to the chauffeur or not. Unfortunately it is not clear what is meant by 'giving orders to the chauffeur'. Does this mean only to him personally? Or can they be given via someone else? The semantic distinction is very far from clear, yet the syntax depends upon making that distinction. It is not then a matter of ORDER belonging to two verb classes, but that the distinction between these two classes is not valid for ORDER.

[iii] There is a different problem with BELIEVE. It is that this verb (as well as other verbs of reporting) can occur with main clause passivization, in spite of the fact that the NP is not semantically the object of the verb, *eg*:

The doctor is believed to have examined John.

The active sentence (possibly a little unnatural) would be:

I believe the doctor to have examined John.

But, although with PERSUADE, the meaning was 'I persuaded the doctor', the meaning here is not 'I believe the doctor'.

Semantically, then, BELIEVE is not like ORDER. For, where with ORDER there was passivization of the main clause, it could be argued that ORDER was like PERSUADE (and that it could also be like WANT). But in terms of meaning at least, it would seem that BELIEVE is not like PERSUADE and occurs only with construction 2, like WANT, where the NP is not the object of the verb of the main clause. Yet the main clause may be passivized. One way of accounting for this was the device known as 'subject raising', where the subject of a subordinate clause is 'raised' to a higher or main clause. On this interpretation *the doctor* would be the subject of the subordinate clause in underlying structure, but would then be raised to be the object of the main clause. It would then become its subject when the sentence is passivized.

[iv] There is a further problem with EXPECT. It appears at first sight to be of the same type as WANT (even occurring with construction 1):

> *I expect to examine John.*
> *I expect the doctor to examine John.*
> *I expect John to be examined by the doctor.*

Yet passivization of the main clause is possible, which suggests rather that the verb is like PERSUADE:

> *The doctor was expected to examine John.*

There is a semantic explanation available again. We may either expect someone to do something (expect it of him that he will do it) or expect that someone will do something. With the former meaning EXPECT is syntactically and semantically like PERSUADE, with the latter like WANT.

Yet this does not fully account for the behaviour of EXPECT. Passivization of the main clause is possible, as in the sentence illustrated, even where there is no expectation directed at someone: it is not necessarily true that we are talking about expecting (*ie* requiring) the doctor to take action. It would seem that with EXPECT sometimes the NP is the object of the main clause and so permits normal passivization, but that sometimes it is the subject of the subordinate clause so that passivization is possible only after 'subject raising'. Other verbs are no less problematic, *eg* INTEND and MEAN, where passivization is possible but rarer:

> *It was intended to be seen.*
> *?John was intended to be examined by the doctor.*
> *John was meant to come at four.*
> *?The doctor was meant to examine John.*

There is a great deal of indeterminacy here; the best we can do is to state the facts – that there are verbs that may occur with either construction, *ie* may or may not have the NP as the object of the main clause, though often with no clear distinction between the two, and that there are others such as BELIEVE that permit main clause passivization, even though semantically the NP is not the object of the main clause.

[v] There is a different though less problematic situation, with PROMISE:

> *I promised John to go.*

This is not:

> NP₁ V NP₂ [(NP₂) V]

This would imply that the meaning was that I promised John that he would go. It is rather:

> (4) NP₁ V NP₂ [(NP₁) V]

This shows that the meaning is that I promised John that I should go.

The verb PROMISE is unique in this respect. It alone produces a structure that looks superficially exactly like that of PERSUADE, etc, but is quite different in its identity relations. There are verbs with prepositions that seem similar (see 9.1.4).

> *I agreed with John to go.*
> *I undertook with John to go.*
> *I offered to John to go.*

But here, of course, *John* is not the object of the verb, and the construction is one with no intervening NP, but the subject of the subordinate verb is still to be identified with the subject of the main verb (and PROMISE would not be unique if it too required *with* or *to* (*I promised with/to John to go).

[vi] There is an apparent problem with:

> *I don't advise doing that.*
> *I don't recommend going there.*

Here the subject of the subordinate clause is semantically not *I* but *we* or *you* or even 'anyone'. (See 9.2.7, 9.3.4.)

[vii] Another addition to the list of structures is required by:

The boy needs to wash.
The clothes need washing.

These are not like:

The boy began to wash.
The boy began washing.

With NEED, *to wash* appears to be active, but *washing* appears to be passive. Alternatively with *need washing* the subject of the main clause is the object of the subordinate clause, the subject being unstated (and indicated by a blank):

NP₁ V [NP₁ V]
NP₁ V [– V NP₁]

There are only a very few verbs of this kind (see 9.2.8).
[viii] A different problem is provided by sentences such as:

John seems to have seen Mary.
Mary seems to have been seen by John.

Here there is passivization of the whole sentence as if it were a single clause (*ie* with a simple verb phrase) with *John* as the subject and *Mary* as the object. It was precisely passivization of this kind that was used as evidence in the arguments about the status of the modals.

Several solutions have been proposed. The simplest is that these verbs function like auxiliaries and are marginal members of the class of auxiliary verbs. In terms of voice neutrality, at least, they form part of a simple rather than a complex phrase. Other solutions again use the notion of subject raising. It might seem possible to analyse the sentence as:

NP₁ V [(NP₁) V NP₂]
John seems [John to have seen Mary].

But this would not account for the passivization of the whole sentence. An alternative solution is that the subordinate clause is the subject (not the object) of the main clause, *ie*:

NP₁ V [(NP₁) V NP₂]
[John to have seen Mary] seems.

John is then raised to subject position in the main clause to become the subject of *seems* to give the required sentence. For the passive sentence, the subordinate sentence is first passivized:

[NP₂V$_{pass}$ by NP₁] V
[Mary to have been seen by John] seems.

The subject of the subordinate clause is now *Mary* and it is this that is raised to the subject position in the main clause to become the subject of *seems*. (None of these solutions, however, is adopted in more recent syntactic theory.)

There are a few verbs that follow the pattern of SEEM as well as the more usual pattern of the other catenatives, *eg* BEGIN in:

John began to read a book.
The rain began to destroy the flowers.

For the first sentence cannot be passivized, but the second can:

*The book began to be read by John.
The flowers began to be destroyed by the rain.

Any analysis in terms of raising must treat these as quite different in their structure although the semantic difference rests only on the rather vague issue of whether or not the subject of the active sentence was fully responsible for the action. On the other hand, an analysis in terms of auxiliary-like characteristics would actually relate to the semantic issue: the more the initiation was associated with the subject, the less likely is a near-auxiliary interpretation, and the less likely, therefore, the possibility of voice neutrality.

9.1.4 Prepositions in the structure
Many of the verbs being considered may be followed by a preposition plus an NP. There are several possibilities, however, some of them problematic.

[i] Many 'futurity' verbs (9.2.1) occur with the NP₁ V[(NP₁)V] construction, but not with NP₁ V [NP₂V]. Indeed, the number that occur with both is very small. There is a contrast:

I want to come.
I want John to come.
I long to come.
*I long John to come.

WANT, but not LONG, enters into both constructions. However, the apparent gap is filled by using a construction with *for*:

> *I long for John to come.*

The identity relations are exactly the same as with *want*: *John* is here the object of *come*.

[ii]   With some verbs a prepositional phrase, often containing *with*, may come after the catenative:

> *I undertook to come.*
> *I undertook with John to come.*

If the prepositional phrase is simply ignored, these verbs occur only with construction I, with the subject of the subordinate clause identical with that of the main clause. But as was noted in 9.1.3[v], they are, in a way, like PROMISE.

[iii] PLEAD is similar but more idiosyncratic:

> *I pleaded to come.*
> *I pleaded with John to come.*
> *I pleaded with John to be allowed to come.*

Obviously the first means that I pleaded that I should come, but the second is much more likely to mean that I pleaded with John that he should come, yet the third (with a passive form) again means 'I pleaded that I should be allowed to come'. If the preposition is ignored, the second is like PERSUADE, the third like PROMISE.

[iv]   There are verbs that require prepositions when followed not by subordinate clauses but by NPs with nouns:

> *He hoped for a victory.*
> *He escaped from prison.*
> *He decided on the proposal.*

These, however, occur as catenatives without prepositions:

> *He hoped to win.*
> *He escaped jailing.*
> *He decided to go.*

The occurrence of the preposition in these cases is, thus, hardly relevant to the analysis of the catenatives.

[v]   There are many verbs that always occur with a preposition. These are very like the catenatives, but will not be discussed further in this book, *eg*:

I reacted against going there.
I insisted upon going there.
He persisted in going there.

9.1.5 Semantics
As has been seen, there are at least three set of criteria available
for the classification of the catenatives: the type of non-finite
form, the identity relations and the features of tense, phase,
aspect and voice.

Any attempt to use all of these in a classification would lead
to a vast number of classes. It would, indeed, be preferable
simply to approach the problem lexically, to list the verbs and
to state for each individually, its characteristics in terms of the
criteria. Yet an attempt to use just one of the sets of criteria
would lead to many, possibly most, verbs being placed in more
than one class. A particular difficulty is that there are borderline
cases.

The only simple solution is to adopt a basically semantic classification. This will not ignore the formal characteristics; indeed,
often there will be close correspondence. For instance, one class
is that of the 'futurity' verbs. These all refer to actions contemplated for the future – planned, foreseen, ordered, etc.
Formally they are distinguished by the possibility of the occurrence of adverbials of future time in the subordinate clause:

I hope to come tomorrow.
I want John to come tomorrow.
I persuaded John to come tomorrow.
I promised John to come tomorrow.

These exemplify the three basic constructions that were proposed
plus the more unusual construction associated with PROMISE:

NP$_1$ V([NP$_1$)V]
NP$_1$ V [NP$_1$ V]
NP$_1$ V NP$_2$ [(NP$_2$) V]
NP$_1$ V NP$_2$ [(NP$_1$) V]

Semantically this is easily explained. For, first, one can plan for
the performing of an action by oneself or by someone else. (NP$_1$
or NP$_2$ in the subordinate clause). Secondly, one can involve
someone else in the planning (NP$_2$ in the main clause) or not
(no NP$_2$ in the main clause). Hence the four possibilities. The last
construction is, of course, unique to PROMISE. The third, the only
other one that involves NP$_2$ in the main clause is required for

only two other sets of verbs, those of causation and process (9.2.2, 9.2.5). For although passivization of the main clause is also possible with verbs of reporting, some other solution, *eg* subject raising, is more appropriate.

Within each class it is possible to see further semantic/formal subclasses. For the verbs of futurity, for instance:

[i]   verbs of persuading, inducing, etc, that occur only with the NP₁ V NP₂ [(NP₂) V] construction, where some person is persuaded, induced, etc to act (*eg* PERSUADE).

[ii] verbs of ordering, compelling, etc, that occur with both the NP₁ V NP₂ [(NP₂) V] and the NP₁ V [NP₂ V] construction, where someone is ordered, etc or the action is ordered without reference to the recipient of the order (*eg* ORDER).

[iii] verbs of asking, etc that occur with the NP₁ V NP₂ [(NP₂) V] and the NP₁ V [(NP₁) V] constructions, where we ask someone to do something or ask that we may do it (*eg* ASK).

But this is not an exhaustive list. The details will be discussed in the appropriate subsection.

9.1.6 Homonyms

The classification of the catenatives specifically takes into account the fact that one verb may occur with more than one construction or with more than one non-finite form. But some verbs have to be listed in two sections or subsections. Putting them in different places essentially treats them as different verbs, *ie* as homonyms. It must be said, however, that this is to use the term 'homonymy' in a very narrow sense, for a particular purpose. In a more general lexical account the verbs concerned would be treated in terms of polysemy ('one word with several meanings') rather than homonymy ('different words with the same shape'). There can be no clear principle for the decision, but there are some obvious guidelines.

First, the fact that a verb occurs both with and without NP but with predictable identity relations is not treated as evidence of homonymy. Nor is the fact that it occurs with different non-finite forms that either mark aspect or have little or no semantic difference. (There is some arbitrariness: SEE clearly marks aspect with the bare infinitive and *-ing* form, but the position with START, LIKE and INTEND is less clear – 9.1.2)

Nor is there homonymy with verbs such as BEGIN and ORDER, even though these verbs have different constructions clearly established by the passivization tests (9.1.3). For not only can this be accounted for in semantic terms, but, more importantly, it is

not always possible to draw a clear line between the two semantic/
syntactic types.

But there are some problem cases. There are some further
distinctions to make with SEE. In addition to the (perception)
meaning 'observe', it has the (reporting) meaning 'see that',
especially in the passive. Consider:

He was seen walking away.
He was seen to walk away.
He was seen to be walking away.

The first has the perception meaning, but the other two the
reporting 'see that' meaning. Notice that *He was seen to walk
away* is not the non-progressive correlate of *He was seen walking
away*; in the passive the perception SEE does not mark aspect as
it does in the active (see 9.1.2, 9.2.4).

There is yet another SEE, meaning 'imagine', as in:

I can't see him ever owning a house.

This is different again since there is no possibility of marking
aspect with this SEE:

**I can't see him ever own a house.*

The *-ing* form is not here an indication of the progressive. This
is conclusively proved by the fact that it occurs as in this example
with a 'non-progressive' verb, OWN (4.6).

How many SEE verbs are there? In fact, almost all the verbs
of perception may also function as verbs of reporting:

I heard him coming.
I heard him to be very foolish.
I found him working in the garden.
He was found to have been stabbed.

Instead of distinguishing homonyms for every one of these verbs,
it may be stated, as a generalization, that they have this double
function. This does not, account for the 'imagine' SEE, which has
to be treated as an isolated case. It is semantically and syntactically different, and so a different verb.

The status of FEEL is a little more doubtful. Semantically it
might seem that there is FEEL$_1$ (= have tactile sensations) and
FEEL$_2$ (= believe instinctively). But formally it is merely a verb
of perception with the function of a verb of reporting as well, like
SEE, etc. The semantic difference between perception and
reporting seems greater, but formally there is no case for
distinguishing two verbs here.

A more extreme example is TRY. This verb is unique in having the meaning 'attempt to do something' with the *to*-infinitive and 'test the usefulness of' with the *-ing* form. Since no kind of general statement about these alternatives can be made, it would seem sensible to identify two verbs TRY$_1$ and TRY$_2$.

More difficult is REMEMBER. With the *-ing* form it means 'to remember that one performed' the action; with the *to*-infinitive it means 'remember and therefore to perform' the action, as in:

I remembered doing it.
I remembered to do it.

There is no obvious general statement that can be made about the *to*-infinitive and *-ing* form carrying such a distinction in meaning (unlike for instance, the distinctions with SEE). The pattern is also found with FORGET and REGRET (9.2.3, 9.2.6, 9.2.7.):

I regret to tell you.
I regret telling you.

HATE also functions in this way, but not, LIKE. The semantic-syntactic patterns are found, separately, with other verbs – HASTEN with *to*-infinitive, MISS with *-ing* forms.

A verb that seems to have several homonyms is GET:

I got to see that I was wrong.
I got them to see that they were wrong.
I got working hard at the project.
I got them working hard at the project.
I got hurt in the crash.

The first has the meaning 'eventually saw' and is like COME in *came to see*. The second means 'caused them to see' and belongs with PERSUADE. The third and fourth are examples of a process verb like KEEP. The fifth is the alternative passive marker dealt with in 5.3.

The decision to recognize homonymy for any particular verb is essentially a practical one, and often fairly arbitrary, for it depends upon the number of sections and sub-sections that are to be set up. Where a verb is dealt with in more than one place, subscript numerals, *eg* SEE$_1$, SEE$_2$, are used to identify and distinguish them. The verbs handled in this way are CHANCE (9.2.7, 9.2.9), FANCY (9.2.4, 9.2.7), FORGET (9.2.3, 9.2.6), GET (9.2.2, 9.2.5, 9.2.6), IMAGINE (9.2.3, 9.2.4), REGRET (9.2.6, 9.2.7), REMEMBER (9.2.3, 9.2.6), SEE (twice in 9.2.4), TRY (9.2.5, 9.2.6), and WANT (9.2.2, 9.2.8).

9.2 Catenative classes

At least nine classes of catenative can be established, together with a number of sub-classes, largely on semantic criteria combined with differences in basic structure.

9.2.1 Futurity

The first class of verbs refers semantically to plans, etc for the future and is formally distinguished by the possibility of adverbials of future time in the subordinate clause. With the exception of one subclass these verbs occur only with the *to*-infinitive (and so may mark both aspect and voice).

[i] WISH. WISH and DESIRE, occur with 1 and 2 (NP₁ V [(NP₁) V], NP₁ V [NP₂ V]) only:

> *I wish to meet Mary.*
> *I wish John to meet Mary.*
> *I wish Mary to be met by John.*
> **John is wished to meet Mary.*

Phase/tense may be marked in the subordinate clause:

> *I wish to have finished before she comes.*
> *I wish John to have finished before she comes.*

It would be reasonable to add here the forms of LIKE *I would like, should like* with the meaning 'wish':

> *I should like to meet Mary.*

These differ from other forms of LIKE in that they do not occur with the *-ing* form. Otherwise LIKE is a verb of attitude (9.2.7).

[ii] DECIDE. There are many verbs that occur only with construction 1:

> *He decided to come tomorrow.*
> **He decided John to come tomorrow.*

Semantically all the verbs in this group refer to plans, hopes, wishes, etc for future activity by the subject of the main clause. A list is ACHE, AIM, ASPIRE, CHOOSE, CONDESCEND, DECIDE, DECLINE, DETERMINE, ELECT, FEAR, HESITATE, HOPE, LONG, LOOK, LUST, PLOT, PREPARE, REFUSE, SCORN, SWEAR, YEARN. Phase/tense may be marked with some of these verbs. It seems to be unlikely with those verbs that refer to specific acts of planning, etc, but much more likely with those of more general attitude:

I aim to have finished it by tomorrow.
I hope to have finished it by tomorrow.
?I decline to have finished it by tomorrow.
?I choose to have finished it by tomorrow.

Two verbs that fit into the same formal pattern, but differ semantically, are STAND (= 'be likely to') and (CAN'T) AFFORD:

I stand to lose a lot of money.

HAVE in its meaning of obligation (6.6) could also have been included here.

Although none of these verbs occur with construction 2, it is possible with most of them to refer to future activity by others by introducing *for*:

*I hope John to come.
I hope for John to come.
*I long John to come.
I long for John to come.

With a few verbs it is less likely that there will be reference to the activity of others, *eg* HESITATE and, perhaps, SCORN. With these there is no place for a *for* construction.

PLAN, PROPOSE and possibly VENTURE are like DECIDE in referring to future plans by the subject, but, except for IN-TEND, which appears in [v], they are alone among the futurity verbs in occurring with the *-ing* form as well as the *to*-infinitive:

I plan going there tomorrow.
I plan to go there tomorrow.

There is little or no difference in meaning.

A number of verbs, *eg* AGREE, ARRANGE, OFFER, UNDER-TAKE occur with prepositional phrases:

I agreed with John to come the next day.
I offered to John to see him the next day.

These are, however, to be regarded as a sub-class of the verbs that occur with no intervening NP, since the subject of the subordinate clause is identical with the subject of the main clause, though PLEAD is an exception (see 9.1.4).

[iii] PERSUADE. There is a large class of verbs that occurs only with construction 3 (NP$_1$ V NP$_2$ [(NP$_2$) V]:

I persuaded John to meet Mary.
!I persuaded Mary to be met by John.
John was persuaded to meet Mary.

All these verbs refer, semantically, to inducing someone to act. Obvious members are ACCUSTOM, ADVISE, APPOINT, ASSIST, BRING (often with *self*), CHALLENGE, COAX, COERCE, COMMISSION, COMPEL, DIRECT, DRIVE, ENTICE, ENTREAT, FORCE, INVITE, LEAD, LEAVE, MOTION, OBLIGE, PRESS, REMIND, REQUEST, TEACH, TELL, TEMPT, TROUBLE, URGE, WARN, WORRY and GIVE (in GIVE . . . TO UNDERSTAND only).

[iv]   ORDER. Some verbs occur with constructions 2 and 3 and seem to be simultaneously members of both the WANT and PERSUADE class:

I ordered the chauffeur to fetch the car.
The chauffeur was ordered to fetch the car.
I ordered the car to be fetched by the chauffeur.

All refer to the notion of 'making' or 'letting' someone perform an action. The problem of these has already been discussed in detal (9.1.3[ii]). Phase is not normally marked. Members of the class include ALLOW, CAUSE, COMMAND, ENABLE, FORBID, ORDER, PERMIT.

[v]   EXPECT. There are a few verbs that occur with constructions 2 and 3 like ORDER, but also with 1.

I expect to meet Mary.
I expect John to meet Mary.
I expect Mary to be met by John.
John is expected to meet Mary.

Other verbs are INTEND and MEAN, though INTEND is rare with main clause passivization. Phase may be marked normally:

I expect to have seen Mary by tomorrow.

[vi]   ASK. Several verbs of asking occur with constructions 1 and 3:

I asked to meet Mary.
I asked John to meet Mary.
!I asked Mary to be met by John.
John was asked to meet Mary.

Semantically this pairing of constructions is a little odd. The pairing of 1 and 2 is obvious enough: one can plan for an action by oneself or by someone else. But 3 also involves someone else in the planning (it is here John who is asked) whereas 1 does not. Yet it is clear that semantically even with 1 we ask someone else that we may act. We seem almost to have the further construction:

NP₁ V (NP₂) [(NP₁) V]

But this is unnecessary. The person involved is not mentioned, and ASK here functions like AIM, CHOOSE, in construction 1. It is interesting to compare these verbs with those of [i] (*eg* WISH). Whereas wish does not appear to have any NP as object, but simply relates to an action by oneself or by someone else, ASK obviously has an object in construction 3, and would also seem to have an unstated object with construction 1 ('I ask someone to allow me to meet Mary'). Indeed, it could be argued that there is a further construction:

NP₁ V (NP₂) [(NP₁) V]

But this is an unnecessary complication. Since the person asked is not mentioned, the pattern is that of construction 1. In that ASK does not occur with construction 2, it is like the verbs of [ii] (AIM, CHOOSE, etc); like them it can refer to activities by others with the introduction of *for*:

I asked for John to meet Mary.
I asked for Mary to be met by John.

Verbs in this group are ASK, BEG, PRAY, REQUIRE and possibly DARE (it belongs formally, but it may not be semantically appropriate).

[vii] PROMISE. This verb is unique in that it occurs with construction 4 as well as 1:

I promised to meet Mary.
I promised John to meet Mary.
*John was promised to meet Mary.
!I promised Mary to be met by John.

Yet it has been noted (9.1.4[ii]), that there is something similar in:

I undertook with John to come.

Here the subject of the subordinate clause is identical with the subject of the main clause.

9.2.2 Causation
This is a good place to deal with some very common verbs that are all concerned with getting or helping someone to act:

[i]   HELP occurs with construction 1 and bare infinitive and with construction 3 with both bare infinitive and *to*-infinitive:

> *You can help push the car.*
> *He helped them build the house.*
> *He helped them to build the house.*

With main clause passivization only the *to*-infinitive is possible:

> *They were helped to build their house.*

[ii] MAKE occurs with construction 3 and bare infinitive, but with *to*-infinitive when the main clause is passivized:

> *He made the boy finish his work.*
> *The boy was made to finish his work.*

[iii] LET occurs with NP and bare infinitive alone:

> *I'll let them stay a while.*

Semantically this would seem to be construction 3, but main clause passivization is not normal:

> *They were let (to) stay a while.*

[iv] There is one use of HAVE that was not discussed in Chapter 8, causative HAVE, which occurs with NP and bare infinitive, the *-ing* form and the *-en* form. Main clause passivization is not possible:

> *He had them come early.*
> *He had them all singing.*
> *He had all the prisoners punished.*

However, two other verbs, GET₁, and WANT, occur in a very similar set of constructions differing only in that they require the *to*-infinitive instead of the bare infinitive:

> *He got them to cut down the tree.*
> *He got them cutting down the tree.*
> *He got the tree cut down.*
> *I want them all to sing the songs.*
> *I want them all singing the songs.*
> *I want all the songs sung.*

9.2.3 Report

There is a group of verbs of 'reporting', 'saying', 'believing', etc
that can be formally distinguished by the fact that there is an
alternative construction with *that*:

> *I believe John to be clever.*
> *I believe that John is clever.*

Moreover all of these verbs occur with NP and *to*-infinitive and
most of them with both main clause and subordinate clause
passivization (for the problematic status of the constructions see
(9.1.3[iv], 9.2.1[v]).

With the *to*-infinitive there are two common characteristics:

(*a*) Main clause passivization is not merely possible, but is
normal:

> *John is believed to be clever.*

With SAY it is obligatory:

> *John is said to be clever.*
> **I say John to be clever.*

(*b*) Phase/tense may be marked with HAVE, but the most common
pattern is for the subordinate clause verb either to be
prefect/past with HAVE (usually past) or progressive, or to
consist of the copula:

> *John is assumed to have gone.*
> *He was thought to be working at the time.*
> *John is considered to be clever.*

With the HAVE forms in particular, main clause passivization
is likely. Other verbal forms are much less likely, the *that*
construction being preferred:

> **I believe Mary to arrive tomorrow.*
> *?Mary is believed to arrive tomorrow.*
> *I believe that Mary arrives tomorrow.*

[i] ALLEGE. Many of these verbs occur only with NP and the
to-infinitive:

> *The boy was alleged to have taken the car.*

Verbs of this type include ACCEPT, AFFIRM, ALLEGE,
ANNOUNCE, ARGUE, ASSERT, CERTIFY, CONJECTURE, ESTIMATE,
KNOW, PROVE, READ, RECKON, REPORT, REPRESENT, RUMOUR,

SAY, STATE, SURMISE, SUSPECT, TAKE, THINK, UNDERSTAND and also almost all of the verbs of perception (9.2.4).

[ii] CONSIDER. Some verbs occur not only with NP and the *to*-infinitive but also with NP and the *-en* form, often with the reflexive *-self* as the NP:

> *They considered him to be a rogue.*
> *They considered themselves beaten.*
> *The chairman considered the meeting closed.*

It is not possible to draw a clear line between this group and the preceding one, but obvious members are BELIEVE, CONSIDER, DECLARE, DISCOVER, IMAGINE₁, SUPPOSE, and, to some extent, there is a semantic difference in that verbs of this group are all 'private', referring to private thoughts, beliefs, etc, while those of the previous group are public, referring to public expressions of such thoughts and beliefs.

With main clause passivization SUPPOSE is semantically like EXPECT (9.1.3[iv], 9.2.1):

> *He is supposed to come tomorrow.*

The perception verbs also occur with NP and *-en* form (see 9.2.4).

[iii] ADMIT. There are a few verbs that occur without NP and with the *-ing* form as well as with NP and the *to*-infinitive (and so with the identity relations of constructions 1 and 2):

> *I admit being a fool.*
> *I admit John to be a fool.*
> *John is admitted to be a fool.*

With the first construction phase/tense may be marked with or without HAVE:

> *I admit seeing John.*
> *I admit having seen John.*

Verbs of this type are ADMIT, ACKNOWLEDGE, CONFESS, DENY. But ADMIT and CONFESS often occur with the preposition *to* when followed by the *-ing* form:

> *I admit to being a fool.*

DENY is rare with NP and the *to*-infinitive.

[iv] CLAIM is a verb of reporting, but is like WANT in that it occurs with constructions 1 and 2:

> *He claims to be descended from Napoleon.*
> *He claims his father to be Napoleon's great grandson.*

PROFESS and AFFECT are similar, but may occur (rarely) with the *-ing* form with construction 1 only:

> *He professes being a good scholar.*
> *He professes to be a good scholar.*

[v]   Verbs concerned with memory, of which REMEMBER is an obvious example, occur with and without an intervening NP. The most common constructions are illustrated by:

> *I remember coming to see you.*
> *I remember having come to see you.*
> *I remember my father going to London.*
> *I remember my father to have been kind.*

A striking feature about these is the contrast between forms with and without HAVE. This is not a distinction in terms of time, since in all cases what is remembered is in the past. Without HAVE the meaning is that the actual event is remembered; with HAVE what is remembered is the fact that the event took place. Thus *I remembered coming* means 'I remember the action of coming', while *I remembered having come* means 'I remembered that I came'. In the construction 1 with no NP, only the *-ing* form occurs. With construction 2 with NP the *to*-infinitive is more likely with HAVE, but the *-ing* form is possible (*I remember my father having been kind*). Surprisingly, perhaps, there is no main clause passivization. It is not possible to say:

> **My father is remembered being kind.*
> **My father is remembered to have been kind.*

Besides REMEMBER₁ the other verbs are RECOLLECT, RECALL and FORGET₁ in the negative (all verbs of memory):

> *I shall never forget coming to see you.*
> *I shall never forget having come to see you.*
> *I shall never forget my father going to London.*
> *I shall never forget my father to have been kind.*

9.2.4 Perception

There is a formally quite distinct set of verbs, involving sensation and imagination that occur with NP and bare infinitive, *-ing* form and *-en* form, marking thereby both aspect and voice. These form the basic set [i] below, but there are some others that seem also to belong here:

[i]   SEE₁. The full range of patterns is illustrated by SEE:

I saw the children eat their lunch.
I saw the children eating their lunch.
I saw the children beaten by their rivals.

Aspect in the passive may, further, be marked by the participial:

I saw the children being beaten by their rivals.

Main clause passivization is possible, but there is in the subordinate clause contrast of voice, active and passive, but not of aspect:

The children were seen eating their lunch.
The children were seen being beaten by their rivals.

It might be thought that these exemplify progressive forms that correspond to:

The children were seen to eat their lunch.
*The children were seen beaten.
or *The children were seen to be beaten.*

But one of these forms (asterisked) does not occur and the other two are to be interpreted not as perception, but as reporting, verbs. For almost all the verbs of perception function also as verbs of reporting:

He saw the children to be eating their lunch.
The children were seen to be eating their lunch.
He saw that the children were eating their lunch.

The *to*-infinitive forms illustrated above can all be handled in terms of reporting. The verbs that belong to this group are BEHOLD (archaic), FEEL, FIND, HEAR, NOTICE, OBSERVE, PERCEIVE, SEE₁, SMELL and WATCH, but with the exception of HEAR and SEE there are some restrictions and probabilities:

(*a*) Only FEEL, HEAR, SEE, SMELL and WATCH occur regularly with the bare infinitive (SMELL mostly with BURN).

(*b*) Only HEAR, SEE and WATCH regularly occur with the *-en* form and FEEL if the NP is a reflexive *-self* form (SMELL does not occur at all), *eg*:

She felt herself overcome by the fumes.

As has been observed, almost all these verbs are also reporting verbs though SMELL and WATCH are exceptions:

?I heard him to be famous.

I noticed them to have come early.
*I smelled the meat to have burnt.
*I watched them to have come into the house.

[ii]   IMAGINE. There are some verbs that occur only with the *-ing*
form and make no aspect distinction. This point is clearly
shown by the occurrence of the *-ing* form with non-
progressive verbs:

I can't imagine him knowing all that.

The verbs of this type are semantically of two kinds, imag-
ining – CONCEIVE, ENVISAGE, FANCY₁ (only in the imperative,
eg Fancy him knowing that), IMAGINE₂, SEE₂ (see 9.1.6) and
portraying – DEPICT, DESCRIBE, PORTRAY. All of these verbs
function also as verbs of reporting.

[iii] KNOW. KNOW belongs here as well as with the reporting
verbs in that it occurs with the bare infinitive with NP and
with the *to*-infinitive when the main clause is passivized. It
is in this respect like a perception verb, although it does not
occur with *-ing* or *-en* forms:

Have you ever known them come on time?
They have been known to get very angry.

The KNOW of reporting also occurs, of course, with main
clause passivization and *to*-infinitive, but normally only with
HAVE (phase/tense) or BE:

They were known to be foolish.
They are known to have been there.

These could be treated as two distinct verbs KNOW₁ and
KNOW₂, but it is better to say that there is a verb of
reporting functioning (partly) as a verb of perception, the
reverse of the usual pattern, but accounted for in the same
way.

9.2.5 Process
There are several types of verb concerned with processes,
starting, stopping, continuation, etc.

[i]   KEEP. A few verbs occur with or without NP and with *-ing*
form, and permit main clause passivization:

He kept talking.
He kept them talking.
They were kept talking.

Only GET₂, KEEP and STOP belong to this group.

[ii]   START. Another group has the same pattern as KEEP except that without NP it also occurs with *to*-infinitive and seems, by this, to mark aspect (see 9.1.2[ii]):

> *He started to talk* (but was interrupted).
> *He started talking* (and carried on for an hour).
> *He started them talking.*

BEGIN and START are the only members of this group but are unlikely to occur with main clause passivization:

> **They were started talking.*

[iii] FINISH. There are a number of verbs of two semantic kinds, of 'ending and avoiding' and of 'effort', that occur only without NP and with the *-ing* form:

> *He finished talking at four.*
> *You should try working a bit harder.*

Verbs of these types are AVOID, COMPLETE, DELAY, ESCAPE, EVADE, FINISH, POSTPONE, QUIT, and SHUN; PRACTISE and TRY₁. GO belongs formally here too:

> *He went fishing.*

[iv]   CEASE. CEASE is like FINISH but also occurs with the *to*-infinitive:

> *He ceased to worry me, when he became older.*
> *He ceased worrying me, when he became older.*

There is again the semantics of aspect in this distinction.

[v]   LEAVE. A few verbs occur with NP and the *-ing* form and with the possibility of main clause passivization:

> *He left them standing in the street.*
> *They were left standing in the street.*

The verbs are CATCH, LEAVE, SEND and SET. SEND usually occurs with verbs implying motion: SEND PACKING, SEND FLYING, etc. CATCH rarely occurs with bare infinitive:

> *? You won't catch him do it twice.*

This would place it among the sensation verbs, rather than here.

[vi]   PREVENT. This verb occurs with NP and *-ing* form only. With main clause passivization a preposition, *from*, is required:

He prevented the men leaving.
The men were prevented from leaving.

Besides PREVENT, HINDER functions in this way. FORBID rarely occurs with NP and *-ing* form; its normal place is with the verbs like PERSUADE (9.2.1[iii]).

9.2.6 Achievement
Another set of verbs is largely concerned with effort, failure and success.

All these verbs occur only without NP and with the *to*-infinitive:

You should try to work a bit harder.
He managed to come.
He failed to see the truth.

Verbs that are clearly concerned with effort are ATTEMPT, ENDEAVOUR, STRIVE, STRUGGLE, TRY$_2$ (see 9.2.5[iii] for TRY$_1$). Verbs concerned with success or failure are COME, FAIL, GET$_3$, MANAGE, NEGLECT, OMIT, PROCEED and SERVE.

REMEMBER$_2$ and FORGET$_2$ are very similar in that they indicate that the event referred to was or was not carried out, with the assistance or failure of memory:

I remembered/forgot to tell him about it.

HASTEN too means 'act with haste', but again indicates that the action took place. Thus some verbs merely indicate the circumstances in which an event did or did not take place. For that reason HATE$_1$ and REGRET$_1$ should also be included:

I regret to tell you this.
I hate to do this to him.

The meanings are 'I tell you with regret' 'I do this to him with great distaste'.

Semantically and in terms of the *to*-infinitive construction the verbs of chance belong here too. But they have such idiosyncratic characteristics that they require a separate section (9.2.9).

9.2.7 Attitude
Verbs of attitude are at one extreme end of the catenatives, with most object-like subordinate clauses. This is shown by two facts:
(*a*) there is never main clause passivization involving the intervening NP;
(b) the intervening NP may be replaced usually by a possessive – *him* by *his*, etc:

I can't contemplate John coming tomorrow.
I can't contemplate John's coming tomorrow.
*John can't be contemplated coming tomorrow.

With all these verbs phase/tense can be marked with HAVE to mean 'the fact that . . . has/did . . .', etc. But the HAVE forms are less common and with some verbs most unlikely.

[i] LIKE. The more common verbs of this type occur with or without NP and with either the *to*-infinitive or with the *-ing* form.

I like to go to the theatre.
I like going to the theatre.
I like the children going to the theatre.
I like the children to go to the theatre.

With these verbs the possessive form is most unlikely:

*I like his going to the theatre.

Verbs of this type are ABHOR, (CAN'T) BEAR, HATE₂, LIKE, LOVE, PREFER. There are other verbs that would normally not occur with the *to*-infinitive except in unfulfilled conditions:

I couldn't stand to wait for three hours.
?I can't stand to wait for three hours.
I can't stand waiting for three hours.
I should dislike the children to gamble.
?I dislike the children to gamble.
I should dislike the children gambling.

The *to*-infinitive, that is to say, has a conditional meaning. The verbs of this type include DISLIKE, LOATHE, (CAN'T) STAND.

[ii] MISS. Other verbs occur without or with intervening NP but only with the *-ing* form:

I miss going to the theatre.
I miss them coming to see me every week.

The possessive is possible with the latter construction. Verbs of this type are CHANCE, CONSIDER, CONTEMPLATE, COUNTENANCE, DETEST, DISCUSS, ENJOY, (DON'T) FANCY₂, (CAN'T) HELP JUSTIFY, (DON'T) MIND, MISS, (DON'T) RELISH, RESENT, RISK, WELCOME. In addition to those listed, others normally occur with a negative – CAN'T CONTEMPLATE, DON'T WELCOME, etc. There are many others with prepositions –

COUNT ON, DELIGHT IN, THINK ABOUT, etc.

REGRET₂ also belongs here, except that the events referred to are always in the past:

I don't regret doing that.

As with the verbs of memory (9.2.3[v]), with or without HAVE, the *-ing* form must be interpreted as past.

[iii] DEPLORE. The least catenative-like of all are the verbs that occur only with NP and the *-ing* form. These are commonly found with the possessive; some may occur also with no NP but with no identity relations (9.1.3[vi]).

I deplore them doing that.
I deplore their doing that.
I don't advocate you going there tomorrow.
I don't advocate your going there tomorrow.
I don't advocate going there tomorrow.

Verbs of this type are ADVOCATE, ANTICIPATE, DEPLORE, DEPRECATE. There are a few others with prepositions – APPROVE OF, DISAPPROVE OF.

9.2.8 Need
The contrast between the *to*-infinitive and the *-ing* form with NEED was noted in 9.1.3[viii]:

The boys need to watch.
The clothes need washing.

An obvious way of dealing with this is to say that the *to*-infinitive is active and the *-ing* form passive (giving the meaning 'The clothes need to be washed').

Alternatively, it could be said that, with the *to*-infinitive, there is identity between the subject of the main clause and the subject of the subordinate, but, with the *-ing* form, between the subject of the main clause and the object of the subordinate. The only clear member of this class besides NEED is DESERVE. WANT₂ also occurs with the *-ing* form, with almost the same meaning as NEED:

The clothes want washing.

WANT with the *to*-infinitive, however, is not similar to NEED, but is to be identified with WANT₁, only with the sense of WISH or DESIRE (9.2.1[i]).

9.2.9 Appearance and chance
Verbs such as SEEM and HAPPEN are (see 9.1.3[viii]) in some

respects like the achievement verbs of 9.2.6. But they are different from all other catenatives in that they permit the passivization of the whole sentence:

John seems to like Mary.
Mary seems to be liked by John.
The boy happened to meet her in the street.
She happened to be met in the street by the boy.

In this respect these complex phrases are very like simple phrases. The verbs themselves are somewhat like modals; in particular SEEM and HAPPEN often occur in the present with a *have* form of the following verb.

He happens to have been there.
He seems to have seen her.

These can be paraphrased 'It happens that he was there', 'It seems that he was there'. There is reference to a past event, but to present 'happening' or 'seeming', where the remarks relate to present circumstances, *eg* in a context where it is denied or questioned whether he was there. However, unlike epistemic modals these verbs may occur in the past tense, if the 'happening' or 'seeming' is past:

He happened to be there.
He seemed to be there.

SEEM has a further peculiarity in CAN'T SEEM *eg*:

I can't seem to do it.

This means 'It seems that I can't do it'. Semantically *can't* belongs to the subordinate clause. The chief verbs in this class are of two semantic types. SEEM and APPEAR are concerned with appearance and are, therefore, very close to epistemic modals, but HAPPEN and CHANCE$_2$ are concerned with CHANCE. TEND could be added on formal grounds but it will not usually occur with the present tense + *have* construction mentioned above. In terms of sentence passivization alone other verbs, especially those of process such as BEGIN, might also be included. The dividing line is by no means clear.

9.3 Further issues

There are some further issues of a descriptive or theoretical nature.

9.3.1 Related and contrasting structures

There are some sequences that are superficially exactly like catenative constructions, but are not to be treated as complex phrases at all:

> *I ran to catch the train.*
> *The car hit the boy running across the street.*
> *We eat our meat cooked.*

These are to be contrasted with:

> *I want to catch the train.*
> *The man saw the boy running across the street.*
> *We had our meat cooked.*

No contrast with bare infinitive is possible since this does not occur except in the complex phrase.

Most of the problems concern the *-to*-infinitive.

[i]   It is clear enough that we want to exclude all 'infinitives of purpose':

> *I ran to catch the train.*
> *I caught the train to go to London.*

The occurrence of the *to*-infinitive is totally independent of the preceding verb and it always expresses purpose. The whole clause can, moreover, be transposed to initial position, though sometimes rather unnaturally:

> *To catch the train, I ran.*
> *To go to London, I caught the train.*

There is even contrast of infinitives of purpose and catenative forms with the same words (the written language indicates the distinction with a comma, speech by timing):

> *I promise to make you happy.*
> *I promise, to make you happy.*
> *I told him to keep him quiet.*
> *I told him, to keep him quiet.*

(Notice that with the complex phrase the two *him* forms cannot refer to the same person, but they do so with the infinitive of purpose.)

But there is a problem with WAIT. It is by no means clear whether there is a clear distinction between:

> *I'm waiting to hear your answer.*
> *I'm waiting, to hear your answer.*

WAIT seems to be a catenative of the futurity type but it is not entirely distinguished from WAIT with an infinitive of purpose.

[ii] Also to be excluded are 'infinitives of result':

I ran all the way to find that he had gone.

But it is not clear whether this is the best interpretation of:

He woke to find he was alone.
He lived to be ninety.

It would be possible to handle WAKE and LIVE here as catenatives of the 'achievement' kind.

[iii] With verbs of emotion the *to*-infinitive occurs:

He rejoiced to hear the news.
I grieve to tell you this.

There is the nursery rhyme too:

The little dog laughed to see such fun.

Clearly these verbs are very like REGRET, etc among the achievement verbs of 9.2.6. But they are also very like constructions with adjectives:

He was happy to hear the news.
I am sorry to tell you this.

This is again a borderline area. It might be possible to put all verbs of emotion into the achievement class, but it would not be easy to define them: in appropriate contexts there would be a case for including not only GRIEVE, LAUGH, REJOICE, but also SMILE, YELL, ROAR, WHISTLE, etc.

There is very little to be said about the *-ing* form. There is no reason to include here such sentences as:

He arrived puffing and panting.

This is no more an example of a complex phrase than:

He arrived hot and miserable.

But there is a problem with:

She sat talking.
We stood talking.

SIT and STAND are semantically not far from KEEP and could be treated as catenatives of the process type (9.2.5).

9.3.2 Simple and complex phrases

It has been argued that catenatives occur in complex phrases, with subordination. One of the reasons for this is that there may be an intervening NP, which is not possible with auxiliaries in a simple phrase. The essential criteria, however, for the distinction of simple and complex phrases are the TNP tests (2.3.1, 6.1.3).

[i]   Verbs in many of the classes (9.2.1, 9.2.3, 9.2.4, 9.2.7, 9.2.9) may mark tense (or phase) in the subordinate clause (with HAVE).

[ii] Negation may be independently marked in both the main and the subordinate clause:

> *He did not agree to do anything.*
> *He agreed not to do anything.*
> *I don't like having a television set.*
> *I like not having a television set.*

The bare infinitive and the *-en* form are not often negated, but there is no absolute restriction:

> *Have you ever known him not come?*
> *I don't like children not taught road safety.*

Where there are restrictions they seem to be semantic rather than grammatical:

> **He helped not wash up.*
> **He failed not to come.*
> **She got not hurt in the accident.*
> *?She saw the children not crossing the road.*

We do not help, fail or get negative actions or states and are unlikely to see non-events.

[iii] Only the verbs of appearance and chance, and, in some circumstances, verbs such as BEGIN, are voice neutral. It was noted that, in this respect, they have something in common with the epistemic modals.

In general, then it is clear that the catenatives are not auxiliaries and that they occur in complex clauses.

9.3.3 Verbal nouns and adjectives

There is a traditional classification of the non-finite forms into verbal nouns and verbal adjectives, a result of the view that all words must belong to one of the parts of speech. On this interpretation the bare infinitive, the *to*-infinitive and some of the *-ing* forms (now called 'gerunds') are nouns, while the *-en* forms (the 'past participles') and the remaining *-ing* forms (the 'present participles') are adjectives.

The plausibility of this rests largely on the similarity of their forms to other nouns and adjectives. Compare:

I want to read.
I want a book.
I like reading.
I like books.

It can be argued that *to read* and *reading* have the same function as *a book* and *books*, that they are noun forms, and objects of the sentence. Similarly compare:

He keeps reading.
He keeps quiet.
He got hurt.
He got hot.

Reading and *hurt* are, it can be said, exactly like *quiet* and *hot*, adjectives functioning in predicative position. A further argument in favour of this position is the observation that the forms seem to have nominal and adjectival functions in other constructions. The infinitive and gerund may function as the subject of the sentence (though the infinitive is rare in colloquial English) and the participles may act as noun modifiers:

To err is human.
Reading is a pleasant relaxation.
A sleeping child.
A hurt child.

There are, however, great difficulties in accepting this classification.

[i] It breaks down with such sentences as:

I saw them eating.
I saw them eaten.
I saw them eat.

Eating and *eaten* are presumably present and past participles and, therefore, adjectives. (*Eaten* cannot be anything else and *eating* is clearly its active counterpart.) But *eat* is an infinitive and so usually treated as a noun. Yet the three forms all have exactly the same function in these sentences, marking only difference of voice and aspect. The noun/adjective distinction would obscure this identity of function.

[ii] Some of the verbal nouns and adjectives must be allowed to have objects. This establishes them as a most unusual kind of noun or adjective, so unusual that there seems to be little point in retaining this classification:

> *I want to read a novel.*
> *I like reading novels.*
> *He keeps reading novels.*

This is true even where the relevant clause is not part of a complex phrase:

> *To read novels is a waste of time.*
> *Reading novels is a waste of time.*
> *Children eating biscuits make a lot of noise.*

It will also be necessary to say that the verbal noun or adjective may have a subject:

> *I want John to read a novel.*
> *I saw the children crossing the street.*

[iii] The issue also relates to a problem that worried many of the traditional grammarians, that of:

> *I don't like him doing that.*
> *I don't like his doing that.*

With the noun/adjective distinction *coming* in the first is an adjective modifying *John*, with a construction like that of *Children singing* in *Children singing are a wonderful sound*. In the second, *coming* is a noun preceded by a possessive, to be compared with *John's coming* (or *John's arrival*) in *John's coming* (*arrival*) *surprised us*. The grammarian Henry Sweet (1903:121) suggested that *coming* was a 'half gerund', because he did not feel that *coming* in *I do not like him coming* modifies *him* in the same way as it does in *I saw him coming*. Jespersen (1909–49: V, 146), though insisting on the distinction, said 'sometimes it is nearly immaterial whether an *-ing* after a noun (or pronoun) is to be taken to be a gerund or participle'. But Jespersen also realized that treating the *-ing* form as an adjective where the syntax allowed this would make nonsense of the semantics. It 'cannot be applicable to Galsworthy's *I hate people being unhappy*, nor to Thackeray's *I have not the least objection to a rogue being hung*, for he has no objection to the rogue, whether he is hung or not.'

9.3.4 Status of the subordinate clause

A more sophisticated view than that proposed in the last subsection sees not the verbal form, but the whole subordinate clause, as nominal, and so as the object of the catenative. It was noted in 2.1.4 that even the modals have been thought to have objects, *swim* being the object of *can* in *I can swim*. This was rejected, but is a similar proposal for the catenatives more acceptable? In *I like playing the piano, playing the piano* might well be regarded as the object of *like* and in *I want to go to London, to go to London* as the object of *want*. If the whole clause is the object of the finite verb, the problem of verbal nouns and adjectives does not arise. The forms function as verbs in the subordinate clause which may have a subject and an object; their non-finiteness marks subordination. Compare:

John reads novels.
I don't like John reading novels.

This treatment of subordinate clauses as themselves composed of clause elements is clearly correct. But it is not so clear that the clauses should be treated as the object of the main verb.

[i]   There are a few forms where the *-ing* form, though not itself adjectival, seems to mark an adjectival clause. Compare:

   He kept talking.
   He kept quiet.

These are quite clearly different from:

   He kept a dog.

But although it would seem plausible to argue that KEEP is followed by an adjectival clause, this will not work for the almost synonymous CONTINUE:

   He continued talking.
   *He continued quiet.
   He continued the conversation.

The evidence suggests that CONTINUE is followed by a nominal, not an adjectival, clause.

However, it must be noted that the construction that occurs with any particular verb has to a large extent to be stated lexically for each verb (though there are general semantic-syntactic classes). Sometimes there is a choice of structure:

   He began talking.

> *He began to talk.*
> *He continued talking.*
> *He continued to talk.*

Sometimes (with no obvious semantic explanation) there is no choice:

> *He stopped talking.*
> *!He stopped to talk.* (a different sense)
> *He kept talking.*
> **He kept to talk.*

[ii]   There are many verbs that do not normally have objects yet are followed by subordinate clauses with *to*-infinitives or *-ing* forms (especially *to*-infinitives):

> *I hope to see you.*
> **I hope a fine day.*
> *He decided to go.*
> **He decided the plan.*
> *I intend to come.*
> *I intend coming.*
> **I intend my arrival.*

The argument that the subordinate clauses are objects rests largely on the fact that they function like other noun objects. Here they occur with verbs that do not take objects. It is true that some of these verbs occur with prepositions (HOPE FOR, DECIDE ON) and may be followed by noun phrases. But not all of them do: INTEND, for instance, does not. In any case this does not support the argument, for the prepositions show that the verbs are *not* simple transitive verbs.

[iii] An argument that has been put forward to support the view that some verbs have objects and others do not is based upon what is called the 'pseudo-cleft construction'. This construction is exemplified by comparison of:

> *I offered a prize.*
> *What I offered was a prize.*

The interrogative form is, for the purpose intended, just as relevant:

> *What did I offer?*

The point is that these constructions may occur where the verb has an object which is referred to by *what*. With the catenatives the constructions are:

> *I asked to come early.*
> *What I asked was to come early.*
> *What did I ask?*
> *I advised him to come early.*
> *What I advised him was to come early.*
> *What did I advise him?*

But with some this is not possible, or less likely:

> *I offered to come early.*
> *?What I offered was to come early.*
> *!What did I offer?*
> *I forced him to come early.*
> **What I forced him was to come early.*
> **What did I force him?*

This, it is argued, proves that ASK and ADVISE take the subordinate clause as their object (and that these are, therefore, nominal) while OFFER and FORCE do not.

But this test is not a very useful one. First, it is very difficult to draw any clear lines where pseudo-clefting is or is not possible. There is no 'Yes'/'No' division, but a range of acceptability. In the examples above, FORCE is almost certainly impossible without *to do*, but OFFER is more dubious, while with both ASK and ADVISE the occurrence of *to do* would make the sentence appear a little more natural. Secondly, the test does not seem to correspond to a semantic distinction (compare OFFER and ADVISE, both of which seem to require objects semantically) or to any other general syntactic characteristics of the verbs.

However, it must be said that some verbs, *eg* those of attitude (9.2.7), seem more appropriately described in terms of having objects, *eg* DISLIKE in:

> *I dislike his actions.*
> *I dislike his doing that.*
> *I dislike his having done that.*
> *I dislike him doing that.*
> *I dislike him having done that.*

Points of relevance are:
(a) the *his/him* relationship (discussed in 9.3.3);
(b) the fact that there are few restrictions on phase/tense in the subordinate clause;
(c) the fact that the subject of the subordinate clause is, with some verbs at least, not identified with the subject of the main clause (9.2.7[iii]).

A similar solution is possible for verbs like ADVISE, RECOM-
MEND in such sentences as:

I don't advise/recommended doing that.
I don't advise/recommend hasty action.

Again the subject of the subordinate clause is not identical
with the subject of the main clause. The *-ing* forms might
plausibly be regarded as nominal objects, or markers of
nominal object clauses.

Chapter 10

Phrasal and prepositional verbs

Any dictionary of English must account for the large number of combinations of verb and particle (a word that may be variously identified as an adverb or a preposition) such as: GIVE IN, LOOK AFTER, CARRY ON, PUT UP WITH, as illustrated by:

The enemy finally gave in.
He looked after his aged father.
She carried on the family tradition.
I can't put up with that noise.

These are extremely common, especially in spoken English. Some of their more obvious characteristics are:

[i]   There is probably a limited number of particles that can rightly be included in the combinations. Some of the more obvious are DOWN, IN, OFF, ON, OUT, UP, and although there may be no obvious limit to the verbs, some, such as PUT, TAKE, GET, MAKE, combine most freely.

[ii] The combinations are not all freely formed; there are severe collocational restrictions. This is clearly seen if the particles in the examples are replaced by particles that are generally opposite in meaning. The result would be sentences of a very different kind. With two of them there would be sequences of verb and particle that can hardly be interpreted as combinations at all; for although we can *look after* someone, we cannot similarly *look before* him, and although we can *put up with* something, we cannot *put down with* it (or *put up without* or *put down without*) it. GIVE OUT and CARRY OFF are similar combinations, but with meanings that are not the opposites of GIVE IN and CARRY ON.

Both have literal meanings deducible from the meanings of the verb and particle, and also have (respectively) the meanings 'run short' and 'win' (*eg* a prize).

[iii] All of them can be replaced, with little change of meaning, by single word verbs, GIVE IN by YIELD, LOOK AFTER by TEND, CARRY ON by CONTINUE, PUT UP WITH by TOLERATE. In all cases the single word is less colloquial; TEND in particular belongs to a literary style.

[iv] All of them (except, naturally, the intransitive GIVE IN) have passive forms:

His father was looked after by the nurse.
The family tradition was carried on by the son.
She's a person who simply can't be put up with.

10.1 Classification

In the main, the characteristics considered in the last section are indications of the idiomatic nature of the verb + particle combinations. Yet idiomaticity is essentially a lexical feature, something to be dealt with in the lexicon or dictionary rather than the grammar. If this was all that had to be discussed, there would be no place for these forms in this book. But there are syntactic features that mark off some of these combinations as grammatical units. (See especially Bolinger 1971.)

10.1.1 Grammar and lexicon

The grammatically defined combinations that are to be discussed will be referred to as 'prepositional verbs' and 'phrasal verbs' – depending on whether the particle is identified as a preposition or as an adverb. This contrasts with other analyses where the terms are used (*eg* Quirk *et al* 1985:1150) only for the idiomatic combinations, the non-idiomatic ones being referred to simply as 'verb + preposition' and 'verb + adverb'. Idiomatic/non-idiomatic pairs are:

GIVE IN and COME IN	*The enemy gave in.*
	The guests came in.
TAKE TO and GO TO	*I didn't take to him.*
	I didn't go to London.
MAKE UP and BRING UP	*She made up the whole story.*
	She brought up a book (to a child in bed).
PUT DOWN in two different meanings	*The ruler put the rebellion down.*
	The teacher put the book down.

The issue of idiomaticity is closely tied up with 'transparency' or literalness (but see 10.2.4). The meaning of a combination can be said to be transparent (or literal) if it can be deduced from the meaning of the individual parts (here the verb and the particle). If it cannot, it is opaque.

The main reasons for using the terms to include both non-idiomatic and idiomatic forms are, first, that it is possible to establish fairly clearly defined formal classes that include both non-idiomatic and idiomatic forms, which are distinct from other combinations of verb and preposition or adverb; second, that idiomaticity is a semantic rather than a grammatical feature; and third, that there is no clear dividing line between idiomatic and non-idiomatic, idiomaticity being a matter of degree, as can be seen from considering the combinations:

put about   (a rumour)
put back   (the clock)
put down   (a resolution, a revolt)
put up   (a candidate)
put in   (an application)
put out   (a pamphlet)
put over   (an idea)
put off   (a meeting)

10.1.2 Preposition and adverb
The term 'particle' has been used in order not to distinguish, as yet, between preposition and adverb. For although it is possible to decide in almost any sentence whether a particle is an adverb or a preposition, a striking characteristic of many, but not all, of the particles is that they can function as either. Examples are IN and UP in:

John sat in the chair.
John came in.
He climbed up the tree.
She got up early.

There are, however, a few particles that can function only as prepositions, *eg* AT and FOR in *eg*:

He looked at the picture.
*He looked at.
He looked for his glasses.
*He looked for.

There are also a few that function as adverbs and also as parts of complex prepositions, but not as prepositions alone. The most obvious one is AWAY:

> *He walked away.*
> **He walked away the crowd.*
> *He walked away from the crowd.*

(But most sequences of adverb and preposition can be interpreted as two independent elements.)

The most important type, then, for consideration here is the one that has both prepositional and adverbial function.

It might be plausible to argue that English does not, in fact, have two word classes adverb and preposition, but a single class 'particle' or, perhaps, 'prepositional-adverb'. For there is considerable similarity in their function. Often the adverb can be replaced, with little or no change of meaning, by the preposition plus a noun phrase:

> *He got across.*
> *He got across the river.*
> *He came down.*
> *He came down the hill.*

Indeed, if the relevant noun phrase had already been mentioned, it would be semantically redundant and therefore normally omitted:

> *He walked to the hill and ran up* (the hill).
> *He ran to the fence and crawled under* (the fence).

Even when it has not already been mentioned, the relevant noun phrase can be deduced:

> *She took the sheets off* (the bed).
> *He put his clothes on* (himself).

Such examples as these are, however, at one extreme. It would be less easy to supply the missing noun phrase in:

> *The canvassers handed out leaflets.*
> *The secretary gave in her notice.*
> *They set up a temporary office.*

Nevertheless, there is even here some implication of motion towards some object. The leaflets are handed out from the point at which the canvassers are standing, the secretary gives her notice into the central office, the temporary office is set upon some site or other. In other words, the possible object of a prepositional phrase may be, in varying degrees, unspecified.

Yet it is not so easy to see what kind of direction could be implied by the particles in:

The enemy gave in.   ('surrendered')
The contestant gave up.   ('retired')
The old car gave out.   ('stopped working')

Or compare:

She took the washing in.
She took the homeless children in.
She takes in washing.
The conjuror took the whole audience in.

In the first *in* clearly means into the home; in the second its meaning is a little vaguer – it is more 'into her home' with all that home implies; in the third the meaning is largely idiomatic though there is some direction; in the fourth the meaning is wholly idiomatic and no direction can be inferred. Nevertheless, it is clear that, with non-idiomatic forms, the notion of direction is part of the essential characteristic of the phrasal verb at least, and that, even with idiomatic forms, a sense of direction in a metaphorical sense, can often be inferred.

10.1.3 Formal contrasts
In spite of the similarity of the function of adverb and preposition, in any one sentence they can be formally distinguished. An often quoted pair of sentences is:

He ran up a hill.
He ran up a bill.

The second of these differs from the first in being idiomatic; indeed it is very restricted in this use, referring only to increasingly incurring debt. Moreover, for reasons that will become apparent later the definite article *the* is preferable here. A better pair of examples is, then:

He ran up the hill.
He ran up the flag.

It would usually be said that in the first of these *up* is a preposition and in the second an adverb. There are three fairly obvious grammatical differences:

[i] The adverb, but not the preposition, may occur after the noun phrase:

  He ran the flag up.

*He ran the hill up.

This is not, however, an absolute test. There are some combinations of verb plus adverb that are certainly idiomatic, where the adverb is unlikely to occur after the verb:

The car picked up speed.
*The car picked speed up.
She gave up hope.
*She gave hope up.

However, the adverb may occur after the adverb in the same combination, but with a different sense:

The car picked the hitchhikers up.
She gave her boy friend up.

[ii] Much more precisely, if there is an object pronoun the adverb occurs after the pronoun and the preposition before it:

He ran it up.   (the flag)
He ran up it.   (the hill)

[iii] It follows from the nature of adverbs and prepositions that the adverb can never occur before relatives or interrogative forms, whereas the preposition can (but need not):

*The flag up which he ran.
The hill up which he ran.
(The hill (which) he ran up.)
*Up which flag did he run?
Up which hill did he run?
(Which hill did he run up?)

[iv] If the particle occurs in final position in the sentence, the adverb will normally be accented, but the preposition may or may not be:

That is the flag he ran úp.

That is the hill he $\begin{cases} \text{rán up.} \\ \text{ran úp.} \end{cases}$

However, this is complicated by at least three things. First, there may be contrastive stress:

This is the hill he ran úp, not dówn.

Secondly, two-syllable particles such as OVER, UNDER are likely to be accented even when they are prepositions.

Thirdly, the variation with prepositions applies only to those with prepositional verbs. Independent prepositions that merely indicate location will not normally be accented (see 10.3.1).

The differences can be further illustrated by comparing OVER as a preposition and as an adverb in LOOK OVER. If the sense is that of a spectator looking over someone's shoulder in order to see more clearly, OVER will be a preposition, but if the sense is that of 'examine', *eg* by a doctor, OVER is an adverb. Hence:

[i]   *The spectator looked over my shoulder.*

$$\text{The doctor} \begin{cases} \textit{looked over my shoulder.} \\ \textit{looked my shoulder over.} \end{cases}$$

[ii] *The spectator looked over it.*
      The doctor looked it over.

[iii] *Over which shoulder did the spectator look?*
      Which shoulder did the spectator look over?
      Which shoulder did the doctor look over?

[iv] $\textit{This is the shoulder the spectator} \begin{cases} \textit{lóoked over.} \\ \textit{looked óver.} \end{cases}$

      This is the shoulder the doctor looked óver.

Another possible restriction is that with an adverb, but not a preposition, the sentence can be freely passivized:

The flag was run up.
*The hill was run up.

However, this is not an absolute restriction, since it is possible to say (with the preposition):

I don't like my shoulder being looked over at football matches.

It is even possible to have passives such as:

He's being looked after.
I'm being stared at.

But this depends, in part at least, on idiomaticity (see 10.3.3).

Finally, there is a point about IN and OUT as prepositions and adverbs. Both function as adverbs, but the corresponding prepositional forms are commonly INTO and OUT OF, which are essentially complex prepositions:

He walked in.
He walked into the house.

> *He walked out.*
> *He walked out of the house.*

But there are two complications. First, IN and OUT may be used
as prepositions where there is reference to an opening:

> *He walked in the door.*
> *He walked out the door.*

Here, in fact, *He walked into the door* would mean he collided
with the door. But even here OUT OF would be preferred to OUT
in a formal style. Secondly, IN (but not OUT) is regularly used as
a 'free' or locational preposition, quite distinct from *into* (see
10.3.1):

> *We walked in the countryside.*

10.2 Phrasal verbs

Phrasal verbs consist of a verb plus a particle that is clearly to be
treated as an adverb. There are two types, transitive and intransitive. So far only transitive ones have been considered, since it
is those that have to be distinguished from prepositional verbs.
Intransitive phrase verbs have no following noun phrase. The two
types are clear enough in:

> *The plane flew in.*
> *The pilot flew the plane in.*
> *The opposition gave up.*
> *The opposition gave up their gains.*

10.2.1 Transitive forms

Formally the only serious issue is whether a phrasal verb can be
clearly distinguished from other combinations of verb and
adverb.

In fact the only test, and it is not an absolute one, is that with
a phrasal verb the adverb may precede the noun phrase, whereas
with adverbs it may not. Thus there is a contrast:

> *He pulled the rope up.*
> *He pulled up the rope.*
> *He pulled the rope upwards.*
> **He pulled upwards the rope.*

This test will only work, however, with a simple definite noun
phrase, with no modifiers. It is possible to say:

He pulled downwards the larger of the two ropes.

Compare similarly:

He pulled down the blind.
*He pulled downwards the blind.
He pulled downwards all the blinds there were.

There is also the complication that some combinations do not permit the adverb to precede the verb as in:

She cried her eyes out.
*She cried out her eyes.
She laughed her head off.
*She laughed off her head.

But these, unlike the DOWN/DOWNWARDS examples, are all highly idiomatic.

There is, then, some formal support for the decision to treat the combination of verb plus a limited set of adverbs (those that also function as prepositions) as phrasal verbs.

It may be further noted here that the combination of verb plus adjective functions like a phrasal verb in:

I cut open the melon.
He made clear his intentions.
They cut short the interview.

This is clear from the position of the adjective – before the object noun phrase (though it may also occur after it). But whether the adjective may occur here or not depends upon the semantics of both verb and adjective. Thus we find:

They packed tight the wadding.
*They packed loose the wadding.

Yet the reason for the acceptability of the first, but not of the second, is clearly related to the semantics of the particles of the phrasal verb – resultant condition, and more specifically, completeness. For one aims usually to pack tight. Packing loose is to fail to complete the task (see 10.2.3).

10.2.2 Intransitive forms

The definite noun phrase test works only, of course, for transitive phrasal verbs, *ie* those with object nouns. But there are many verb plus particle combinations that are intransitive, yet seem to belong to the class of phrasal verbs. Consider, for instance, the verbs in:

The plane flew in.
The enemy finally gave in.
Term breaks up next Wednesday.
She broke down when she heard the news.

There are, both syntactic and semantic reasons for associating these forms with the transitive phrasal verbs. Syntactically these forms can be related to their transitive counterparts in three ways.

[i]   Some of them can be regarded as identical with transitive forms, but with the object 'deleted' or 'understood'. The relationship is, that is to say, like that of *He was eating* and *He was eating his lunch*:

> *They carried on.*
> *They carried on the business.*
> *He turned over.*
> *He turned over the page.*

[ii] Some of them are related to transitive phrasal verbs in terms of the transitivity relation of the familiar type exemplified by such verbs as BREAK in *It broke* and *He broke it* (5.4.1), one being semantically active, the other passive:

> *The house blew up.*
> *They blew up the house.*
> *The chimney-pot blew down.*
> *The wind blew the chimney-pot down.*

[iii] An extension of the relationship considered in [ii] involves the use of different lexemes, but with, otherwise, the same syntactic and semantic relationships:

> *He brought about his own downfall.*
> *His downfall came about.*
> *He brought in his friend.*
> *His friend came in.*

10.2.3 Semantics

In all the phrasal verbs with a literal meaning there is a verb of motion and the particle indicates the direction of the motion. There is a further semantic feature of the phrasal verb as a whole, that of indicating a final resultant position. Consider once again:

> *He ran the flag up.*
> *The pilot flew the plane in.*

The operations were completed: the flag was up (up the pole), and the plane was in (in the airport). This accounts for the difference between:

> He pulled up the rope.
> *He pulled upwards the rope.

To pull up means to pull to final up position; to pull upwards does not. Hence the first, but not the second, is semantically (as well as formally) a phrasal verb.

This is a natural consequence of the relationship between adverb and preposition noted in 10.1.2, and supports the suggestion that phrasal verbs always contain an adverb that may also be a preposition.

Yet there are problems with some phrasal verbs that seem to be non-idiomatic. For consider the difference between the following pairs:

> She washed out the stain.
> She washed out the clothes.
> She wiped out the dirt.
> She wiped out the sink.

In the first of each pair there is the normal relationship – the adverb can be replaced by a preposition plus noun phrase:

> She washed the stain out of the clothes.
> She wiped the dirt out of the sink.

In the second of each pair, however, the noun phrase that follows the preposition in this extended version (the clothes, the sink) actually occurs. Prima facie it might seem that out is here a preposition (out (of) the clothes, out (of) the sink) and that it is the object of the verb (the stain, the dirt) that has been omitted. But this is clearly wrong – out even here is an adverb as shown by the pronoun test:

> She washed it out.
> She wiped it out.

A similar pair is:

> She tidied up the room.
> She tidied up the mess.

There is a difference, in that in neither case can the adverb be replaced by a preposition plus a noun phrase. But the semantic relation of room and mess is like that of clothes and stain, sink and dirt.

These phrasal verbs seem to provide counterexamples to what was said (10.1.2) about the relation between preposition and adverb. But they are not alone in having two different patterns in relation to the choice of direct object; there are also single-word verbs such as PRESENT:

They presented the prize to John.
They presented John with the prize.

We can present a prize or present a person; equally we can wash out stains or wash out clothes.

There are many phrasal verbs which do not have the literal (transparent) directional meaning, but nevertheless share with the literal ones a notion of final result, a meaning not at all unlike the meaning of the perfect in English. The possible variations depend upon the particle. For UP some of the possibilities are shown by:

The work piled up.
Has he turned up yet?
The ice broke up.
We can't just give up.
They speeded up.

The first indicates simple direction and result (even though in a non-concrete sense). The second extends the directional use of UP to indicate proximity to the speaker (just as students, especially at Oxford or Cambridge, COME UP and GO DOWN). In the third, there is perfectivity, in the sense of resultant condition. The fourth is perfective in the sense of completion and the fifth in a further extension of meaning – high intensity. Similar statements, can be made for the other particles.

10.2.4 Idioms

It was noted in 10.1 that it is difficult to distinguish between literal and idiomatic phrasal verbs. In the previous section it was suggested that there is a range of meanings from the most literal (directional) to the most abstract, associated with most of the particles. But the term 'idiomatic' is not a very clear one. With the phrasal verbs there seem to be three ways in which it may be used.

First, it is clear that there is some collocational restriction upon the combinations. It is possible to think up explanations for some of these restrictions, but not possible to give any general rules concerning them. Compare the possible and impossible pairs:

I helped him out.

I aided him out.
He yielded up all his property.
He abandoned up all his property.
Can you fit out this expedition?
Can you equip out this expedition?

Secondly, 'idiomatic' could be used to refer to all the combinations that are not literal in the sense of being directional. But these non-literal combinations are still very largely (though in varying degrees) transparent, *ie* their meaning can be inferred from the meaning of the parts. A native speaker of English would have no difficulty in understanding or forming new combinations using the adverb in one of its aspectual senses even with a new verb. If, for instance, there were a verb *ACIDIZE meaning 'to burn with acid', there would be no problem with:

He acidized out a hole.
He acidized up the body.

The third possible use of 'idiomatic' would be simply for those combinations that are totally opaque (non-transparent), *ie* whose meanings cannot be inferred from the meanings of the individual words (though there is no absolute cut-off point between these and the last type); examples are GIVE UP, GIVE OUT, BREAK UP, BREAK DOWN. Some verbs have various degrees of idiomaticity. One can *make up* a bed, a fire, a face or a story. Only with the last of these does MAKE UP with the meaning of 'invent' seem to be a complete idiom. With TAKE IN there are four possibilities (10.1.2).

Being idiomatic in the last two senses of the term is wholly a semantic, not a syntactic, matter. (Whether it is so in the first sense is debatable.) Yet it has an effect on the syntax. In general the more closely related semantically are the verb and adverb, the less likely they are to be separated. This may be illustrated in three different syntactic patterns.

[i] An inverted structure with the adverb in initial position is possible only where there is no idiomatic use.

> *Down he sat.*
> *In he went.*
> *Down he broke.*
> *In he gave.*

As always, idiomaticity is a matter of degree. Where there is, even metaphorically, a sense of direction inversion is possible:

> *Out went the light.*
> *Up went a great cry.*

[ii] An ordinary adverb may much more easily separate the elements of the phrasal verb if it is not idiomatic:

> *The money he gave happily away.*
> **The subject he brought angrily up.*
> *The troops marched briskly in.*
> **The troops fell briskly in.*

[iii] With transitive phrasal verbs there is a greater likelihood of the particle preceding the noun phrase if idiomatic, and of following it, if not:

> *They covered up the crime.*
> *They covered the body up.*

There are some idiomatic forms that permit no separation at all (or very rarely):

> *He put up a good fight.*
> **He put a good fight up.*
> *They found out the truth.*
> *? They found the truth out.*

Conversely the non-idiomatic LEAVE UP allows only position after the noun phrase:

> *Leave the flap up!*
> **Leave up the flag.*

But there is no strict rule. Examples were noted earlier (10.1.3) of PICK UP and GIVE UP each with two idiomatic senses. Yet in one of the senses (*picked up speed, gave up hope*) the particle always appears before the noun phrase, while in the other (*picked up hitchhikers, gave up her boyfriend*) position is optional. Moreover with *cried her eyes out, laughed his head off* the particle can occur only in final position.

There is one final point. TO occurs as part of phrasal verb only in COME TO and BRING TO ('return to consciousness' in an intransitive and a transitive sense); TO, moreover, in BRING TO can occur only after the noun phrase:

> *The doctor brought the unconscious man to.*

AT, by contrast, never occurs as an adverb.

10.3 Prepositional verbs

As with phrasal verbs, there is a need to define prepositional verbs more precisely.

10.3.1 Free prepositions

Before a discussion of prepositional verbs, it is necessary to distinguish and exclude simple sequences of verb and preposition. For almost any verb can be followed by a prepositional phrase. One can *work, sit, sleep, live, die, cry, shout* etc, *in a house, under a tree* or *on a beach*. Clearly such sequences are of no interest here.

Prepositional verbs form much closer combinations and, as noted in 10.1.3, are often paralleled by phrasal verbs, *eg*:

> *He came down.*
> *He came down the stairs.*
> *He ran the flag up.*
> *He ran the flag up the flagpole.*

Moreover, with the prepositional verbs, as with phrasal verbs, there is usually a sense of direction, and often a terminal point.

It is not difficult to find a trio of sentences, one illustrating a phrasal verb, one a prepositional verb and one a sequence of verb plus prepositional phrase:

> *The pilot flew in the plane.*
> *The sparrow flew in the plane.*
> *The passenger flew in the plane.*

The last of these is a sequence of verb and preposition, merely indicating where it was that the passenger did his flying. It is no different in kind from *The passenger slept in the plane*. Admittedly the prepositional verb here would more naturally contain *into* – *The sparrow flew into the plane*, but there are other possible contrasts with other prepositions:

> *We walked under the trees.*

This can either mean that we walked to a place under the trees (prepositional verb) or that we did our walking under the trees (verb plus preposition). There is similarly a three-fold ambiguity in:

> *He ran down the road.*

This can mean he disparaged the road (phrasal verb), descended

the road at a rùn (prepositional verb) or did his running somewhere down the road (verb plus preposition).

There is a potential difference between prepositional verb and
verb plus preposition in terms of final accent, *eg* (with a phrasal
verb also illustrated):

> (*This is the plane the pilot flew in*)
> *This is the plane the passenger fléw in.*
>
> *This is the plane the sparrow* $\begin{Bmatrix} \text{fléw in.} \\ \text{flew ín.} \end{Bmatrix}$

Similarly:

> *These are the trees we wálked under*
>   (took a walk)
> *These are the trees we* $\begin{Bmatrix} \text{wálked under.} \\ \text{wálked únder.} \end{Bmatrix}$
>   (walked to a position under)

With the verb plus preposition the preposition, if it occurs in final
position, will not have an accent, but with the prepositional verb
the accent may fall on either verb or preposition. Moreover, the
particle of the prepositional verb can always appear in final
position, but the independent preposition would be unusual
there:

> *?This is the road he rán down.*
>   (did his running)
> *This is the road he* $\begin{Bmatrix} \text{rán down.} \\ \text{ran dówn.} \end{Bmatrix}$
>   (descended at a run)

For the purpose of contrasting prepositional verbs with verbs
plus preposition only intransitive verbs have been considered so
far. But the contrast is equally valid for transitive verbs:

> *He ran the flag up the pole.*
> *He cultivated a garden up the hill.*

There is potential ambiguity again in:

> *He drove the car down the road.*

The formal contrast of accent is again available, though it is
difficult to find satisfactory identical sentences:

> *This is the place he taught the children*   (verb and
> *in.*   preposition)

This is the place he drove the shéep in.
This is the place he drove the sheep in.   (prepositional verb)

10.3.2 Semantics

It is, above all, the semantics of the prepositional verbs that
make it worthwhile treating them as a special class. All the prepositional verbs that we have been considering have two characteristics. First, the verb is a verb of motion and secondly, the
preposition has a meaning similar to that of the adverb of the
phrasal verbs, motion plus terminus. Obvious examples are:

He walked across the bridge.
He ran up the hill.

In these there is the motion-act of walking or running in relation
to the bridge or the hill, and the terminus position, across the
bridge, up the hill.

Bolinger (1971:28) suggests that prepositions in such cases are
'adpreps' since they combine the functions of preposition and
adverb. They can be compared both with the prepositional
complexes and with sequence of adverb and preposition:

He walked through the door.
(*He walked through, through the door*)
He walked into the house.
He walked down across the street.

In the first of these, preposition and adverb are fused to a single
form; in the second, they make a complex preposition, in the
third; they remain apart.

The same points hold for prepositional verbs with objects:

He took the children through the door.
(*He took the children through, through the door*)
He took the children into the house.
He took the children down across the street.

10.3.3 Intransitive forms

The prepositional verbs so far discussed have been semantically
transparent and fairly free syntactically. There are many other
combinations that are semantically and syntactically more
restricted, and since the semantics and syntax are inter-related
issues of grammar and idomaticity will be considered here. The
issues are somewhat different for intransitive and transitive
forms; this section will deal only with intransitives.

A number of different types may be distinguished:

[i]   There are some combinations that have both a literal meaning and a non-literal one, *eg*:

> *He came across the road.*
> *He came across the missing papers.*
> *He ran into the house.*
> *He ran into an old friend.*

[ii] There are some combinations where the non-literal meaning is a fairly obvious extension of the literal one:

> *You can't see through the glass.*
> *You can't see through his deception.*
> *They went into the house.*
> *They went into the affair.*

There are borderline cases between [i] and [ii]. It is debatable how transparent are:

> *He came into a fortune.*
> *He came by a fortune.*

[iii] There are some combinations with several meanings in varying degrees of transparency:

> *The thieves broke into the shop.*
> *The children broke into a rash.*
> *The athlete broke into a trot.*

[iv] There are some combinations that are as common as prepositional verbs, but could be interpreted literally, though only as verb plus preposition, *eg*:

> *I'm looking for John*
> *He looked after his father.*
> *She went for him* (*ie* attacked).

It is possible to interpret these in appropriate contexts in terms of 'looking on John's behalf', 'looking after his father did', 'going on his behalf'.

[v]   There are some combinations that occur only as prepositional verbs, *eg*:

> *I can do without all the worry.*
> *I didn't take to that young man.*

Literal meanings would be possible here only for transitive DO and TAKE followed by a free preposition – *do the work without help, take a book to John.*

[vi] There are some combinations where the verb does not

normally occur with any other than one preposition. These are more collocationally restricted than idiomatic:

I can cope with that rogue.
You can rely on me.
She dotes on her husband.

Of these COPE may occur with no preposition, but not the others (perhaps DOTE marginally):

I can cope all right.
*You can rely.
?She is one to dote.

There are no very clear formal tests that set these apart from the other prepositional verbs, though in general the combination functions more like a single unit. Two possible but not wholly conclusive tests are separation and passivization.

The test of separation may be applied by using a relative clause. This works fairly well for the [i] examples:

The road across which he came.
*The missing papers across which he came.
The house into which he ran.
*The old friend into whom he ran.

But this formation is today a rather unnatural one. Attempts to produce it are liable to result in oddities such as the (actually attested):

*. . . with whom we could not do without.

With [ii] it seems only that the less literal forms are a little less natural.

The glass through which they could see.
?The deception through which they could see.
The house into which they went.
? The affair into which they went.

This may, perhaps, distinguish COME INTO from COME BY (the latter as more idiomatic):

The fortune into which he came.
*The fortune by which he came.

With [iii] only BREAK INTO in its first sense seems to allow separation:

The shop into which they broke.
*The rash into which the children broke.

The trot into which the athlete broke.

This is, of course, the most transparent of them; it suggests breaking a door or window to get in. Similarly with [iv] and [v] only the fairly transparent LOOK FOR seems to permit separation:

The teacher for whom I was looking.
The father after whom he was looking.
The man for whom she went in a fit of temper.
All the worry without which I can do.
The young man to whom I didn't take.

All the [vi] examples allow separation; the test does, then, to some degree indicate those combinations that are less idiomatic.

The passivization test produces rather different results. With [i] the literal forms seem to have no passives:

The road was come across.
The house was run into.

One of the non-literal forms is marginal, the other most unlikely:

?*The missing papers were soon come across.*
The old friend was run into.

With [ii] only one seems not to passivize:

The glass can be seen through.
The deception can be seen through.
The house was gone into.
The affair was gone into.

There is a contrast between:

A fortune is not easily come into.
A fortune is not easily come by.

With [iii] only one passivizes:

The shop was broken into.
A rash was broken into.
A trot was broken into.

With [iv] and [v] only the two LOOK examples passivize easily:

The teacher is being looked for.
His father was looked after.
He was gone for.
?*All this worry can be done without.*
The young man wasn't taken to.

Moreover, there are sequences of verb and preposition that are not prepositional verbs, yet have passives:

She slept in the bed.
The bed was slept in.
They sat on the chair.
The chair was sat on.

More marginal, but possible, examples are:

?This office has never been worked in.
?The hill was run down by everyone.

Passivization then seems to have only partly to do with idiomaticity. Another factor is that we passivize when the relevant noun phrase is naturally seen as undergoing the action. Shops get broken into, but not rashes or trots. Beds are slept in, chairs sat on, but houses not usually said to be run into or gone into.

Finally there are some prepositional verbs that collocate with particular noun phrases to produce a completely idiomatic combination:

He came off his high horse.
She went for him in a big way.
She went for him hammer and tongs.

Because of the idiomatic unity, there can be neither separability nor passivization, just as there can be no passive with the colloquial idiomatic KICK THE BUCKET (= 'die').

10.3.4 Transitive forms

As with the intransitive forms there are plenty of combinations that are semantically transparent and syntactically fairly unrestricted. But there are other types too.

[i]   There are very few transitive prepositional verbs that are clearly idiomatic. Possible examples are TAKE (*someone*) FOR, PLY (*someone*) WITH:

  He took me for a man he knew.
  The host plied his guests with drink.

[ii] More commonly the combination involves collocational restrictions between verb and preposition, but remains transparent, *eg* DEPRIVE OF, CONFINE TO:

  They deprived the children of their rights.
  You should confine yourself to the issue in question.

[iii]   There is a whole group of sequences of verb, preposition and object noun phrase that are collocationally closely linked, *eg* MAKE A MESS OF, SET FIRE TO, GIVE WAY TO; most of these are fairly transparent:

> *He made a mess of his speech.*
> *They set fire to the house.*
> *You should give way to oncoming traffic.*

The test of separation does not show any of these as very idiomatic except TAKE FOR which normally has an indefinite noun phrase following:

> **The man for whom he took me.*
> *(The man he took me for).*

The test of passivization is more interesting. [i] and [ii] passivize freely:

> *I was taken for a man he knew.*
> *The children were deprived of their rights.*

But there are various possibilities with [iii]. Some have two possible passives, either making the object NP or the NP after the preposition the subject of the passive verb:

> *A mess was made of his speech.*
> *His speech was made a mess of.*

Other examples are provided by TAKE CARE OF, TAKE ADVANTAGE OF, PAY ATTENTION TO:

> *Care should be taken of the matter.*
> *The matter should be taken care of.*
> *Advantage should be taken of his offer.*
> *His offer should be taken advantage of.*
> *Attention should be paid to his remarks.*
> *His remarks should be paid attention to.*

It may be added though that TAKE CARE OF is used in both a fairly transparent sense and in a less transparent sense of 'deal formally with'. In this second sense the whole combination is treated as a unit for passivization giving the second example above (which is most likely to be interpreted as 'This matter must be dealt with'). Other combinations, though fairly transparent, have one passive only, with the NP following the preposition as the subject of the passive, *eg* SET FIRE TO, CATCH SIGHT OF:

> *The house was set fire to.*
> **Fire was set to the house.*

The boys were caught sight of.
**Sight was caught of the boys.*

Others have no passives at all (or very rarely), *eg* GIVE WAY TO, KEEP PACE WITH:

??Oncoming traffic should be given way to.
**Way should be given to oncoming traffic.*
??He can't be kept pace with.
**Pace cannot be kept with him.*

10.3.5 'Postpositions'

It has been argued that sometimes prepositions may follow rather than precede the noun phrase (and so are 'postpositions'). For these the test of order obviously fails. Examples are:

He has travelled the world over.
I pass their arguments by.
They ran him over.
Will you look it over for me?

The reason for thinking that these are prepositions rather than adverbs is the fact that they may, with little or no change of meaning, precede the noun phrase in sentences where they are much more plausibly to be regarded as prepositions:

He has travelled over the world.
I pass by their arguments.
They ran over him.
Will you look over it for me?

In the first set of sentences, it is suggested, the preposition has been postposed. But this argument is not at all convincing. For with the first sentence the preposition can be omitted:

He has travelled the world.

Although this is not possible with the second, the verb PASS is often used without a particle in a very similar (but literal) sense:

I passed the old buildings.

This suggests that the particle is not a preposition, but an adverb, for adverbs, but not prepositions, are freely omitted.

Implicit in the argument, no doubt, is the fact that the particles appear to be semantically prepositional – 'over the world', 'by their arguments'; but semantic relationships of this kind are not a good guide, as the examples of 10.2.3 show.

Admittedly, even if these particles are adverbs in final position

they are prepositions in non-final position (as the pronoun test
will show). In this sense they are unusual, since the adverbs
usually occur also before the noun phrase and are there in
contrast with prepositions. But this shows only the marginal
nature of these verbs, RUN OVER in particular, seems to be in the
process of becoming a phrasal verb, but does not yet fully
contrast with the homonymous prepositional verb. But nothing
is gained by talking about 'postpositions' – these are merely the
adverbial particles of 'marginal' phrasal verbs.

10.4 Phrasal prepositional verbs

There are some combinations of verb plus two particles, one an
adverb, the second a preposition, eg PUT UP WITH, DO AWAY WITH,
GET AWAY WITH:

  I can't put with with her.
  He did away with his wife.

These may be called 'phrasal prepositional verbs'.

These must, of course, be distinguished from sequences of
phrasal verbs plus free prepositions. Thus PUT UP in the sense of
'lodge' is often followed by *with*:

  You can put up with Mrs Brown when you visit Bristol.

Here the phrasal verb is idiomatic. It could be non-idiomatic, eg
WALK UP:

  I walked up with my friends.

GET AWAY WITH can be treated as either a phrasal verb plus preposition or as a phrasal prepositional verb with the sense of 'carry
out without punishment':

  The thief got away with her purse.
  He can get away with anything.

The separation test clearly shows the unity of the phrasal prepositional verbs. Only as a joke is it possible to say:

  The woman with whom I cannot put up.
  The wife with whom he did away.
  That is something with which he cannot get away.

Even more clearly ruled out (because UP and AWAY are not free
prepositions) are:

  *The woman up with whom I cannot put.

*The wife away with whom he did.
*That is something away with which he cannot get.

The passives also display their unity:

She can't be put up with.
The wife was done away with.
It can't be got away with.

The phrasal verb plus prepositional sequences do not similarly passivize:

Mrs Brown can be put up with. ('lodged with')
*My friends were walked up with.
*The purse was got away with by the thief.

There are also some very collocationally restricted combinations of transitive verb with adverb and preposition that may be seen as transitive phrasal prepositional verbs, eg FOB OFF WITH, PUT DOWN TO:

He fobbed me off with a feeble excuse.
I can put my success down to hard work.

The only passive here is the normal one:

I was fobbed off with a feeble excuse.
My success can be put down to hard work.

In addition to combinations like SET FIRE TO, etc (discussed in 10.3.4), there are other combinations of three elements that do not fit the description of phrasal verb, prepositional verb or phrasal prepositional verb, but share many of their idiomatic characteristics, eg GET RID OF, PUT PAID TO, HAVE DONE WITH, MAKE DO WITH. Some eg the first two, allow passivization of the entire verbal element:

They soon got rid of the property.
The property was soon got rid of.
I soon put paid to that nonsense.
The nonsense was soon put paid to.

The other two have no passives.

Chapter 11

Morphology

All the auxiliaries and some of the main verbs exhibit irregularity in their morphology.

11.1 The auxiliaries

The auxiliary verbs differ morphologically from the other verbs in several ways. First, none of them have a present third person singular form that differs from other present forms only by having a final -s [s], [z] or [iz] (11.2.2). Most of them have no distinct third person form (*I can, he can*) at all, while the forms *is*, *has* and *does* [dʌz] cannot (in spoken form) be interpreted phonologically as *am* (or *are*), *have* and *do* [duː] respectively, plus -s. The verb BE has other idiosyncratic forms too. Secondly, most of them have negative forms; there is indeed a good case for talking about 'a negative conjugation', since negation is essentially morphological; though *not* occurs commonly in writing, the form [nɒt] rarely follows an auxiliary form in speech. Thirdly, most of the auxiliary verbs have 'weak' forms, as well as 'strong' forms, the former occurring only when unstressed.

11.1.1 Irregular forms

Apart from the negative and weak forms the auxiliary verbs have a number of forms that do not follow the pattern of the full verbs and are in this sense irregular.

[i]   The verb BE has five wholly irregular finite forms.

(a) In the present tense there is a distinct form, *am* [æm], for the first person singular; for all other verbs the form is identical with the plural form.

(b) The third person singular and plural form of the present tense are wholly idiosyncratic −*is* [ɪz] and *are* [ɑː].

(c) There are two past tense forms *was* [wɒz] (in my own speech [wʌz]) and *were* [wɜː]; these are again idiosyncratic in form. Moreover, no other verb has distinct past tense forms for singular and plural; a further peculiarity is that the first person singular form is identical with the third singular (*was*) – in all other paradigms, apart from the present tense of BE, the first person singular form is identical with the plural forms and it is the third person singular that stands alone – *I love, they love*, but *he loves*.

[ii] The third person singular present tense form of HAVE is *has* [hæz], not *haves (the past tense form *had* too is irregular, but so too are many such forms of full verbs).

[iii] The third person singular present tense form of DO is *does* [dʌz] not *[duːz], in spite of *do* [duː]. Even as a full verb DO has the irregular form (see 8.3 and 11.4).

[iv] Apart from BE, HAVE and DO, none of the auxiliaries has a distinct form for the third person singular of the present – no form in *-s*. (*Dares* and *needs* are not to be regarded as forms of the auxiliary, see 2.2.8.)

11.1.2 Negative forms

The auxiliaries have negative forms ending in orthographic *n't*, phonetically [nt], but the relations between the positive and the negative forms are of several kinds:

[i] The negative form differs only in the addition of [nt] in the case of *is, are, was, were, has, have, had, does, did, would, should, could, might, ought, dare* and *need*.

[ii] The negative form lacks the final consonant of the positive form in the case of *must* [mʌst] [mʌsnt]. This is also true of USED (8.4), which will be included in the discussion in this chapter, [juːst] [juːsnt].

[iii] The negative form has a different vowel from that of the positive form in the case of *do* [duː] [dəʊnt].

[iv] The negative form has a different vowel from that of the positive form and lacks the final consonant in the case of *will* [wɪl] [wəʊnt], *shall* [ʃæl] [ʃɑːnt], *can* [kæn] [kɑːnt]. With these three the differences are paralleled by differences in the orthography too – *won't, shan't* and *can't* (not **cann't*).

[v] *Am* has no negative form in statements; the negative form of a sentence containing *am* contains the form *not* [nɒt]:

I'm going. [aɪm gəʊɪŋ]   *I'm not going.* [aɪm nɒt gəʊɪŋ]

In questions with inversion, however, there is a negative form [ɑːnt]:

Am I? [æm aɪ]   [ɑːnt aɪ]

The only possible orthographic form of this is *Aren't I?*, but in a formal style this is avoided presumably because it is felt to be the negative of *are* and not of *am; Am I not?* is used in its place. But the form is no stranger than *can't, won't* or *shan't* either in transcription or in orthography. Similarly, as was noted in 2.2.2, there is, for many speakers, no negative form corresponding to *may* (**mayn't*) and *usedn't* is uncommon. There is no negative form corresponding to *be*, though by analogy with the imperative form *don't*, one might expect **ben't* (see 3.1.1).

Finally, with *can't, won't, shan't* and *don't* the final nasal and stop may be homorganic with the following consonant. Their place of articulation, that is to say, is wholly determined by the initial consonant of the following word. This may be shown by using transcriptions such as [kɑːmp], [kɑːŋk]:

[aɪ kɒːmp biː ðeə]   *I can't be there.*
[ʃɪ wəʊŋk keə]   *She won't care.*
[aɪ ʃɑːmp peʃ]   *I shan't pay.*
[wɪ dəʊŋk gəʊ ðeə]   *We don't go there.*

Often, however, the final stop seems to be absent, and all that remains is the homorganic nasality:

[aɪ dəʊn θɪŋk səʊ]   *I don't think so.*
[aɪ kɒːm bɪ ðeə]   *I can't be there.*
[ʃɪ wəʊŋ keə]   *She won't care.*

11.1.3 Weak forms

Most of the auxiliaries have forms that occur only in unstressed positions. These are the so-called 'weak' forms. Some of these are non-syllabic; the others are syllabic but contain vowels of the kind that are associated with absence of stress in English – most commonly [ə], or a syllabic consonant:

[aɪl kʌm]   *I'll come.*   *Cf* [aɪ wɪl kʌm]
[dʒɒn kən kʌm]   *John can come.*   *Cf* [dʒɒn kæn kʌm]

It must not, however, be supposed that strong forms do not occur in unstressed position. Indeed strong forms often occur initially, even without stress (though this raises fundamental problems regarding the nature of stress, for it could be argued that the occurrence of a strong form in an environment where a weak form is possible is itself an exponent of stress):

[hæv juː siːn hɪm]   *Have you seen him?*
[kæn aɪ kʌm]   *Can I come?*

In clause-final position, when the verb is acting in 'code' function, the weak form does not occur at all; though the form is unstressed the form is always the strong one:

He's working harder than I am. [aɪ æm]
She can't do it but he can.   [hiː kæn]

The weak forms are difficult to describe because 'weakness' is not a 'yes or no' characteristic, but a 'more or less' one. There are degrees of weakness, and a whole gradation of forms. For instance, there are a number of forms corresponding to orthographic *we are* that differ phonetically between [wiː ɑː] and [wə]. Only some of the gradation may be represented phonetically – [wiːə*] [wɪə*] [wɪ*] and [wə*]. Even when it is important to contrast two forms phonetically, it is not certain that the contrast will always be observable. For instance it is usually possible to distinguish the vowel sequences of orthographic *key will* and *he will*:

He'll be waiting.   [hiːl] or [hɪl]
The key'll be waiting.   [kiːəl] or [kɪəl]

But it would be rash to maintain that the difference is always maintained. The statements that follow are thus only approximations. Not only is the number of distinctions based on an arbitrary (though now traditional) choice, but it is not supposed that all the distinctions that are shown are always clear.

One important classification of the forms, is into those that are syllabic and those that are not. The forms are set out in the following table. The asterisk indicates that there is a 'linking r' before vowels:

ORTHOGRAPHIC	STRONG	WEAK SYLLABIC	WEAK NON-SYLLABIC
am	æm	əm	m
is	ɪz		z, s
are	ɑː*	ə*	*
was	wɒz	wəz	wz
were	wəː*	wə*	w*

ORTHOGRAPHIC	STRONG	WEAK SYLLABIC	WEAK NON-SYLLABIC
have	hæv	həv, əv	v
has	hæz	həz, əz	z, s
had	hæd	həd, əd	d
shall	ʃæl	ʃəl, ʃ!	ʃl
should	ʃʊd	ʃəd	ʃd
will	wɪl	əl, l	l
would	wʊd	wəd, əd	d
can	kæn	kən, kn, kŋ	kn
could	kʊd	kəd	kd
must	mʌst	məst, məs	ms
do	duː	du, də	d
does	dʌz	dəz	dz
did	dɪd		dd, d
be	biː	bɪ	
been	biːn	bɪn	

The basic problem is to state the conditions under which the non-syllabic form occurs. This depends on no less than five factors:

(a) position of the form in the sentence;
(b) the verbal form itself (they do not all function in the same way);
(c) whether the preceding word is (a form of) a noun or a pronoun;
(d) whether the preceding form ends in a consonant or a vowel;
(e) if the preceding form (noun forms only) ends in a consonant, the place of articulation of that consonant.

The types of weak form that occur medially in the clause are different from those that occur initially. The two types are therefore dealt with separately.

In terms of the patterns of weak forms in medial position the auxiliaries fall into three main classes.

[i] The forms corresponding to orthographic *is* and *has* may be non-syllabic, except where the final element of the preceding word is a sibilant or palatal consonant. Where this condition does not apply the auxiliary form is 'fused' with the preceding noun or pronoun form, the whole piece having the phonological characteristics of a single word. Phonetically the form may be voiceless or voiced – [s] or [z]:

[ðə kæts kʌmɪŋ]   *The cat's coming.*
[ðə dɒgz kʌmɪŋ]   *The dog's coming.*

But the absence or presence of voice is shared by both the sibilant and the final element of the preceding noun or pronoun form. The auxiliary is phonetically identical with the *-s* of plurality and the possessive *-'s* (these occur with nouns only). In all cases the final element is a sibilant accompanied by voice or voicelessness, but this final voice or voicelessness is essentially a characteristic of the noun in all its forms:

[dɒgz]   *dog's (dog is, dog has) dogs dog's, dogs'*
[kæts]   *cat's (cat is, cat has)   cats cat's, cats'*
[biːz]   *bee's (bee is, bee has) bees bee's, bees'*

With pronouns there are only:

[hiːz]   *he's (he is, he has)*
[ʃiːz]   *she's (she is, she has)*
[ɪts]   *it's (it is, it has)*

The element with which the auxiliary is 'fused' is not necessarily the head of the noun phrase:

The girl with the ticket is waiting for you.   ([tɪkɪts])

If the noun ends in a sibilant or a palatal the auxiliary must have a syllabic form. With *is* this can only be [ɪz], while with *has* it is commonly [əz], *eg*:

[tʃɜːtʃ ɪz]   *church is*
[tʃɜːtʃ əz]   *church has*
[fens ɪz]   *fence is*
[fens əz]   *fence has*

Yet it is misleading to write the forms in phonetic script as two words. For the pattern is the same as that of the forms with *s* plural and *'s* possessive except that the *has* form has a central vowel (and this is not important since the vowel qualities of both forms show considerable variation):

[hɔːsɪz]   *horse's (horse is)   horses horse's, horses*
[hɔːsəz]   *horse's (horse has)*

[ii] The forms corresponding to orthographic *am, are, will, would, have* and *had* have a similar feature when preceded

by pronoun forms ending in a vowel. The pronoun and
verb forms again have the phonological characteristics of
one word. They are best set out paradigmatically; indeed
there is a strong case for treating them as if they were
comparable to the paradigms of inflected languages. For
completeness the table that follows includes *he* and *she*
with *is* and *has*, which were dealt with under [i]:

am/(*is*)/*are*	*had or would*	*will*	*have*/(*has*)
aɪm	aɪd	aɪl	aɪv
(hiːz)	hiːd	hiːl	(hiːz)
(ʃiːz)	ʃiːd	ʃiːl	(ʃiːz)
wiə*, wi*, wə*	wiːd	wiːl	wiːv
jʊə*, jɔː*, jə*	juːd	juːl	juːv
ðeiə*, ðeə*, ðə*	ðeid	ðeil	ðeiv

Two points are to be noted: first, the degrees of 'weakness' (not all of them shown) that may be indicated for
some of the forms, and secondly the vowels of [jɔː*] and
[ðeə*], where the pronoun is 'fused' with the auxiliary.

This fusion is restricted to pronouns plus finite form. It
is not characteristic of all sequences of pronoun form plus
have, etc. [aiv], for instance, does not occur in:

Should I have gone.   ([aɪ əv])

Here *have* is an infinitive and not the finite form with *I*
as the subject. The auxiliary forms now being considered
are normally syllabic when preceded by forms of nouns or
the pronoun form *it*, the 'weakest' forms being [ə*], [l̩],
[əv] and [əd], though *would* is usually [wəd] and so distinct
from *had*. In spite of [mænz] (*man is, man has*), there is
no [*mænd] (*man had, man would*), but only [mæn əd] or
[mæn wəd]. Similarly a contrast can be made with *she* and
the diminutive of Sheila written here as *Shei*:

[ʃiː əl bɪ kʌmɪŋ]	*Shei'll be coming.*
[ʃiːl bɪ kʌmɪŋ]	*She'll be coming.*
[ʃiː wəd bɪ kʌmɪŋ]	*Shei'd be coming.*
[ʃiːd bɪ kʌmɪŋ]	*She'd be coming.*

But there is no difference between *She's* and *Shei's* (except
in the different feature that the former may be unstressed).

[iii] Nothing yet has been said about the forms with two consonants: *can, could, shall, should* and *must*. After a final

consonant these must be syllabic. But there may be non-syllabic forms after a vowel, especially after pronoun forms (thus patterning with the forms considered under [ii]); a set of contrasts between *Shei* and *she* can again be made. But we are again faced here with the problem of degrees of weakness. Consider:

[aɪ kd ɑːsk]   *I could ask.*

This unfortunately does not indicate that [k] here is released and is different from the unreleased [k] of:

[laɪk dɑːts]   *Like darts.*

The release of the [k] may then be treated as a mark of a syllable – and in that case the problem is not one of syllabic versus non-syllabic forms, but of degrees of syllabicity. A further point to be noted is that *can* may occur as [kŋ]. Yet since there is homorganic nasality, there is no release of the [k] before the [ŋ]. But if [ŋ] is not syllabic it will occur in phonologically impossible positions (syllable initially and in the middle of a cluster of consonants):

[aɪ kŋ ɑːsk ɪm]   *I can ask him.*
[juː kŋ teɪk wʌn]   *You can take one.*

There are two other points to be noted. First, among the syllabic forms of *can* we may note [kəm] and [kəŋ] with nasality that is homorganic with the following consonant:

[aɪ kəm peɪ]   *I can pay.*
[aɪ kəŋ gəʊ]   *I can go.*

But statements of this kind ought not to be considered as special statements about certain of the forms; they are rather indications of the limits of phonetic transcription. There are similar features with all the forms, but they are more difficult to show. Secondly, nothing has been yet said about the non-finite forms *be, been* and *being*. In unstressed position *be* and *been* have weak forms. It is sometimes stated that *being* has no weak form, and it is always written [biːɪŋ], but in fact it also seems to occur as [biːŋ] and even perhaps [bɪŋ].

With the exception of forms of do, syllabic forms are more common at the beginning of a sentence:

[kən aɪ kʌm]   *Can I come?*   (not *knaɪ)
(wəd juː gəʊ)   *Would you go?*   (not *djuː)

The forms of HAVE are those with initial [h]:

[həv juː siːn ɪm]   *Have you seen him?*
[həz iː gɒn]   *Has he gone?*

A non-syllabic form of *do* is common, often linked phonologically to the following consonant:

[dwiː nəʊ ðəm]   *Do we know them?*
[dʒə wɒnt tʊ]   *Do you want to?*   (Palatal affricate)
[dðei sei səʊ]   *Do they say so?*   (Interdental [d])

A similar feature may be noted for *does* especially when followed by *she*:

[dzʃɪ wɒnt tʊ]   *Does she want to?*

Did may be represented by an initial voiced alveolar stop alone; its duration may often, but not always, justify the transcription [dd]:

[dd ai sei səʊ]   *Did I say so?*
[dai sei səʊ]

There can be no confusion with *Do I* which must always have rounding – a rounded vowel or [w] – [du ai], [dwai]. But there is the possibility of ambiguity in:

[dðei sei səʊ]   *Do they say so?*   or   *Did they say so?*

The forms of *can* that have homorganic nasality with the following consonant occur initially too:

[kəm bɒb kʌm]   *Can Bob come?*
[kəŋ keit kʌm]   *Can Kate come?*

11.2 Full verbs: *-ing* and *-s* forms

There is little to be said about the morphology of the *-ing* form. In all cases it differs from the simple form only by the addition of [ɪŋ]:

cut [kʌt]   *cutting* [kʌtɪŋ]

In rapid conversation style the final nasal is often alveolar [n] instead of velar [ŋ]. Forms with the alveolar nasal are often regarded as substandard but they certainly occur in my speech and that of others.

The *-s* form differs from the simple form by the addition of an alveolar fricative (a sibilant). Phonetically there are three possibilities:

[i]   a voiceless sibilant [s] where the final element of the sim-
      ple form is voiceless and is not sibilant or palatal,
[ii] a voiced sibilant [z] where the final element of the simple
      form is voiced and is not sibilant or palatal,
[iii] a voiced sibilant [z] preceded by the vowel [ɪ] where the
      final element of the simple form is sibilant or palatal.

The alternation is wholly determined by the phonetic–
phonological environment and English orthography, quite rightly, makes no distinction between them:

[i]   *hate* [heɪt]   *hates* [heɪts]
[ii] *love* [lʌv]   *loves* [lʌvz]
      stay [steɪz]   *stays* [steɪz]
[iii] *miss* [mɪs]   *misses* [mɪsɪz]

For BE, HAVE and DO see 11.4. Apart from these there is only
one verb in English that is irregular in respect of its -*s* form –
SAY, whose -*s* form, though spelt *says*, is [sez] not [*seɪz].

11.3 Full verbs: past tense and -*en* forms

For most of the verbs the past tense and -*en* forms are identical;
even when they differ they are often related by a simple phonological feature. It is clearly convenient to handle them together.
     There is one 'regular' or 'productive' formation that would
apply to any word newly introduced into English; this is the
'regular -*ed* formation' of *lick/licked, like/liked, sin/sinned*
(11.3.1). The other formations might seem to be all irregular,
but in fact many of them belong to the 'secondary -*ed* formation', which differs from the regular one in having three simple
phonological rules (11.3.2). A third small class can be dealt with
in terms of a specific kind of vowel change (11.3.3), while a
fourth actually has the suffix -*en* for its -*en* forms (11.3.4). Between them there are four classes accounting for the vast majority of the verbs. There are a few that are wholly idiosyncratic
(11.3.5).

11.3.1 Regular -*ed* formation

For most verbs the past tense and -*en* forms are formed by the
addition of an alveolar plosive. This has, *mutatis mutandis*, the
same kind of characteristics as the alveolar sibilant of the -*s*
forms. The alveolar plosive will be:

[i]   voiceless [t] when the final element of the simple form is a
      voiceless consonant that is not an alveolar plosive, *eg*:

like [laɪk]   *liked* [laɪkt]

[ii] voiced [d] when the final element of the simple form is
      a voiced consonant that is not an alveolar plosive or is a
      vowel, *eg*:

        love [lʌv]   *loved* [lʌvd]
        stay [steɪ]   *stayed* [steɪd]

[iii] a voiced consonant [d] preceded by the vowel [ɪ] when the
      final element of the simple form is an alveolar plosive [t]
      or [d], *eg*:

        hate [heɪt]   *hated* [heɪtɪd]

      With both the *-s* form and the *-ed* form there is

(a) assimilation in terms of voicing such that the suffix is voice-
     less after a voiceless consonant and voiced after a voiced
     one;
(b) a special kind of dissimilation that prevents the immediate
     co-occurrence of two consonants of the same type of arti-
     culation: the sibilant does not immediately follow a sibilant
     or palatal, or the alveolar plosive another alveolar plosive.
     They are always separated by a vowel [ɪ], and the suffix is
     voiced because the vowel is voiced).

11.3.2 Secondary *-ed* formation
There are many other verbs whose formation can be handled in
terms of the addition of an alveolar plosive together with three
phonological rules that are not applicable to the regular formation.

(a) With a number of verbs that end in a lateral [l] or an alveo-
     lar nasal [n], there is a rule of 'devoicing' in that the
     suffixed alveolar plosive may be voiced as in the regular
     formation (since laterals and nasals are voiced) or voiceless
     eg: burn/burnt [bɜːnt].
(b) The pattern *keep/kept* [kiːp]/[kept] suggests that there is a
     'vowel shortening rule' whereby the 'long' vowel [iː] is re-
     placed by the 'short' vowel [e] when the suffix is added.
     This is plausible in the light of the identical vocalic pattern
     of such pairs as *serene* [səriːn] and *serenity* [sərenɪtɪ], and,
     with different vowels [eɪ]/[æ], *profane* and *profanity*, or
     [aɪ]/[ɪ], *revise* and *revision*. It is worth noting that the
     orthography indicates the relationship while the phonetic
     transcription does not. There is only one small class of
     verbs, all with the same vowels as KEEP, that exhibit this fe-

ature alone, but there are other verbs whose formation is to be accounted for by this feature plus some other (see in particular the next paragraph).

(c) There are about twenty verbs in English that appear to have no past tense/-*en* form suffix at all, *eg* HIT. But all of these end in an alveolar plosive – either [d] or [t]. Since English phonology does not permit within the word either the sequence [dt] or [tt] (or, indeed, any similar combination of consonants) it may be argued that the suffix is deleted in this context. This is preferable to simply saying that these verbs have 'zero' past tense/-*en* form suffix for two reasons. First, it gives an explanation for the forms themselves: they are not just irregular – their final consonants are significant. Secondly, it helps to generalize the formation of such forms as *bleed/bled*. Here there is vowel shortening, but vowel shortening takes place when a suffix is added. Since this verb too ends in an alveolar plosive it can be argued that the suffix is added but then deleted. This feature is 'consonant reduction'.

Six classes of verb may be recognized, each involving either one or two of these phonological features.

[i] Devoicing alone is found in:

> *smell* [smel] *smelt* or *smelled* [smelt]

The verbs that belong to this class (all ending in an alveolar nasal or a lateral) are BURN, LEARN, SMELL, SPELL, SPILL, SPOIL and the now slightly archaic DWELL. In the orthography the ending is either -*t* or -*ed*.

[ii] Vowel shortening alone is found in:

> *keep* [kiːp] *kept* [kept]

All the verbs in this class have the same vowels and final consonant CREEP, KEEP, LEAP, SLEEP, SWEEP, WEEP. The voicelessness of the suffix is in accordance with the regular pattern. FLEE is the only verb of the type:

> *flee* [fliː] *fled* [fled]

Here vowel shortening takes place when the suffix is added, but not before two consonants and the alveolar plosive is voiced in accordance with the regular pattern.

[iii] Consonant reduction alone is found in:

> *hit* [hɪt] *hit* [hɪt]

The verbs that belong here (all with final alveolar plosive) are BET, BURST, CAST, COST, CUT, HIT, HURT, LET, PUT, QUIT, RID, SET, SHED, SHUT, SLIT, SPLIT, SPREAD, THRUST, UPSET. WET functions either like these or in the regular formation.

[iv] Devoicing and vowel shortening together are found in:

mean [miːn]   *meant* [ment]

All the verbs of this class have the vowel [iː] and [e] and, with one exception, end in an alveolar nasal or lateral (and thus combine the characteristics of the verbs of [i] and [ii]) – DEAL, FEEL, KNEEL, LEAN, MEAN. The exception is DREAM which ends in a bilabial, not an alveolar, nasal.

[v] Devoicing and consonant reduction together are found in:

bend [bend]   *bent* [bent]

The verbs that belong to this class end in an alveolar nasal or lateral plus alveolar plosive (and thus combine the characteristics of the verbs in [i] and [iii]) – BEND, BUILD, LEND, REND (now rather archaic) SEND and SPEND. GIRD might be added, but it does not have the same final consonants, and is now obsolete.

[vi] Vowel shortening and consonant reduction together are found in:

bleed [bliːd]   *bled* [bled]

The verbs that belong to this class all end in an alveolar plosive and have the vowels [iː]/[e] (and so combine the characteristics of the verbs of [ii] and [iii]) – BLEED, BREED, FEED, LEAD, MEET, READ, SPEED. A different pair of vowels is found in:

light [laɪt]   *lit* [lɪt]

The only verbs in this group are LIGHT and SLIDE.

There are a few other verbs that are best dealt with in this section. Vowel shortening involving different vowels (plus consonant reduction in the first example) is to be seen in:

shoot [ʃuːt]   *shot* [ʃɒt]
shoe [ʃuː]   *shod* [ʃɒd]

This is a less common vowel pattern but found in, *eg: lose/loss.* Otherwise these verbs are like BLEED and FLEE. SHOOT and SHOE are the only examples. Finally are both types of vowel shortening exemplified in:

leave [liːv]   *left* [left]
lose [luːz]   *lost* [lɒst]

The idiosyncratic feature of these is the devoicing of the final consonant [v] → [f] and [z] → [s], LEAVE and LOSE are the only examples.

Overall there is a remarkable regularity. Even these last few examples, though apparently totally irregular at first sight, are evidence of the existence of the patterns.

11.3.3 Back vowel formation

There is another kind of vowel change that involves a change from a front vowel in the simple form to a corresponding back vowel in one or both of the other forms.

[i] The most striking pattern is that of:

drink [drɪŋk]   *drank* [dræŋk]   *drunk* [drʌŋk]

This could be called the 'vowel-triangular formation'. There are three vowels all short and all at the extremes of the vowel diagram front close, open and back close. On purely phonetic grounds one might expect the triangle to be that of [ɪ], [æ] and [ʊ], not [ɪ], [æ] and [ʌ]. But there is a simple explanation: [ʊ] does not occur in English before a nasal, but [ʌ] and [ʊ] are closely related and differ only in the absence or presence of 'rounding', and 'rounding' does not occur before [ŋ]. Hence in this environment [ʊ] is replaced by [ʌ], and the triangle thus is preserved. The verbs that belong to this class are BEGIN, DRINK, RING, SHRINK, SING, SINK, SPRING, STINK, SWIM.

[ii] The same pattern but without a separate [æ] form for past tense is found with:

win [wɪn]   *won* [wʌn]

Verbs in this class are CLING, DIG, FLING, SLING, SLINK, SPIN, STICK, STING, STRING, SWING, WIN and WRING. The same comment about the final nasal applies to all of these except DIG and STICK. But it is also true that [ʊ] does not occur before [g]; it occurs, however, before [k] (*eg: rook*) STICK is, therefore, exceptional.

[iii] A straightforward change is found in:

get [get]   *got* [gɒt]

The two vowels are phonetically both half open; GET is alone in this class.

[iv] A change involving only the last element of a diphthong is found in:

find [faɪnd] *found* [faʊnd]

Verbs in this class are BIND, FIND, GRIND, WIND.

[v]   Less clear-cut cases are:

shine [ʃaɪn]   *shone* [ʃɒn]
SHINE
fight [faɪt]   *fought* [fɔːt]
FIGHT
strike [straɪk]   *struck* [strʌk]
STRIKE
stride [straɪd]   *strode* [strəʊd]
ABIDE (archaic), STRIDE

The simple form has a front diphthong, the other a variety of back vowels. STRIDE is idiosyncratic in that it has no *-en* form: *strode* is past tense only. ABIDE has regular *-ed* forms also.

[vi] Back vowel formation cannot, however, account for all vowel changes. One can do little more than list the following:

sit [sɪt]   *sat* [sæt]
SIT, SPIT
hang [hæŋ]   *hung* [hʌŋ]
HANG
hold [həʊld]   *held* [held]
HOLD

Some have in addition the suffix of the regular formation:

sell [sel]   *sold* [səʊld]
SELL
hear [hɪə]   *heard* [hɜːd]
HEAR
say [seɪ]   *said*]sed]
SAY

[vii] Even more idiosyncratic are the verbs that have a vowel change form for the past tense but an *-en* form that is identical with the simple form:

come [kʌm]   *came* [keɪm]   *come* [kʌm]
BECOME, COME
run [rʌn]   *ran* [ræn]   *run* [rʌn]
RUN

11.3.4 -*en* suffix

There are some verbs that actually have orthographic -*en* or -*n*, phonetic [n] as the -*en* suffix! Apart from this they belong with many of the verbs already considered.

[i]   Within the regular -*ed* formation is:

   sew [səʊ]   *sewed* [səʊd]   *sown* [səʊn]
   SEW, SHOW, SOW and the now archaic HEW.

[ii] In the secondary -*ed* formation with consonant reduction is:

   beat [biːt]   *beat* [biːt]   *beaten* [biːtn]
   BEAT

[iii] In the secondary -*ed* formation with consonant reduction and vowel shortening (the latter applying to the -*en* form as well as to the past tense) is:

   bite [baɪt]   *bit* [bɪt]   *bitten* [bɪtn]
   BITE, HIDE

[iv] With a variety of vowel changes (none strictly in the back vowel formation) are:

   see [siː]   *saw* [sɔː]   *seen* [siːn]
   SEE
   eat [iːt]   *ate* [et]   *eaten* [iːtn]
   EAT
   forbid [fəbɪd]   *forbade* [fəbeid]   *forbidden* [fəbɪdn]
   BID, FORBID, FORGIVE, GIVE
   take [teɪk]   *took* [tʊk]   *taken* [teɪkən]
   FORSAKE, SHAKE, TAKE
   fall [fɔːl]   *fell* [fel]   *fallen* [fɔːlən]
   FALL
   draw [drɔː]   *drew* [druː]   *drawn* [drɔːn]
   DRAW
   grow [grəʊ]   *grew* [gruː]   *grown* [grəʊn]
   BLOW, GROW, KNOW, THROW
   slay [sleɪ]   *slew* [sluː]   *slain* [sleɪn]
   SLAY

[v]   With vowel change (past tense) and vowel shortening when the -*en* suffix is added are:

   ride [raɪd]   *rode* [rəʊd]   *ridden* [rɪdn]
   ARISE, DRIVE, RIDE, RISE, SMITE (now archaic), WRITE

[vi]   There are some verbs that form the past tense by vowel
       change, but the *-en* form by the addition of the *-en* suffix
       to the past tense form, not as in the preceding examples
       to the simple form. The vowel changes are varied, but the
       first two below are clear examples of back vowel forma-
       tion:

         forget [fəget]   *forgot* [fəgɒt]   *forgotten* [fəgɒtn]
         BEGET (archaic), FORGET, TREAD
         break [breik]   *broke* [brəuk]   *broken* [brəukn]
         BREAK, WAKE
         steal [stiːl]   *stole* [stəul]   *stolen* [stəuln]
         CLEAVE, FREEZE, SPEAK, STEAL, WEAVE
         bear [beə]   *bore* [bɔː]   *borne* [bɔːn]
         BEAR, SWEAR, TEAR, WEAR
         lie [laɪ]   *lay* [leɪ]   *lain* [leɪn]
         LIE [= lie down]
         choose [tʃuːz]   *chose* [tʃəuz]   *chosen* [tʃəuzn]
         CHOOSE

[vii] Only one verb has different vowels in all three forms:

         fly [flaɪ]   *flew* [fluː]   *flown* [fləun]
         FLY

[viii] A particularly idiosyncratic verb has a regular past tense
       form but an *-en* form with vowel change:

         swell [swel]   *swelled* [sweld]   *swollen* [swəuln]
         SWELL

11.3.5 Idiosyncratic forms
There are only a few verbs that have peculiarities that have not
been discussed. Yet even these have some shape.

[i]   MAKE would be regular except for the loss of final [k]:

         make [meɪk]   *made* [meɪd]

[ii]   STAND, UNDERSTAND and WITHSTAND would belong with the
       vowel change verbs if the loss of the nasal consonant could
       be accounted for:

         stand [stænd]   *stood* [stud]

[iii] Six verbs, BUY, BRING, THINK, TEACH, SEEK, CATCH (with
       archaic BESEECH like TEACH), all differ in the simple forms
       but have similar past tense/-en forms:

         buy [baɪ]   *bought* [bɔːt]

bring [brɪŋ]	*brought* [brɔːt]
think [θɪŋk]	*thought* [θɔɪt]
teach [tiːtʃ]	*taught* [tɔːt]
seek [siːk]	*sought* [sɔːt]
catch [kætʃ]	*caught* [kɔːt]

[iv]   GO alone has a suppletive past tense form (with a vowel-change -*en* suffix -*en* form):

go [gəʊ]   *went* [went]   *gone* [gɒn]

11.4 BE, HAVE and DO

The full verb BE has exactly the same forms as the auxiliary, including negative and weak forms (8.1.1). It is completely irregular except for its -*ing* form *being*.

The full verb HAVE also has the same forms as the auxiliary (8.2.1); it also has an -*en* form *had* that the auxiliary lacks. The formation is like that of MAKE in that it would be regular if the loss of the final consonant could be accounted for. (This is true of the -*s* as well as the past tense form.)

DO, however, is different. It shares with the auxiliary only the -*s* form and the past tense form. It has no negative or weak forms, but has an -*ing* form that the auxiliary lacks. Its -*s* form *does* [dʌz], its past tense *did* [dɪd] and its -*en* form *done* [dʌn] are all quite irregular.

11.5 Forms with *to*

Some phonological features are associated with the *to* of the *to*-infinitive following an auxiliary or a marginal verb:

[i]   With OUGHT there is loss of a consonant in that there is not in normal conversation a geminate [t] ([ɔːt tə]) as might be expected, but a single consonant [ɔːtə] – see 8.5.

[ii]   With HAVE the final consonant is devoiced before *to* [hæftə] – 6.6.

[iii]   With USED there is both devoicing and 'loss' of a consonant [juːstə] – 8.4.

These are, no doubt, indications of the close relationship between *to* and the preceding word – it is treated phonologically as if it were part of that word. There are at least other forms that exhibit the same close relationship – '*ve got* and *want*:

I've got to go	[aɪv gɒtə gəʊ]
I want to go	[aɪ wɒntə gəʊ]

References and citation index

AUSTIN, J. L. (1962) *How to do things with words*. London: Oxford University Press.

BOLINGER, D. L. (1971) *The phrasal verb in English*. Cambridge, Mass: Harvard University Press.

CHOMSKY, N. (1957) *Syntactic structures*. The Hague: Mouton.

CHOMSKY, N. (1965) *Aspects of the theory of syntax*. Cambridge, Mass: M.I.T. Press.

CRYSTAL, D. (1966) 'Specification and English tenses'. *Journal of Linguistics* 2, 1–34.

DUDMAN, V. H. (1983) 'On interpreting conditionals'. *Australian Journal of Linguistics* 3, 25–44.

EHRMAN, M. (1966) *The meaning of modals in present-day American English*. The Hague: Mouton.

FILLMORE, C. J. (1968) 'The case for case' in Bach, E. and Harms, R. T. (eds). *Universals in linguistic theory*. New York: Holt, Rinehart & Winston. pp. 1–88.

FIRTH, J. R. (1968) *Selected papers of J. R. Firth 1952–59* (ed Palmer, F. R.). London: Longman.

FRIES, C. C. (1925) 'The periphrastic future with *shall* and *will* in modern English'. *Proceedings of the Modern Language Association* 40, 963–1024.

FRIES, C. C. (1927) 'The expression of the future'. *Language* 3, 87–95.

GRANGER, S. (1983) *The be + past particle construction in spoken English with special emphasis on the passive*. Amsterdam: North-Holland.

HILL, A. A. (1958) *Introduction to linguistic structures: from sound to sentence in English*. New York: Harcourt, Brace.

HOFMAN, T. R. (1976) 'Past tense replacement and the modal system' in McCawley, J. D. (ed). *Syntax and semantics 7: Notes from the linguistic underground*. New York: Academic Press. pp. 85–100.

HUDDLESTON, R. D. (1971) *The sentence in written English: a syntactic study based on the analysis of scientific texts*. Cambridge: Cambridge University Press.

HUDDLESTON, R. D. (1976) 'Some theoretical issues in the description of the English verb'. *Lingua* 40, 331–83.

HUDDLESTON, R. D. (1977) 'Past tense transportation'. *Journal of Linguistics* 13, 43–52.

JESPERSEN, O. (1909–49) *A modern English grammar* I–VII. Heidelberg: Karl Winter, and Copenhagen: Einar Munksgaard.

JOOS, M. (1964) *The English verb: form and meaning*. Madison: The University of Wisconsin Press.

LAKOFF, R. (1970) 'Tense and its relation to participants'. *Language* 46, 838–49.

LEECH, G. N. (1969) *Towards a semantic description of English*. London: Longman.

LEECH, G. N. (1971) *Meaning and the English Verb*. London: Longman.

LYONS, J. (1977) *Semantics*. Cambridge: Cambridge University Press.

MCINTOSH, A. (1966) 'Predictive statements', in Bazell, C. E. *et al.* (eds) *In memory of J. R. Firth*. London: Longman. pp. 303–20.

PALMER, F. R. (1974) *The English verb*. London: Longman.

PALMER, F. R. (1977) 'Modals and actuality'. *Journal of Linguistics* 13, 1–23.

PALMER, F. R. (1978) 'Past tense transportation: a reply'. *Journal of Linguistics* 14, 77–81.

PALMER, F. R. (1979) *Modality and the English modals*. London: Longman.

PALMER, F. R. (1983) 'Future time reference in the conditional protasis: a comment on Comrie'. *Australian Journal of Linguistics* 3, 241–3.

PALMER, F. R. (1984) *Grammar* (2 edition). Harmondsworth: Penguin.

PALMER, H. E. and BLANDFORD, F. G. (1939) *A grammar of spoken English on a strictly phonetic basis* (2nd edition). Cambridge: Heffer. (The 3rd edition (1969) has been completely revised and rewritten by Roger Kingdon.)

PULLUM, G. and WILSON, D. (1977) 'Autonomous syntax and the analysis of auxiliaries'. *Language* 53, 741–88.

QUIRK, R., GREENBAUM, S., LEECH, G. and SVARTVIK, J. (1972) *A contemporary grammar of English*. London: Longman.

QUIRK, R., GREENBAUM, S. LEECH, G. and SVARTVIK, J. (1985) *A comprehensive grammar of the English language*. London: Longman.

SVARTVIK, J. (1966) *On voice in the English verb*. The Hague: Mouton.

SWEET, H. (1903) *A new English grammar* III. Oxford: Clarendon.

TWADDELL, W. F. (1965) *The English verb auxiliaries* (2nd edition). Providence: Brown University Press.

VAN EK, J. A. (1966) *Four complementary structures of predication in contemporary British English*. Groningen: Wolters.

VENDRYES, J. (1921) *Le langage*. Paris: La renaissance du livre.

WEKKER, H. (1976) *The expression of future time in contemporary British English*. Amsterdam: North-Holland.

WIERZBICKA, A. (1982) 'Why can you *have a drink* when you can't *have an eat*?'. *Language* 58, 753–99.

ZANDVOORT, R. W. (1957) *A handbook of English Grammar*. London: Longman.

Verb index

The verbs of Chapter 10 are listed under the heading of the verb only.

ABHOR, 203
ABIDE, 254
ABLE TO(BE), 94, 106, 112–15, 121–2
ACCEPT, 196
ACCUSTOM, 193
ACHE, 74, 191
ACKNOWLEDGE, 197
ADMIT, 197
ADVISE, 183, 193, 213–14
ADVOCATE, 204
AFFECT, 198
AFFIRM, 196
AFFORD, 192
AGREE, 183, 192
AIM, 191, 194
ALLEGE, 196
ALLOW, 193
ANNOUNCE, 196
ANTICIPATE, 204
APPEAR, 81, 205
APPOINT, 193
APPROVE, 204
ARGUE, 196
ARISE, 256
ARRANGE, 192
ASK, 193–4, 213
ASPIRE, 191
ASSERT, 196
ASSIST, 193
ATTEMPT, 202
AVOID, 201

BE, 14–16, 18, 21–2, 26, 29, 33–7, 53,
    85, 106, 128, 158–62, 169, 200,
    240–6, 249, 257; *see also* IS TO
BEAR, 203, 256
BEAT, 168, 255
BECOME, 85, 90, 254
BEG, 190
BEGET, 256
BEGIN, 17, 19–21, 66, 81, 83, 185,
    201, 205, 211–12, 253
BEHOLD, 199
BELIEVE, 73, 177, 181–3, 197
BELONG, 71
BEND, 252
BESEECH, 257
BET, 252
BETTER, 170–1
BID, 255
BIND, 254
BITE, 255
BLEED, 251–2
BLOW, 224, 255
BOUND TO (BE), 94, 106, 123–5
BREAK, 90, 224, 226–7, 232–4, 256
BREED, 252
BRING, 80, 193, 216, 224, 228, 256–7
BUILD, 252
BURN, 199, 250–1
BURST, 252
BUY, 256

CAN, 15–16, 18–19, 21, 23, 26, 73,
    95–8, 100–5, 107–23, 125, 132,

138–9, 156, 203, 205, 241–2, 244, 246–7

CARRY, 215–16, 224
CAST, 252
CATCH, 201, 237, 256–7
CAUSE, 193
CEASE, 201
CERTIFY, 196
CHALLENGE, 193
CHANCE, 81, 190, 203, 205
CHOOSE, 191, 194, 256
CLAIM, 197
CLEAVE, 256
CLING, 253
COAX, 193
COERCE, 193
COME, 81, 190, 202, 216, 218, 224, 229, 232–3, 235, 254
COMMAND, 193
COMMISSION, 193
COMPEL, 193
COMPLETE, 201
COMPLICATE, 86
CONCEIVE, 200
CONDESCEND, 191
CONFESS, 197
CONFINE, 235
CONJECTURE, 196
CONSIDER, 197, 203
CONSIST, 71
CONTAIN, 71, 82
CONTEMPLATE, 203
CONTINUE, 211–12, 216
COPE, 233
COST, 82, 252
COUNT, 204
COUNTENANCE, 203
COVER, 228
CREEP, 251
CRY, 223
CUT, 223, 252

DARE, 15, 23–6, 94, 106, 135, 155, 194
DEAL, 252
DECIDE, 178, 186, 191–2, 212, 241
DECLARE, 197
DECLINE, 191
DELAY, 201
DELIGHT, 204
DENY, 197
DEPEND, 71
DEPICT, 200
DEPLORE, 204

DEPRECATE, 204
DEPRIVE, 235
DESCRIBE, 200
DESERVE, 71, 204
DESIRE, 191, 204
DETERMINE, 191
DETEST, 203
DIG, 253
DIRECT, 193
DISAPPROVE, 204
DISCOVER, 197
DISCUSS, 203
DISLIKE, 203, 213
DO, 14–26, 35, 127–8, 159–60, 168–70, 232–5, 238–42, 244, 247–9
DOTE, 233
DRAW, 255
DREAM, 252
DRINK, 253
DRIVE, 193, 230–1, 256
DROWN, 83
DWELL, 251

EAT, 255
ELECT, 191
ENABLE, 193
END, 66
ENDEAVOUR, 202
ENJOY, 178, 203
ENTICE, 193
ENTREAT, 193
ENVISAGE, 200
EQUAL, 82
ESCAPE, 186, 201
ESTIMATE, 196
EVADE, 201
EXPECT, 174, 182, 193, 197

FAIL, 202, 208
FALL, 228, 255
FANCY, 190, 200, 203
FEAR, 191
FEED, 252
FEEL, 73, 75, 189, 199, 252
FIGHT, 254
FINISH, 66, 178, 201
FIND, 199, 228, 254
FIT, 226
FLEE, 251–2
FLING, 253
FLY, 222, 224, 229–30, 256
FOB, 239
FORBID, 193, 202, 255
FORCE, 193, 213

FORGET, 73, 190, 198, 202, 256
FORGIVE, 255
FORSAKE, 255
FREEZE, 256

GET, 89–90, 128, 130, 190, 195,
    201–2, 208, 215, 218, 238–9,
    253–5
GIRD, 252
GIVE, 80, 193, 215–16, 219–20, 224,
    226–8, 236–7
GO, 146, 216, 226, 232–5
GOING TO(BE), 38, 43, 94, 106, 143–9,
    152
GRIEVE, 207
GRIND, 254
GROW, 82, 255

HANG, 254
HAPPEN, 204–5
HASTEN, 190, 202
HATE, 17, 190, 202–3
HAVE, 15–16, 18, 20, 22, 26, 29,
    33–5, 51, 82, 85, 99, 106, 109,
    128, 155, 162–9, 174–5, 177–8,
    192, 195–8, 200, 203, 240–1,
    244–6, 248–9, 257
HAVE(GOT) TO, 94, 106, 126, 128–31,
    168
HEAR, 71, 73, 76, 199, 254
HELP, 195, 203, 208, 226
HESITATE, 191–2
HEW, 255
HIDE, 255
HINDER, 202
HIT, 251–2
HOLD, 254
HOPE, 73, 186–7, 191, 212
HURT, 252

IMAGINE, 73, 190, 197, 200
INSIST, 187
INTEND, 176–7, 182, 188, 192–3, 212
INVITE, 192
IS TO, 144, 160–1
ITCH, 74

JUSTIFY, 178, 203

KEEP, 14, 26, 176–8, 190, 200–1, 207,
    209–11, 237, 249, 251
KNEEL, 252
KNOW, 197, 200, 255

LACK, 81
LAUGH, 207, 223
LEAD, 193, 252
LEAN, 252
LEAP, 251
LEARN, 251
LEAVE, 80, 193, 228, 252
LEND, 252
LET, 171, 195, 252
LET'S 170–1
LIE, 71, 256
LIGHT, 252
LIKE, 26, 176–7, 188, 190–1, 203,
    209–10
LISTEN, 76
LIVE, 71, 207
LOATHE, 203
LONG, 186, 191
LOOK, 76, 191, 215–17, 221, 232,
    234, 237
LOSE, 252
LOVE, 203
LUST, 191

MAKE, 176–7, 195, 215–16, 223, 236,
    256–7
MANAGE, 202
MARCH, 92, 228
MARRY, 82
MATTER, 71
MAY, 15–18, 20, 23, 26, 95, 98–101,
    103–5, 107–23, 125, 136, 242
MEAN, 182, 193, 252
MEASURE, 82
MEET, 252
MIND, 203
MISS, 190, 203
MOTION, 193
MUST, 15–16, 18–21, 23, 26, 95, 97–9,
    103–7, 122–31, 133–4, 136, 155,
    241–2, 244, 246

NEED, 15, 20, 23–6, 95, 103–6, 110,
    122–8, 155, 184, 204, 241
NEGLECT, 202
NOTICE, 199

OBLIGE, 193
OBSERVE, 199
OFFER, 183, 192, 212–13
OMIT, 202
OPEN, 90–2
ORDER, 180–1, 193

OUGHT TO, 15, 18, 20, 24, 26, 95, 106,
    131–4, 241, 257
OWN, 71

PACK, 220
PASS, 237
PAY, 236
PERCEIVE, 199
PERMIT, 193
PERSIST, 187
PERSUADE, 179–83, 187–8, 190, 192–3,
    202
PICK, 220
PILE, 226
PLAN, 73, 192
PLEAD, 186, 192
PLEASE, 71
PLOT, 191
PLY, 235
PORTRAY, 200
POSTPONE, 201
PRACTISE, 201
PRAY, 194
PREFER, 17, 170, 203
PREPARE, 191
PRESENT, 226
PRESS, 193
PREVENT, 201–2
PROCEED, 202
PROFESS, 198
PROMISE, 183, 187, 206
PROPOSE, 192, 194
PROVE, 197
PULL, 222–3, 225, 228
PUT, 215–18, 238–9, 252

QUIT, 201, 252

RATHER, 170–1
REACT, 187
READ, 197, 252
RECALL, 198
RECOLLECT, 198
RECKON, 197
RECOMMEND, 183, 214
REFUSE, 191
REGRET, 190, 202, 204, 207
REJOICE, 207
RELISH, 203
RELY, 233
REMEMBER, 27, 113, 177–8, 198, 202
REMIND, 193
REND, 252

REPORT, 197
REPRESENT, 197
REPUTE, 83
REQUEST, 193
REQUIRE, 194
RESEMBLE, 81
RESENT, 203
RID, 252
RIDE, 256
RING, 90, 253
RISE, 256
RISK, 203
ROAR, 207
RUMOUR, 83, 197
RUN, 92, 219–21, 224, 229–34, 237,
    254

SAY, 83, 196–7, 249, 254
SCORN, 191–2
SEE, 26, 71, 73, 76, 174–5, 177,
    189–90, 198–200, 209, 233–4, 255
SEEK, 256–7
SEEM, 14, 81, 85, 184–5, 204–5
SELL, 92, 254
SEND, 201, 252
SERVE, 202
SET, 201, 236–7, 252
SEW, 255
SHAKE 255
SHALL, 16, 26, 38, 95, 97–8, 136–57,
    241–2, 244, 246
SHED, 252
SHINE, 254
SHOE, 252
SHOOT, 252
SHOULD, 96, 106, 131–5; see also
    SHALL
SHOW, 255
SHRINK, 253
SHUN, 201
SHUT, 252
SING, 253
SINK, 253
SIT, 207, 235, 254
SLAY, 255
SLEEP, 235, 251
SLIDE, 252
SLING, 253
SLINK, 253
SLIT, 252
SMELL, 73, 75, 199, 251
SMILE, 207
SMITE, 256

SOPHISTICATE, 86
SOUND, 76
SOW, 255
SPEAK, 256
SPEED, 226, 252
SPELL, 251
SPEND, 252
SPILL, 251
SPIN, 253
SPIT, 254
SPLIT, 252
SPOIL, 251
SPREAD, 252
SPRING, 253
STAND, 71, 192, 203, 207, 256
START, 66, 81, 176–7, 188, 201
STATE, 197
STEAL, 256
STICK, 253
STING, 253
STINK, 253
STOP, 81, 176, 201, 212
STRIDE, 254
STRIKE, 254
STRING, 253
STRIVE, 178, 202
STRUGGLE, 202
SUFFER, 74
SUPPOSE, 197
SURMISE, 197
SUSPECT, 197
SWEAR, 191, 256
SWEEP, 251
SWELL, 256
SWIM, 253
SWING, 253

TAKE, 197, 215–16, 218–19, 231–2,
    235–6, 255
TASTE, 73, 75
TEACH, 193, 256–7
TEAR, 256
TELL, 80, 193
TEMPT, 193
TEND, 205, 216
THINK, 73, 197, 204, 256
THROW, 255
THRUST, 252

TIDY, 225
TOLERATE, 216
TOTAL, 82
TRAVEL, 237
TREAD, 256
TROUBLE, 193
TRY, 190, 201–3
TURN, 226

UNDERSTAND, 113, 192–3, 256
UNDERTAKE, 183, 186, 197
UPSET, 252
URGE, 193
USED TO, 43, 170, 241

VENTURE, 192, 257

WAIT, 206–7
WAKE, 207, 256
WALK, 92, 218, 222, 229–31
WANT, 14, 17, 19–21, 26, 175,
    178–82, 186–7, 190, 193, 195,
    197, 204, 209–10
WARN, 193
WASH, 92, 225
WATCH, 199
WEAR, 256
WEAVE, 256
WEEP, 251
WEIGH, 82
WELCOME, 203
WET, 252
WHISTLE, 207
WILL, 15, 18, 26, 38, 94–8, 100, 107,
    134, 136–57, 241–4, 246–7
WILLING TO(BE), 94, 106, 121, 140–1
WIN, 253
WIND, 254
WIPE, 225
WISH, 191, 204
WITHSTAND, 256
WORRY, 193
WRING, 253
WRITE, 256

YEARN, 191
YELL, 207
YIELD, 216, 226

Subject index

ability, 97, 101, 109, 112–18, 121, 138
achievement, 202, 205, 207
accent, 8, 21–2, 52, 111, 138, 220–1, 230
actuality, 118, 121–2, 138–40
adjectival, adjective, 56, 85–6, 89–90, 207, 209–11
adprep, 231
adverb, adverbial, 9, 19, 22, 39–41, 47, 49, 56–7, 61–5, 79, 82, 107, 187, 191, 215–19, 220–3, 225–8, 238
adverbial passive, 92–3
adverbial specification, 57, 65
affected subject, 164–8
agency, agent, 77–9, 81, 83–4, 90–1
animacy, animate, 83–4, 112, 138
anomalous finite, 159
appearance, 204–5
aspect, 32–3, 35–6, 47, 51, 54–6, 84, 95, 107, 109, 123, 137, 145–6, 174–8, 187, 189, 191, 198–201, 209
asterisk, 4
attitude, 42, 191, 202–4, 213
auxiliary, *passim esp.* 14–26, 28–31, 240–8

back vowel formation, 253–6
bare infinitive, 13, 24–5, 95, 127, 171, 173–4, 188, 195, 198, 200–1, 206

case, 90–3
catenative, 4, 12, 14, 17, 26–8, 33, 78, 81, 89, 165, 168, 172–214
causal 150, 153

causation, causative, 91, 165, 168, 188, 195–6
chance, 202, 204–5
characteristic, 113, 115–16, 121, 137, 139, 159
circumstance, circumstantial, 102–3, 112–16, 118
clause *see* subordinate clause *and* main clause
code, 14, 19–20, 24–5, 159, 169–70
collocation, 215, 226, 233, 236, 239
commentary, 58, 147
complement, 28
complete, 55–6
complex phase, 12–13, 27–8, 172–4, 184, 205–10; *see also* simple phrase
concessive, 108, 119
conclusion, conclusive, 122, 125, 129, 137
concord, 14
condition, conditional, 18, 45, 51, 72, 94, 96, 120, 132–5, 138, 142–3, 147–57, 203
consonant reduction, 251–2, 255
counter-factual, 150
current orientation, 146
current relevance, 48–51, 68–70

definite noun phrase, 222–3
degree of modality, 97
deictic, deictic shift, 41–4, 46, 65, 70, 117, 124
deontic, 97–105, 107, 109–12, 114, 116–17, 119–20, 123, 125–8, 131–4, 136, 141–2, 156

demonstration, 58–60
devoicing, 251–2
direction, 219, 224–7, 229
disapproval, 64
discourse orientation, 98, 132, 171
displaced, 44
di-transitive, 12, 80
duration, 36, 47, 54–62, 68, 70–1, 95, 107, 123
dynamic (HAVE), 162–4 168
dynamic (modality), 97–103, 112–17, 119–21, 136, 138–40

-ed formation, 249–53, 255
emotion, 207
emphatic, 35, 111
emphatic affirmation, 14, 20–1, 24–5, 159
empty auxiliary, 21, 169
-en form, 16, 33, 37, 85, 87, 166, 173–5, 177, 197, 199–200, 249–57
epistemic, 97–110, 116–17, 119, 122–5, 127, 129, 131, 134, 136–8, 146, 156–7, 205, 208
evaluative, 131, 134–5
exclamation mark, 4
Existential, 113, 116, 120, 167

finite, 11–15, 26, 30, 51, 169, 187, 208, 211, 246
form, 9, passim
form and meaning, 8
free preposition, 222, 229–31, 238–9
full verb, 14–16, 22, 24, 26, 28–31, 127–8, 158–60, 162–4, 168, 170
fusion, 231, 246
future, 38, 54, 56–7, 64–7, 94, 107, 109, 123–4, 136–8, 141–6, 157, 160–1
future in the past, 43, 65, 146
future tense, 36, 38, 142, 144–6
futurity verb, 185, 187, 191–5

gender, 8
gerund, 13, 209
goal, 91
grammar, 5, passim
guarantee, 141–2

habit, habitual, 35, 38, 54, 56–64, 67, 72, 107, 118, 120, 136, 139–40, 153
historic present, 39
homonym, homonymy, 76, 188–90
hypothetical, 45, 154

identity relations, 28, 178–88, 197, 204
idiom, 216–17, 221, 223, 225–8, 233, 235–6, 239
imperative, 13, 21, 34–5, 95, 159, 171, 200
inanimate see animate
inductive, 61
inference, 138, 153
infinitival, infinitive, 3, 13, 15, 34, 57, 95, 174–5, 178, 206–7, 209
infection, inflectional, 1
-ing form, 13, 33–5, 166, 173–8, 188, 190–2, 195, 197–8, 200–4, 207, 211–12, 248–9
insistence, 138
instrument, 191
intention, 147
interrogation, interrogative, 7, 18–19, 22, 105, 111, 115, 119, 124, 126–7, 133, 140, 142, 212, 220
intonation, 6–7, 18–20, 23, 52, 65
intransitive, 71, 82, 90–2; see also transitive
inversion, 14, 18–19, 21, 23–5, 34, 128, 159, 169, 227, 242
invitation, 125
isolating, 1

judgement, 97–8, 105, 122–3, 129, 134–5

kinds of modality, 97, 106, 117

legal, 141
lexeme, 9, 15, 27, 96, 224
lexical passive, 90–2
limited duration, 47, 56–7, 62–3, 72

main clause, 11, 149, 178–80, 182–5, 192, 195–202, 204, 213
main verb, 31, 99, 145
meaning see form and meaning and semantics
memory, 198, 204
mental activity, 73–4
modal, 7, 14–21, 25–6, 27–8, 33, 38, 44, 51, 78, 94–157, 172–3, 205, 211
morpheme, 10
morphology, 5, 240–57
motion, 64, 201, 218, 224, 231

native speaker, 1, 3

necessity, 94–7, 103–4, 106, 110,
    122–3, 125–6, 128, 130, 132–4
need, 130, 204
negation, negative, 5, 14, 16–18, 21,
    23–5, 27, 30–1, 34–5, 84, 88
    98–106, 108–11, 114, 122, 126,
    130, 133, 137–42, 145, 149,
    159–61, 169, 198, 203, 208,
    240–2
negative interrogation, 23, 106, 108–9,
    111, 115, 124, 126–8
neutral modality, 102–3, 112, 114–15,
    121, 125, 129–33
NICE properties, 14–25, 27, 29, 102,
    106, 127, 158, 163, 168–70
non–assertion, 22–3, 25, 104–5,
    108–12, 114–15, 118–19, 123–4,
    126–7, 130, 133, 137, 139–40,
    148–9
non-epistemic see epistemic
non-finite see finite
non-perfect see phase
non-progressive see aspect
non-progressive verb, 58, 70–6, 189
normative, 3
noun, 208–9
noun phrase, 10, 77, 79, 173, 175,
    178–9, 218–20, 222, 228, 236–7
number, 8, 14, 240–1

object, 28, 77, 79, 91, 164, 178–84,
    202, 204, 209–14, 220, 231
obligation, 91, 101–3, 105, 125–6,
    128–30, 132–3, 192
opaque see transparent
orthography, 6

paradigm, 16, 26, 29, 32–5, 38, 94–5,
    102, 106, 151, 174
participle, participial, 13, 16, 34, 51,
    95, 175, 199, 209, 224, 237–8
particle, 215–20
passive see voice
past see tense
past-past, 42, 51–2, 99, 145
perception, 189, 198–200
perfect see phase
performative, 59, 98–100, 105, 126–7,
    141
permission, 98, 101, 105, 107,
    109–12, 125
phase, 27, 32–3, 35–7, 42–3, 46–54,
    68–70, 84, 88, 147, 168, 174–8,
    187, 191, 193, 196–7, 203, 208,
    213, 226

phrasal verb, 215–39
phrasal prepositional verb, 80, 238–9
phrase, 8–10, passim
plan, 143–4, 161, 191–2, 194
plural see number
polysemy, 72, 75, 188
possession, 163, 167
possibility, 94–7, 103–4, 108, 112,
    114–15, 117, 119, 121–3, 132,
    161
postposition, 237–8
power, 138
predictive, 150–2
preposition, 80, 87, 165, 183, 185–7,
    192, 197, 203–4, 212, 215,
    217–23, 225–6, 229–33, 235–8
prepositional verb, 80, 215–39
prepositional-adverb, 218
present see tense
primary, 25–7, 31–93, 95, 170, 172
private verb, 71–6, 113, 118, 121, 197
probability, 38, 134
process, 188, 190, 200–2, 205, 207
progressive see aspect
promise, 97, 141
pronoun, 166, 220, 225, 246
proposition, 98–101, 103–4, 107–8
    110, 112, 123–4, 126, 137, 141,
    149–50, 153, 157
prosodic, 7
pseudo-cleft, 212–13
pseudo-passive, 85–7, 89–90
purpose, 206–7

quantifier, 84
question, 18, 21, 73
question mark, 4

real condition see condition
reasonable, 161
reflexive, 197, 199
refusal, 138–40
relative clause, 233
relevance, 154
remote, 45
reported speech, 40–3, 51, 100, 117,
    124, 131–2, 138, 142, 145
reporting, 188–9, 196–200
request, 112, 115, 119, 140
result, 47–51, 207, 222, 224, 226
root modality, 103

scientific, 116
semantics, 187–8, 224–6, 230

semi-modal, 94, 106, 128–30, 146,
   148, 168
semi-negative, 18, 22–3, 104, 108
semi-passive, 87–8
sensation, 71–6, 113, 198, 201
sentence, 6, 10–11, *passim*
separation, 228, 233–5, 238
sequence of tenses, 40–3, 46, 96
-*s* form, 14, 24, 26, 127, 248–9
simple, phrase, 12, 27–8, 208; *see
   also* complex phrase
simple present, 61–2
singular *see* number
speaker, 102, 105, 108, 110–11, 122,
   125–6, 129–30, 134, 139–41, 153,
   171
speaker oriented, 98
speech and writing, 4–9, 240
sporadic repetition, 57, 62–4
stance, 71–2
statal passive, 88–9
state, 71–2 75, 81
stative, 161–2, 167–8
stress, 6–8, 242–3
strong form *see* weak form
subject, 77–8, 81, 83–4, 91–2, 98,
   101, 171, 178–9, 182–3, 186, 192,
   195, 204, 210–11, 214; *see also*
   affected subject
subject orientation, 101, 112–13, 115,
   132, 135, 138, 171,
subject raising, 182, 184–5, 188
subjunctive, 46, 135
subordinate clause, 11, 13, 29, 42,
   173–4, 179–87, 191–2, 195–6,
   199, 202, 204, 208, 211–14
subordination, 27–8
success, 168
suggestion, 114–15 118–21 139–40
suppletive, 257
syllabic, 243–4

tag, 22–3, 105–6, 111, 124, 132
tense, 2, 27, 30, 32–3, 35–47, 51, 65,
   96, 98–100, 102, 106, 109, 112,
   115, 117, 121–2, 124, 127–8, 130,
132–3, 135, 137, 139, 142, 149,
   155, 160–1, 174–8, 187, 191,
   196–7, 203, 205, 208, 213, 240–1,
   249–57
tentative, 46, 96, 100, 119–20, 130,
   132–3, 135, 140, 142
text, 3–4
thematization, 83–5
threat, 141
time, 2, 30, 36–40, 46–51, 54–5, 65,
   69
timeless, 61
TNP tests, 30–1, 98–103, 208
to-infinitive, 13, 15, 24–5, 81, 95,
   173–7, 190–2, 195–204, 206–7,
   212
token, 9
transformation, 78–9
transitive, transitivity, 12, 79–82,
   90–2, 212, 222–4, 228, 230–2,
   239
transparent, 217, 226–7, 234–6

ungrammatical, 3–4
unreal condition *see* condition
unreality, 37, 44–6, 51, 100, 132, 150;
   see also condition

verb phrase, 1, 10, 12–31, *passim*
voice, 31–3, 36, 50, 77–93, 98–9,
   101–2, 109, 112, 115–16, 124,
   131, 134–5 138, 140, 142, 145,
   149, 163, 165–6, 174–85, 187–9,
   191, 193, 195–202, 204–5, 208–9,
   216, 221, 224, 233–7, 239
voice neutrality *see* voice
volition, 138–9, 145–6, 149
vowel shortening, 251–2, 255

weak forms, 146, 162–4, 168–9, 171,
   242–8
'whenever', 153
willingness, 97, 138, 140
wish, 45
word, 2, 6, 8–10
writing *see* speech and writing